D0256561

ED...........................S

Our Troubles with
FOOD

Our Troubles with

FOOD

FEARS, FADS AND FALLACIES

Stephen Halliday

The
History
Press

EDINBURGH LIBRARIES	
C0043366244	
Bertrams	10/03/2009
	£18.99
CE	TX355

First published 2009

The History Press
The Mill, Brimscombe Port
Stroud, Gloucestershire, GL5 2QG
www.thehistorypress.co.uk

© Stephen Halliday, 2009

The right of Stephen Halliday to be identified as the Author
of this work has been asserted in accordance with the
Copyrights, Designs and Patents Act 1988.

All rights reserved. No part of this book may be reprinted
or reproduced or utilised in any form or by any electronic,
mechanical or other means, now known or hereafter invented,
including photocopying and recording, or in any information
storage or retrieval system, without the permission in writing
from the Publishers.

British Library Cataloguing in Publication Data.
A catalogue record for this book is available from the British Library.

ISBN 978 0 7509 4869 2

Typesetting and origination by The History Press
Printed in Great Britain

Contents

Introduction

Until comparatively recently mankind has had good reason to worry about where its next meal was coming from. In 1585 Queen Elizabeth's Lord Treasurer, William Cecil (1520–98), reflected upon the comparative tranquillity that had marked the first twenty-seven years of the queen's reign and attributed this, at least in part, to the fact that there had been no harvest failures in that time. This was not to last. In the next half century poor harvests occurred regularly and helped to account both for the discontents that marked Elizabeth's last years and the upheavals that led to the Civil War and the death of Charles I. It was not until the early nineteenth century that a national network of canals, and later railways, made it feasible to transport bulky crops from areas of plenty to areas of need, while later in that century new methods of storing and preserving surplus crops made it feasible for the abundance of one year to supplement the shortages of another. Nor were these problems confined to England. Harvest failures in France in the later eighteenth century fanned the discontent that led to the French Revolution. And even when food was available from cheap and abundant sources in America and Australasia much of the British population remained malnourished. In the last years of Victoria's long reign (1837–1901) forty per cent of volunteers to serve in the Boer War were rejected because they were too small as a result of poor nutrition.

By the time of the Boer War the poor condition of the population owed as much to ignorance as to poverty. The mediaeval English diet was a relatively healthy one which was fortunate since most people were required to undertake hard manual work, often as agricultural labourers in small rural communities. Its chief component was 'pottage', a stew of fresh seasonal vegetables, pulses, cereals and, where affordable, a little meat. This was supplemented by milk, seasonal fruit and by bread baked from unrefined flour – that it to say flour which contained most of the bran and other elements which are removed by the refining process which produces flour for white bread. This diet, cheap and strongly vegetarian in character, contains all the nutrients required for healthy, strenuous living including carbohydrates, protein, vitamins, minerals and a little fat. The mediaeval diet was very similar to that provided in a later century for the orphans of the Foundling Hospital, founded in London in 1739 by Thomas Coram. It provided its charges with 'all the produce of the kitchen garden' – vegetables and fruits grown by the children themselves – as well as milk and meat.

In the intervening centuries some members of the British population were less well-nourished than their ancestors had been. A preference for white bread made from refined flour, with much of the bran removed, was established by the end of the sixteenth century and remained in place for 400 years. Only in the late twentieth century was much of the British population weaned off white bread and persuaded to re-adopt the healthier wholemeal bread which their ancestors had eaten through necessity. Another component of the mediaeval countryman's diet, fresh milk, fell from the diets of that substantial proportion of the population which, in the course of Victoria's reign, became town rather than country dwellers. The completion of the railway network in the latter part of the nineteenth century made it possible to deliver milk fresh to distribution points in towns and cities, though it was not until the early twentieth century that its buyers could feel reasonably sure that the milk was free of pollutants, including tuberculosis bacteria.

At the same time that milk depots were being set up by local authorities in cities like Liverpool to ensure that the product was safe to drink, others were fighting to prevent the deliberate adulteration of food in the interests of appearance and profit. The habit of adding alum to bread to give it the desired whiteness; of adding copper to pickles to give them a nice green hue; and of adding lead to vinegar to give a passable wine was widespread until the passing of the Sale of Food and Drugs Act, 1875. Also at this time a small band of scientists was beginning to understand that certain undetectable components of the food supply, known at first as 'accessory food factors' were essential to human health. In 1900 it had been known for three centuries that the consumption of lemons provided protection against scurvy, but it was not until 1912 that the word *vitamin* entered the language. Other connections between diet and disease were soon to be made in the case of conditions like rickets and *beri beri*. An understanding of the role of vitamins in human health was to win many Nobel Prizes in the twentieth century.

In the twentieth century, as we have approached a full understanding of the essential components of the human diet and as agricultural science has enabled mankind to produce enough food for everyone, the issue has been clouded by three further factors. The first is the decline in physical activity in the population of the developed world. The human physique, which has evolved over millennia to cope with hard physical labour, has found itself in developed economies with a rapidly diminishing burden of physical work. Hard labour in the fields and mines has given way to the clicking of a computer mouse or the management of a robot. Walking and cycling to work have been replaced by motoring. At the same time we are encouraged, by the imperatives of a consumer society and its food processors, to eat more than our ancestors and, consequently, much more than we need. The third and most discussed factor concerns the use of chemical additives to preserve our food and to give it colour and taste. This is the issue that has provoked most alarm and criticism from consumer movements and lobbyists particularly, though not exclusively, in the USA.

In 2006 a conference was held in Istanbul by the World Health Organisation which drew attention to the fact that a large and growing proportion of the population of the developed world is overweight or obese, and this was confirmed by a UK government report in 2007. In the course of a century we have moved from the under-nourished Boer War volunteers to overweight citizens of an affluent society. This book examines mankind's faltering journey along that food chain.

1

Fears, Fads and Fallacies

What is it for? How does it work?

A few years hence, when the connection between the poor feeding of mothers
and children and subsequent poor physique and poor health is as clearly understood as the connection between a contaminated water supply and cholera, the
suggestion that a diet fully adequate for health should be available for everyone
will be regarded as reasonable and in accordance with common sense as is the
preservation of our domestic water from pollution.

John Boyd Orr writing in Food, Health and Income, 1937

If thou are dull and heavy after Meat it is a sign that thou has exceeded due
measure; for Meat and Drink ought to refresh the Body and make it cheerful
and not dull or oppress it.

Benjamin Franklin

One of the greatest demonstrations in public health administration that the
world has ever seen.

American Public Health Association, referring to the British diet in the
Second World War

Why Do We Need Food?

When the distinguished nutritionist John Boyd Orr (1880–1971) wrote the words which head this chapter he may have been aware of the struggle which some of his Victorian predecessors had mounted to persuade their contemporaries that polluted water and epidemics of cholera, typhoid and dysentery were connected. Eminent authorities like Edwin Chadwick (1800–1890) and Florence Nightingale (1820–1910) went to their graves believing that epidemics were caused by foul air rather than infected water. In 1949 the by then Baron Boyd Orr won the Nobel Peace Prize for his nutritional research. Yet he cannot have anticipated that he and his fellow nutritionists would have as great a struggle persuading their political masters and their fellow citizens of the need for a healthy diet as had their antecedents in their campaigns for clean water. Many of the difficulties which he and his successors faced arose from widespread ignorance, even amongst the medical profession, of the roles of different foods in human health – of the need for quality as well as quantity in the foods ingested and of the need to understand what 'quality' meant. Many believe that this battle is still being fought.

It is therefore not surprising that the increase in the standard of living and of life expectancy, even amongst the poor, which had characterised the reign of Victoria in Great Britain, was not accompanied by a proportionate improvement in physical well-being. When Victoria came to the throne in 1837 the average lifespan of her subjects was about thirty-eight years. At the time of her death in 1901 this had risen to about fifty-two years. From the 1870s the cost of staple foods fell by as much as 30 per cent as policies of free trade encouraged the importation of cheap foods from Australia, New Zealand, the United States and Europe. During the same period wages rose by 65 per cent[1] so that most Victorians were able to afford more nourishing food than their fathers, if they knew what 'more nourishing' meant. Yet at the end of Victoria's reign, 40 per cent of those volunteering for service in the Boer War were rejected on medical grounds, despite the fact that the minimum height requirement for the army was reduced from 5ft 3in to 5ft,[2] a phenomenon which supports the claim of Boyd Orr's fellow nutritionist Sir Jack Drummond that 'the opening of the twentieth century saw malnutrition more rife in England than it had been since the great dearths of mediaeval and Tudor times'.[3]

Sir Jack Drummond (1891–1952): born in Leicester, gained a first-class degree in chemistry at East London College in 1912 before joining King's

College, London, as a research assistant in 1913 where he undertook studies of human nutrition. During the First World War he worked on the development of margarines as butter substitutes and became interested in the role of vitamins in human diet. In 1920 he argued, successfully, that the word *vitamin* should replace the earlier usage *vitamine* on scientific grounds. In 1922 he was appointed to the new post of professor of biochemistry at University College, London, where he wrote his seminal study of the English diet over five centuries, a task he shared with his secretary and future wife, Anne Wilbraham. It was published in 1939 as *The Englishman's Food: Five Centuries of English Diet* and is still in print, read as a standard text. During the Second World War he worked with John Boyd Orr as adviser to Lord Woolton, Minister of Food, their achievement being not just to maintain but to improve the diet of the British population in the face of wartime privation. In August 1952, Drummond, along with his wife Anne and ten-year-old daughter, were sensationally murdered while camping in France. Gaston Dominici, a peasant farmer on whose land the family was camping, was gaoled for the murder, but later pardoned.

How could it be that the greater abundance of affordable food, accompanied by a rise in wages, coincided with such poor physical condition for much of the population? This paradox can be partly attributed to the problems of adulteration which are examined in chapter six but much of the blame lies with contemporary ignorance of the basic principles of nutrition.

Early Theories of Nutrition

Theories concerning the amounts and types of food needed for humans to thrive are found as early as the works of Hippocrates (*c.* 460–*c.* 380 BC), whose texts were in reality the product of many writers spread over six centuries. His writings postulated, correctly, that the quantity of food necessary for health depends upon the constitution of the individual, the energy expended and the season. However, Hippocrates' theories of nutrition were inextricably bound up with his theory of 'Humours' which were adopted, developed and propagated by Galen (131–201 AD) in Christian Europe and bedevilled the practice of medicine for more than two millennia. Galen, who was Greek by birth and appointed medical attendant to the Roman gladiator school in Pergamon in Asia Minor, was regarded favourably in mediaeval Europe, partly because, as a believer in one God, he was more acceptable to the ecclesiastical hierarchy than were most authorities from the ancient world. Through the influence of Galen,

'Complexions' (better described as personality types) and 'Qualities' were in turn associated with Humours, as shown in the table below.[4]

Complexion	Corresponding Humour	Corresponding Qualities
Sanguine	Blood	Hot and Moist
Phlegmatic	Phlegm	Cold and Moist
Choleric	Yellow or Green Bile	Hot and Dry
Melancholic	Black Bile	Cold and Dry

To these were added the four 'Elements' of earth, fire, water and air, derived from the writings of Aristotle, of which all matter was thought to be composed and which were, in turn, associated with the four Humours. Disorders in any one of the Humours would account for different types of illness and it followed that persons endowed with a certain 'complexion' should favour certain foods which complemented their characteristics and avoid those which exacerbated them. Galen was particularly severe in his view of fruit, claiming that his father had lived to the age of 100 by avoiding their consumption. Moreover, children were considered to be phlegmatic and should avoid foods and drinks categorised as cold or moist, these being deemed to include water, milk, fruits and lamb. Otherwise, it was feared, diarrhoea or worse would follow. For the same reason nursing mothers and wet nurses were advised to avoid these nutrients, advice which, where it was followed, presumably set back the cause of nutrition by centuries. The theories were not unchallenged even in classical times. Thus Cato the Elder (234–149 BC), who is chiefly remembered as a soldier and statesman, expressed the view that the consumption of cabbage was a sovereign remedy for all conditions – or, better still, the consumption of the urine of one who had eaten cabbage. There is no record of his prescription being widely adopted.

The mediaeval English diet, particularly in rural areas, was nutritious, as it needed to be given the hard physical work that it had to sustain. The most common food was 'pottage' consisting of a mixture of seasonal green vegetables, pulses, cereals and sometimes meat, cooked in a pot suspended over an open fire. To these would be added herbs including, from the fourteenth century, rosemary and saffron which had first been imported as medicines and later cultivated locally as foods. Many years later Sir Jack Drummond commended the qualities of a very similar diet consumed by people in developing countries: 'wholemeal cereals, mixed vegetables and dairy produce … Little meat is eaten but the staple diet is a coarse, wholegrained bread, thick vegetable stews and goats' milk cheese'.[5]

By the fifteenth century dried fruits were making their appearance in the form of currants from Spain, together with ginger, cloves and cinnamon and in the following century oranges and lemons, which were becoming available in London and other large towns along with locally grown apricots, spinach, parsley and sauerkraut.[6] By this time lettuce was also available in about a dozen varieties whereas Henry VIII's first queen, Catherine of Aragon, had sought it in vain when she came to England earlier in the century to marry his elder brother. Some foods were regarded as 'wholesome' because they promoted health while 'physic herbs' were seen as medicines to cure disease. One of the earliest English recipe books, *The Widowes Treasure*, published by 'a gentlewoman' in 1585, has as its first concern the use of food as medicine. Sage was considered to be good for the brain and was the subject of poems celebrating its virtues including one by Sir John Harington (1561–1612), better remembered as the inventor of the water closet:

> But who can write thy worth O sovereign sage?
> Some ask how men can die where thou dost grow ...

The theories of Hippocrates, as mediated by Galen, were brought to Europe by one Constantine the African via the Medical School at Salerno. They were propagated by a document called *Regimen Sanitas Salerni*, which may have been compiled at the request of Robert, eldest son of William the Conqueror in the late eleventh century and thereby came to influence English practice.[7] The *Regimen* particularly disapproved of feeding apples, pears and milk to the sick but popularised the practice of bleeding, thereby inflicting great harm on the practice of medicine for centuries. Yet the milk of wet nurses was given to the elderly infirm, one of the beneficiaries being Dr John Caius (1510–73), second founder of Gonville and Caius College, Cambridge.[8] The *Regimen* went almost unchallenged for 500 years though there were occasional sallies on behalf of individual foodstuffs like that made by Cato the Elder on behalf of cabbage. Thus Andrew Boorde (*c.* 1490–1549), who left the Carthusian order in the face of Henry VIII's persecutions, travelled throughout Europe at the behest of the king's minister, Thomas Cromwell, and became convinced that rhubarb was a cure for many conditions – a plant he duly introduced to Henry's kingdom for the first time. Other new foods were given a more hostile reception in some quarters. Thus the potato, introduced to Europe by the Spaniards who brought it from South America in the late sixteenth century, was blamed for an outbreak of leprosy shortly after its arrival in Burgundy.[9] Sugar, being associated with fruit, was also regarded with suspicion though Frederick Slare (1646–1727), a physician, Fellow of the Royal Society and contemporary of Sir Isaac Newton, wrote an essay entitled 'A Vindication of Sugars' in which he observed that the preservative powers of sugars meant that they could not be all bad.[10]

In the following century the work of chemists undermined the theory of the four 'Elements' and, with it, the infrastructure of the 'Humoral' theories of Hippocrates and Galen. Joseph Priestley (1733–1804) showed that Aristotle's element 'air' consisted of more than one chemical, one of which, oxygen, he described as 'dephlogisticated air'. Similarly, Henry Cavendish (1731–1810) discovered hydrogen, which had no place in the ancient theories. Robert Boyle (1627–91) in *The Sceptical Chemist* (1661) made it clear that he disagreed in every way with the theory of the four Elements and all that proceeded from them. There was, however, little to put in their place as a dietary model to promote a healthy population apart from some highly subjective, if patriotic, sentiments such as those expressed by one Robert Campbell in a publication entitled *The London Tradesman*. In it, he declared, in 1747, that 'In the days of good Queen Elizabeth mighty Roast Beef was the Englishman's Food' and went on to complain of 'French Fashion … Spices, Pickles and Sauces, not to relish but to disguise our Food'.[11] Galen's firm opposition to the consumption of fruit continued to hold sway, its 'evil, pernicious qualities' being condemned by a writer called Aubrey who appears to have been a ship's doctor, from which one may infer that any ship's company to whom he administered was exceptionally likely to suffer from scurvy.[12]

Chewing and Chemistry

At about the same time that Boyle was at work, a number of continental writers were studying the processes by which food was absorbed by the human body. Herman Boerhaave (1668–1738) was born near Leiden in Holland and, fortunately for the cause of science, was diverted from his early intention to enter the church in favour of a career in medicine, in which he graduated from Leiden's famous medical school. From 1701 he worked as a lecturer at Leiden and attracted the admiration of Peter the Great, Voltaire and Dr Samuel Johnson, who wrote a biography of him. He suggested that, having been ground by the teeth, food passed into the stomach where it was transformed into *chyle*. This substance was then mixed with blood and carried along the arteries to those parts of the body where it was needed at which point, under pressure from the blood, it was converted into the materials needed to replenish the body. This represents the beginnings of an understanding of how food is converted into energy and tissue.

Rene-Antoine Ferchault de Reaumur (1683–1757) was born in La Rochelle, studied at a Jesuit college and devoted his life to the study of a wide range of scientific subjects including the digestive processes of birds, arguing that digestion was promoted by chemical processes in the birds' digestive systems rather than by the action of grinding, as done by human teeth. Another product of Jesuit education, the Italian Abbé Lazzaro Spallanzani (1729–99) supported this hypothesis, thus leading towards an understanding of the role of gastric juices in the digestive process. The Frenchman Antoine Lavoisier (1743–94), one of the founders of the modern science of chemistry, was carrying out experiments on animals which showed the relationship between food, energy and heat which, if he had been allowed to complete them, could have advanced the understanding of nutrition by decades. Unfortunately, the generous income which enabled him to devote his time to scientific experiment was derived from his position as a 'farmer' of taxes – that is to say a tax-gatherer – and although he appears to have conducted this business with an unusual degree of probity, it was enough to condemn him in the eyes of the revolutionary government which came to power in France in 1793. His pioneering work was ended when he was arrested, tried and executed in one day in May 1794. The judge who presided over his trial, upon learning of Lavoisier's eminence as a scientist, declared that 'the revolution does not need scientists',[13] thereby dealing a blow to the development of the science of nutrition as well as that of chemistry.

Dieting to Death

A more heroic, if misguided test of the role of food for humans was undertaken by an English doctor called William Stark in 1769. He was probably born in the then small town of Birmingham[14] in about 1740 and studied medicine at Glasgow and Edinburgh universities, moving to London in 1765 to study with the distinguished physician John Hunter (1728–93). He was more successful in making influential friends than in obtaining jobs, since he failed to gain the post of physician at St George's Hospital despite being one of its governors. He did, however, befriend Benjamin

Franklin who was in London at the time and also Sir John Pringle (1707–82). Pringle was physician to the army, later to George III, and was a man whose opinions carried much weight in the medical world. He became President of the Royal Society which august body awarded him its prestigious Copley Medal for his confident (if false) assertion that sweet wort, a by-product of the brewing process, mixed with sugar, was a remedy against scurvy.[15] Benjamin Franklin informed Stark that, when a younger man, he had lived on a weekly vegetarian diet of water and bread,[16] expressing his doubts about the value of meat by adding: 'If thou are dull and heavy after Meat it is a sign that thou has exceeded due measure; for Meat and Drink ought to refresh the Body and make it cheerful and not dull or oppress it.'[17] Pringle told Stark that Greeks lived on a diet of currants, adding that one lady of his acquaintance, aged ninety, lived entirely on mutton fat. Such tales survived well into the nineteenth century, sometimes taking more extreme forms. In 1809 Ann Moore, 'The Fasting Woman of Tutbury' in Staffordshire, claimed to have eaten, drunk and excreted nothing for five years and was widely believed. It was probably Pringle's confident advice that aroused Stark's interest in nutrition and led him to undertake the experiment that led to his untimely death.

In June 1769, he announced: 'It will afford me singular pleasure if I can prove by experiment that a pleasant and varied diet is equally conducive to health, with a more strict and simple one'.[18] On 12 June 1769, he embarked upon the diet, a healthy male, aged twenty-nine, weighing 12st 3lb. He kept a daily account of the weather, the food ingested, the change in his weight and 'the number and total weight of my stools'. For ten weeks he lived on water and between 20 and 38oz of bread daily, permitting himself the addition of some sugar for an interval of two weeks. At the end of this time he had lost a stone in weight and his gums were swollen and bleeding – almost certainly as a result of scurvy. This was followed by a period of eighteen days when he consumed a diet of meat, milk and wine and a further period of almost eight weeks when he confined himself to bread, meat and water. He recorded such afflictions as 'blackened gums' with 'foetid white fluff round their edges'. For a further month, taking him to 26 December, he lived off 'puddings' consisting of flour, various oils and water before moving on to a diet of bread, meat and currants, the last of these possibly introduced as a result of Pringle's reassuring advice about the Greek practice referred to above (Pringle was monitoring the experiment). Stark next planned to switch to a diet of fruit and vegetables which would presumably have been his salvation but for unknown reasons he decided instead to confine himself to honey

puddings and Cheshire cheese. On 14 January 1770 his health took a turn
for the worse and he died on the 23rd, racked with scurvy and a martyr to
the cause of science. His last diary entry was: 'Nothing passes through me,
except sometimes a little wind upwards or downwards, and that without
relief'.[19] At no stage in his record does Stark record anxiety or dismay at
the course of events. Rarely can anyone have made such a sacrifice in the
cause of science. Sir John Pringle's reaction to Stark's heroic, if misguided,
experiment is unrecorded.

The Balanced Diet

Further and surer steps towards an understanding of the connections
between diet and health were taken by William Cullen (1710–90). Born in
Lanarkshire, he studied medicine at Edinburgh and Glasgow, at which latter
university he first demonstrated the techniques of refrigeration, though
without applying them in any practical way.[20] It was at Edinburgh that he
became a renowned lecturer in chemistry and medicine, revealing himself
to be a strong opponent of the 'Humoral' doctrines that still prevailed in
many quarters. A friend of Adam Smith and David Hume, his influence
extended far beyond Scotland, not least because he was amongst the first to
attempt a classification (or 'nosology') of diseases in relation to their symptoms. His lectures were published in 1789 as *A Treatise on Materia Medica*, in
which he showed some awareness of the need for what we would now call
a 'balanced diet'. Thus he suggested that vegetables like cucumbers could
'allay the heat of meat' in big flesh eaters. Jonas Hanway (1712–86),[21] in
his *Letters on The Importance of the Rising Generation*, published in 1767, had
noted that some families who could not afford much meat had found ways
of making their portions go further, with beneficial results: 'With the addition of legumens, roots and vegetables, 5lb weight of meat will go as far as
we generally make ten or fifteen and the consumer will be more free of
the scurvy'.[22] What Hanway did not know was that such a diet, resembling
the peasant 'pottage' commended by Jack Drummond, was rich in vitamins
– essential elements of the diet which had to wait a century and a half
before they were identified and understood.
    The concept of the balanced diet revolved around the theories of ases-
cence (acid-bearing) and alkalescence (alkaline) which were emerging at
this time from the comparatively new science of chemistry. Vegetables, and
the formerly suspect fruit, were held to provide acid to the diet while
cheese, eggs and meat, especially red meat, were believed to provide the

alkaline component. In 1776 a Dr William Smith, who besides being a practising doctor was also an author of medical textbooks, wrote *A Sure Guide in Sickness and in Health in the Choice of Food and Use of Medicine*, the title of which carries its own significance since it clearly indicated a connection between diet and health. Smith observed that southern Europeans habitually consumed far more fruit than the English, with no harmful consequences despite Galen's teachings to the contrary. Smith also suggested that 'People in general eat too much', in turn suggesting that his circle was confined to those prosperous citizens who were not constantly worried by poverty. His book also expressed clearly the acid/alkaline theory of the time:

> When a person attempts to live upon flesh meat alone, though it be fresh, his appetite becomes keener, and even ravenous; and nature will crave for some acids and vegetables to correct the alkaline acrimony of the blood. And when he lives upon vegetables alone, whereby the stomach will contract an acid tendency he will find a craving for animal food to temperate the acidities.[23]

The science may not have been wholly correct but neither was it wholly wrong, as Galen had been in eschewing fruit, and Smith was making a case for what later came to be understood as a balanced diet.

As the nineteenth century approached, others attempted to carry out experiments on the effects of diets on animals. The French physiologist Francois Magendie (1783–1855) is most often remembered for his research into the human nervous system and for some brutal exercises in the vivisection of dogs which attracted the criticism of Charles Darwin, but he is also credited with measuring the effects upon dogs of different diets. He discovered, by experiment, that dogs fed on coarse, dark bread thrived while those whose bread was made from high grade wheat flour, producing white bread, soon died. Likewise, dogs fed on boiled egg whites suffered sore skin and loss of hair. Without knowing it, Magendie was observing the effects of a diet deficient in certain vitamins.

'The Man with the Lid on his Stomach'

In June 1822, Alexis St Martin (1794–1880), an employee of the American Fur Company, was accidentally shot on an island in Lake Huron, off the coast of Michigan. St Martin's birth name was Alexis Bidigan *dit* (i.e. known as) St Martin but he was known throughout his long and remarkable career as a human guinea pig by the name St Martin. Born in Canada of French descent, he was working as a 'voyageur' whose job was to paddle cargo-carrying canoes along rivers and carry them over rapids, from which we may conclude that he was reasonably fit and strong. He needed to be. Dr William Beaumont (1785–1853), a US Army surgeon, was at hand and treated the injured man whose wound was thought to be fatal. In Beaumont's words:

> The wound was received just under the left breast and supposed, at the time, to be fatal. A large portion of the side was blown off, the ribs fractured and openings made into the cavities of the chest and abdomen, through which protruded portions of the lungs and stomach, much lacerated and burnt … The diaphragm was lacerated and a perforation made directly into the cavity of the stomach, through which breakfast food was escaping.

Beaumont cleaned and dressed the wound and predicted that St Martin would be dead within thirty-six hours. Nevertheless St Martin made a slow recovery and within four weeks was eating and digesting his food normally. The wound eventually healed in such a way as to leave a permanent hole (a *gastric fistula*) in the side of St Martin's body which had to be plugged with a dressing to prevent his meals exiting from his body by this unconventional route. St Martin entered Beaumont's household, working as a handyman, while enabling the doctor to observe the processes of digestion and to carry out experiments on gastric juices. As Beaumont himself wrote in the *American Medical Recorder* in 1825:

> This case affords a most excellent opportunity of experimenting upon the gastric fluids and the process of digestion. It would give no pain, nor cause the least uneasiness, to extract a gill of fluid every two or three days, for it frequently flows out spontaneously in considerable quantities; and one might introduce various digestible substances into the stomach and easily examine them during the whole process of digestion. I may therefore be able hereafter to give some interesting experiments on these subjects.[24]

There is some dispute about whether Beaumont's scientific curiosity overcame his medical ethics. It has been suggested that Beaumont could have operated on St Martin to close the fistula but left it open, closed only by a dressing, so that he could carry out his experiments. Beaumont, however, claimed that this was 'an operation to which the patient would not submit'.[25] It should, however, be noted that St Martin lived to the age of eighty-six, married and sired six children, so his peculiar physiognomy does not appear to have acted as an inhibiting influence on his life. Nevertheless, he tired of his life as a medical curiosity and in 1826 made his way back to his Canadian home, but was persuaded to return to the care of Beaumont who by this time was in Wisconsin. St Martin, at Beaumont's behest, was eventually enrolled as a sergeant in the US Army on a salary of twelve dollars a month, his only duty being to make himself available to Beaumont for his experiments. He became known amongst his fellow soldiers as 'the man with the lid on his stomach'.[26] This new status did not prevent St Martin from deserting on at least one occasion on account of the fact that his wife was homesick, but so great was the interest in his case that such eccentricities were tolerated and he was subjected to no disciplinary procedures.

His co-operation enabled Beaumont, in 1833, to publish *Experiments and Observations on the Gastric Juice and the Physiology of Digestion*, containing the results of 240 experiments conducted on the famous stomach. It made the reputation of Beaumont as an authority on digestion. For centuries doctors had debated whether digestion was a chemical or physical process, an issue which was summarised, but not resolved, by the great English physician William Hunter when he wrote that 'Some physiologists will have it that the stomach is a mill, others that it is a fermenting vat, others, again, that it is a stew pan. I say that it is a stomach'.[27] Beaumont's experiments resolved the matter.

William (1718–83) and John (1728–93) Hunter: William Hunter was born in Lanarkshire and worked with William Cullen before moving to Paris to study anatomy and surgery. In 1744 he set up a practice in surgery and midwifery in London but became better known as a lecturer on dissection, advertising his services by explaining that 'Gentlemen may have the opportunity of learning the Art of Dissection during the whole winter season in the same manner as in Paris' – that is to say by dissecting human corpses. In 1749 he moved with his brother John to Covent Garden and later to a specially equipped residence and anatomy theatre in Great Windmill Street nearby. He became physician extraordinary to Queen Charlotte, wife of George III, in 1762 and a Fellow of the Royal Society (FRS) in 1767. A wealthy but reputedly miserly man, he enjoyed the friendship of David Hume, Henry Fielding and Tobias Smollett and assembled a collection of anatomical specimens which he left to form the Hunterian Collection in Glasgow. His younger brother John first assisted William in his work in London, not least by using his less exalted friends to obtain cadavers for William's dissection classes. He became an army surgeon during the Seven Year War (1756–63) and bought an estate at Earl's Court, in the countryside outside London, where he assembled a huge collection of animal skeletons, including cadavers from the royal menagerie. He became a surgeon at St George's Hospital, then situated at Hyde Park Corner, where his first pupil was Edward Jenner, future discoverer of the process of vaccination. He was elected FRS a few months before William in 1767 and fell out with his brother in 1780 in a dispute over precedence in certain discoveries of the properties of the placenta. In 1769 he is believed deliberately to have infected himself with gonorrhoea in order to study the course of the disease. He was a friend of Joseph Banks, Captain James Cook and Joshua Reynolds and assembled a huge collection – 13,682 specimens – of natural history and comparative anatomy which he stored in his large mansion in Leicester Square and which formed the Hunterian Collection in London, much of which was destroyed by bombing in May 1941. He is commemorated by a statue in Leicester Square, near the site of his former home and by the Hunterian Museum at the Royal College of Surgeons in Lincoln's Inn Fields.

In *Experiments and Observations* Beaumont described in some detail both the experiments he carried out and the fifty-one 'inferences' he had drawn from them over a period of about six years. They represented a significant advance on previous knowledge of the ways in which substances were converted from food to tissue and energy, and many of his conclusions, which led the science of nutrition in new directions, remain axioms. Thus he remarked that most reasonably well-to-do people, then as now, ate more than was good for them: 'The system requires much less than is generally supplied to it ... Dyspepsia is oftener the effect of over-eating and over-drinking than of any other cause'.[28] A selection of his 'inferences' follows, numbered as Beaumont numbered them, in his own words and with his italics:

1. That *animal* and *farinaceous* elements are more easy of digestion than *vegetable*.
4. That the *ultimate principles* of aliment are always the same, from whatever food they may be obtained
8. That *bulk* as well as nutrient, is necessary to the articles of diet.
30. Pure gastric juice, when taken out of the stomach of a healthy adult ... is a clear, transparent fluid; inodorous, a little saltish, and very perceptibly acid ... an effectual solvent of the *materia alimentaria* ... powerfully antiseptic, checking the putrefaction of meat. [This suggests that Beaumont had himself tasted the output of St Martin's stomach.]
45. That the motions of the stomach produce a constant *churning* of its contents and *admixture* of food and gastric juices.

He supported the earlier hypothesis of the Italian biologist Lazzaro Spallanzani[29], who had identified the role of gastric juices in the digestive system and added some comments on the process of 'chymification' by which food is converted into chyme, a liquefied substance that is passed from the stomach into the small intestine. There, enzymes from the pancreas, liver and gall bladder work with those of the small intestine itself to turn food into nutrients, which enter the circulatory system and pass thence to cells where they are used as energy, for repair or for growth. Beaumont stated, correctly, that '*Chymification* is effected in the stomach. It is the first stage, proper, of the conversion of aliment into blood', though he could have added that it is converted into other things as well. Twentieth-century scientists like Sir Hans Krebs, referred to below, would develop these concepts further.

In the same year, 1833, that *Experiments and Observations* was published, St Martin returned to Canada and resisted all attempts by Beaumont and others to induce him to leave his family and co-operate with further experiments. These included a group of vegetarians in Boston who hoped to disprove Beaumont's conclusion (inference 1) that meat was more easily digested than vegetables; and the prestigious Medical Society of London who offered him £300 to travel to London and show them his celebrated hole. The nearest he came to Europe was when a bottle of his gastric juices was sent to a Swedish chemist in 1834 but the five-month voyage, in the heat of summer, ensured that the sample was not analysed in time for the publication of Beaumont's book.

Following Beaumont's death in 1853 from a fall on icy steps, St Martin fell into the hands of an exhibitionist charlatan calling himself Dr Bunting (the doctorate awarded by Bunting himself) who took the human guinea pig on a freak show tour of eastern cities. Alexis St Martin died in Quebec in 1880 and his family refused all requests from scientists and doctors for the body to be made available for an autopsy and research. They even buried him at a greater depth than usual to deter 'resurrectionists' who might be tempted to disinter the body.

'Count Rumford' and Justus von Liebig

No account of the development of the science of nutrition in the eighteenth and nineteenth centuries would be complete without some reference to the work of 'Count Rumford' and Justus von Liebig, though the latter's work is covered in more detail in a later chapter. Count

Rumford (1753–1814) was born Benjamin Thompson in Massachusetts where he showed an early interest in science which benefited from his marriage to a wealthy widow, leaving him leisure time to pursue his studies. He made good use of a quality described in his entry in the *Dictionary of National Biography* which records that, 'Among Thompson's many talents, the capacity to recommend himself to the mighty was prominent'.[30] He became a major in the New Hampshire Militia but, being out of sympathy with the aims of the American Revolution, left for England where he entered government service and was elected a Fellow of the Royal Society for his work on explosives and heat. He was knighted in 1784 and from that year until 1795 he worked in the service of the Elector of Bavaria, who conferred on him the title Count von Rumford, taking his title from the small town of Rumford (now Concord), New Hampshire, where Thompson met his first wife. He invented the *Rumford Stove*, an effective means of cooking food either in the kitchen or on the field of battle, and the *Rumford Fireplace*, a thermally efficient means of heating a room and, while in the Elector's service, made a contribution to the science of nutrition as a result of a misapprehension.

Rumford believed that water was itself a nutrient and that manure, rather than feeding plants itself, simply prepared water to perform its nutritious task.[31] He reasoned that soup could fulfil the same role for humans, the solid content being the means by which the water was able to nourish the human body. He concentrated on creating a soup that was tasty and produced a recipe which contained 'pearl barley, pease, potatoes, wheaten bread, vinegar, salt and water' – again a nutritious meal similar to the 'pottage' later commended by Sir Jack Drummond and observed by Jonas Hanway.[32] It was easily prepared and digested by the Elector's soldiers and the Elector's poorer subjects.[33] Rumford later married the widow of Antoine Lavoisier,[34] his own wife, whom he had abandoned in America, and he founded the Royal Institution in partnership with Sir Joseph Banks, appointing Humphrey Davy as its first lecturer.

In 1837 the British Association asked the eminent German professor Justus Von Liebig (1803–73) 'to prepare a Report on the present state of our knowledge in regard to Isomeric Bodies',[35] a rather convoluted way of asking Liebig to explain the chemistry of agricultural production. This Liebig was well qualified to do since he was the world's leading authority on the application of science to agriculture from his base at the university now named after him at Giessen, Hesse. The result of his enquiry was the seminal work, *Chemistry in its Application to Agriculture and Physiology*, which explained how crops drew carbon dioxide from the air and nitrogen from the roots and turned both into nutrients, an analysis which has stood the test of time. Liebig was an entrepreneur as well as a professor. In 1865 he formed the Liebig Extract of Meat Company operating from Fray Bentos in Uruguay. The product had a curious origin. Liebig was friendly with the distinguished English chemist and industrialist James Muspratt (1793–1886), whose chemical business eventually became Imperial Chemical Industries. Muspratt's daughter stayed with Liebig in Munich when she was seventeen and became ill with scarlet fever. Alarmed, Liebig minced some chicken, heated it in water and pressed the juice from the chicken for feeding to the stricken girl. Her weakened appetite and digestion were able to absorb the readily digestible nutrients and she made a quick recovery.[36] The extract was later adopted by hospitals in Munich. The beef product from Fray Bentos involved removing fat, sinew and bone from meat, chopping up the remainder into a pulp and heating it in water for thirty minutes. Following this, any remaining fat was removed and the remaining extract was cut into cubes of which it was claimed that '1lb of extract of meat contains the soluble elements of 30 to 32lb of lean fresh beef' and further that 'if boiled with a few slices of bread, potatoes and a little salt, is sufficient to make broth for 120 men [i.e. soldiers] in the field'.[37]

Liebig's claims provoked a lengthy and sometimes acrimonious correspondence in *The Lancet* for much of 1865, involving contributions from Liebig in Munich and a Frenchman called Parmentier (not the earlier inventor of potato soup) as well as a number of English pharmacists. Parmentier, a military doctor, was quoted as stating of Liebig's meat extract that, 'Dissolved in a glass of wine, it is a powerful restorative, rendering severely wounded soldiers, however weakened by loss of blood, capable of bearing removal to the nearest field hospital'. The pharmacists on the whole disagreed, pointing out that the heating process would cause many nutrients to be lost in the water, while some of those who marketed the product weighed in with denials that reputable organisations would adulterate the product by adding salt, as some correspondents claimed was happening. The controversy did no lasting damage to the company which sold 12,000 jars in a year to London's St Thomas's Hospital and, after Liebig's death, became Brooke-Bond Liebig and named the meat extract product Oxo.

The Chemical Composition of Foods

Following Liebig's description of how plants grow and become nutritious, the systematic analysis and publication of the chemical composition of foodstuffs, with its implications for human diet, had to wait until the following century and is inseparably associated with the names McCance and Widdowson.[38] Robert McCance (1898–1993) was born in Ireland, served in the Royal Naval Air Service in the First World War and subsequently studied natural sciences at Cambridge. In 1926 he moved to King's College Hospital, London, with an annual grant of £30 from the Medical Research Council[39] to calculate the carbohydrate content of cooked fruit and vegetables, a matter that was, at that time, of concern to those treating diabetics, the results being published in 1929.[40] This was followed by a further study of meat and fish which was published in 1933.[41] During the course of this work McCance met Elsie Widdowson (1906–2000) in the kitchens of King's College Hospital where she was studying dietetics and where he was seeking the assistance of the chefs in cooking one of the large joints of meat that was an object of his study. She had completed a PhD on the carbohydrate content of apples. A mutual interest in the chemical composition of the human diet led to their agreement to work together, an arrangement that was not without its hazards. Robert McCance was a man whose determination to achieve results sometimes outran his diplomatic skills. Elsie Widdowson later said of their close working relationship that he was the acid and she the neutralising base.[42]

An investigation into the effects of salt deficiency tempted Robert McCance to experiment upon himself, causing him to pass out, a state from which he was rescued by Dr Widdowson before the onset of brain damage which could otherwise have occurred,[43] but this did not discourage him from carrying out other strenuous experiments upon himself and colleagues, described below. In 1945 McCance was appointed to the new Professorship of Experimental Medicine at Cambridge and Elsie Widdowson joined him there in his research to begin a lifetime collaboration. Their partnership led to a series of groundbreaking discoveries. For example, they discovered that newborn babies excrete a far smaller proportion of the nitrogen that they ingest than adults, this being due to the fact that, whereas adult kidneys filter out the nitrogen when they are working properly, babies' kidneys do not do so because the nitrogen is used to fuel the babies' growth. In Robert McCance's own words, 'growth was by far the most important influence in maintaining a normal internal environment'.[44]

In the 1930s they, with others, completed a series of studies of the nutritional content of fruits, vegetables, meat, fish, nuts, cereals, dairy products, beverages and preserves. The result of this collaboration was their definitive study of human foods, *The Chemical Composition of Foods*,[45] published in 1940 and in print ever since, the most recent edition being issued in 2002. In the 1940 edition they wrote that, 'A knowledge of the chemical composition of foods is the first essential in the dietary treatment of disease', and their original work continues to be updated as new foods are added to the human diet and as changes in farming methods bring about changes in nutritional values. It remains the most authoritative and widely used source of information about the nutritional value of foods and is used throughout the world by dieticians, caterers, food scientists, health professionals, schools and others concerned with the human diet. The latest edition comprises 370 pages of tables analysing foodstuffs according to the quantities they contain of such dietary elements as carbohydrate, protein, fat, energy, vitamins and minerals. It also contains twenty-six pages of recipes.[46] Such is the reputation of its original authors that the volume is still, after their deaths, referred to not by its title but as *McCance & Widdowson*, rather as *Wisden* is in cricketing circles or *Bradshaw* by Sherlock Homes when looking up the times of trains.

The Chemical Composition of Foods is the achievement for which they are best known but some of their most important work was done during and immediately after the Second World War. In the early days of the war the government, mindful of the problems posed by the undeveloped U-Boats of the time, was very anxious about its ability to ensure an adequate supply of food. Rationing was introduced to cover such staples as meat, butter, cheese, eggs and other items that were taken for granted as part of the weekly diet. Robert McCance and Elsie Widdowson, with the assistance of some younger colleagues, decided to test the effects of the proposed diets upon themselves. In Robert McCance's own words, 'This was fun', though an examination of the processes to which he subjected himself and others could lead a more pampered generation to other conclusions. Potatoes, along with wholemeal flour for cooking and breadmaking, were unrationed, but otherwise the McCance diet consisted of exiguous allowances: for example, 4oz per week of fat; 5 of sugar (including that in jam); one egg; 4oz of cheese; 16oz of meat and fish combined; and 6oz of fruit. The milk ration amounted to a quarter of a pint each day. Despite the predictions of their friends and colleagues that they would become ill and weary, after three months 'we decided to go to the Lake District to test our physical fitness'.[47]

They did not travel by train. Just after Christmas 1940, in the coldest season, Robert McCance and a younger colleague, James Robinson, who later became a distinguished professor of physiology in New Zealand, 'started by cycling to Langdale against a northerly wind. We got there in two and a half days, the latter half of the distance over snowy roads.'[48] At each stop the food they consumed would be carefully weighed to ensure that they stuck to the diet. Elsie Widdowson wisely followed by car together with McCance's son, Colin, and (later Sir) Andrew Huxley, future winner of the Nobel Prize for Medicine and grandson of T.H. Huxley, 'Darwin's Bulldog'. For the next nine days the party stayed in a cottage called Robin Ghyll in Langdale, of distinctly Spartan character, which belonged to the celebrated historian G.M. Trevelyan, where they were subjected to a ruthless programme of diet and physical exertion. A 6 a.m. start was followed by thirty-six miles a day on foot.[49] Scafell Pike was ascended on more than one occasion together with Langdale Pikes, Borrowdale, the fearsome Hardknott and Wrynose Passes, Great Gable, the Old Man of Coniston and other similar obstacles. A glance at the map will demonstrate to the armchair traveller the degree of exertion required for these exercises. However, additional rigour was introduced in the form of rucksacks filled with bricks weighing 15–20kg. And of course the weather was far from welcoming. Calorific intake was measured each day and the conclusion was drawn from the exercise that the proposed diet would deliver a healthy population able to withstand the rigours of war provided that calcium carbonate (chalk) was added to wholemeal bread – as it has been ever since, despite the early opposition of some baking and consumer interests. This was necessary to offset the loss of calcium caused by the rationing of dairy products. These studies contributed to the work of Jack Drummond and John Boyd Orr when, during the Second World War, they advised the Minister of Food, Lord Woolton, on the provision of an adequate diet for the British population in the face of shortages of every kind. As a result of such work the average citizen was better fed during the war than before (or in many cases since), an achievement described by the American Public Health Association when presenting an award to Jack Drummond as 'one of the greatest demonstrations in public health administration that the world has ever seen'.[50] After the war Drummond continued to campaign for better nutrition and argued against the use of pesticides in farming, a campaign which, if successful, could have significantly altered for the better the eating habits and nutritional welfare of affluent western consumers. A recent author has argued that Drummond's untimely death would have suited the interests of food processors and agronomists. Even the KGB has been offered as a possible culprit and more than one person 'confessed' to his murder. There is virtually no evidence to support these theories, which in any case overlook the fact that Drummond's attitude towards business interests was sufficiently benign for him to accept a post as director of research for Boots Pure Drug Company.[51]

Andrew Huxley, having survived the ordeal to win his Nobel Prize and become Master of Trinity College, Cambridge, referred to the conclusions of the report which resulted from the exercise: 'In conclusion, we would draw attention to the value of experiments such as this in planning relief diets for starving populations in stricken areas'.[52] At the end of the war this proposition was put to the test when Elsie Widdowson travelled to Germany to supervise the diets of children at orphanages in Wuppertal, near Cologne. She concluded that malnourished children would thrive on a diet of wholemeal or white bread provided that it was fortified with calcium carbonate (chalk), and also made some perceptive observations on the effect of children's psychological states on their welfare. She noted that some children who were given extra food failed to put on weight as rapidly as those on the basic German ration. Further enquiry revealed that the failure of the children to thrive on their supplemented rations coincided with a change of housemother. The imposition upon them of an unkind and unpleasant woman in place of a kind and sympathetic one had had a damaging effect upon their ability to benefit from the extra food, this insight adding further to Elsie Widdowson's contribution to an understanding of the human condition.[53]

Their work continued after the war, Elsie Widdowson carrying out a study of the effects of poor nutrition in childhood which led her to conclude that, the earlier the malnutrition occurred, the longer and more pronounced would be its effects. Robert McCance's research continued in Cambridge as did his rigorous programme of exercise, where the instal-lation of a milometer on his beloved bicycle revealed that, between 1939 and 1969, he cycled 200,000 miles.

Human Metabolism

While McCance and Widdowson were revealing the nutritional content of foods, other scientists were investigating the processes by which that nutrition was conveyed to the human body via *metabolic pathways*. Some of these are *anabolic* pathways by which complex molecules are created through the use of energy, while *catabolic* reactions break down foodstuffs into simple molecules by the release of energy. One of the better known of these processes is the *Krebs Cycle,* which takes its name from Sir Hans Krebs (1900–81). Hans Krebs was born in Hildesheim, near Hanover in Germany, and educated at German universities before engaging in research at the University of Freiburg which led to important discoveries in the field of human metabolism. In 1933 he lost his post at Freiburg because of his Jewish ancestry[54] and went to work in Cambridge, England, at the invitation of Frederick Gowland Hopkins who, four years earlier, had won the Nobel Prize for Physiology for his work in connection with vitamins. After working at Cambridge, Krebs, who in 1939 became a British subject, went to Sheffield University and identified the process by which carbohydrates, proteins and fats are chemically converted into useable energy. The process is also known as the *citric acid cycle* and, together with other similar cycles,[55] demonstrated how the human body converted food into tissue and energy. For this discovery Krebs himself received the Nobel Prize for Physiology in 1953.

Sir Frederick Gowland Hopkins (1861–1947): born in Eastbourne and later educated at the City of London School, he had a scientific paper published in *The Entomologist* upon leaving school, aged only seventeen. After working for a short time as an insurance clerk he attended University College, London, gaining a BSc before going to Guy's Hospital as a medical student where he quickly distinguished himself, gaining a prize for chemistry and later working as a lecturer in physiology and toxicology. He then moved to Cambridge where he virtually created the discipline of biochemistry, eventually being appointed professor. In 1912, Hopkins published an article entitled 'Feeding Experiments Illustrating the Importance of Accessory Food factors in Normal Dietaries', and in the same year the word *vitamine* (thus spelt) was used by a Polish researcher called Casimir Funk to describe these substances, as yet unidentified, whose inclusion in the human diet were essential to good health. In 1929 Hopkins was awarded the Nobel Prize for Medicine in connection with his work in identifying the role of vitamins in the human diet. In 1925 he was knighted, became President of the Royal Society in 1930 and was awarded the Order of Merit in 1935. Chapter four discusses in more detail the diseases arising from vitamin deficiencies and the work of Hopkins and his colleagues in identifying the causes and cures.

Thus by the 1950s the science of nutrition was set upon firm foundations. It had come a long way since Hippocrates had correctly proposed a link between diet and energy while his mediator, Galen, had encouraged the belief that fruit was noxious, a theory that long promoted a mistaken over-confidence in the properties of meat as the basis of a healthy diet. Jonas Hanway's advocacy of vegetables owed at least as much to their cheapness and availability as to their nutritional qualities, and it was only towards the end of the eighteenth century that writers like Dr William Smith advocated the inclusion of vegetables and fruits in the novel concept of a balanced diet. Wise though this advice was, it was dependent upon observation and anecdote rather than upon any rigorous scientific understanding of the processes of digestion. This had to wait for Alexis St Martin to suffer his unfortunate shooting accident and for the ruthless Dr William Beaumont to observe, extract, analyse and evidently taste St Martin's gastric juices. In the twentieth century Frederick Gowland Hopkins and others identified the role of vitamins in the human diet while Robert McCance and Elsie Widdowson discovered and published the nutritional values of human foods. Others, like the refugee Hans Krebs, showed the processes by which they entered and nourished the human body. And thanks to such advances in understanding, British citizens, despite the privations of war, were better nourished in 1945 than they had ever been and perhaps better nourished than they would be in a more affluent future, a paradox examined in chapter seven.

2

The Staffs of Life

The Dolphin or Grand Junction Nuisance Proving that Several Thousand Families in Westminster and its Suburbs are Supplied with Water in a State Offensive to the Sight, Disgusting to the Imagination and Destructive to Health.

Title of a pamphlet published in London, 1827

Her face oblong, fair but wrinkled, her eyes small, yet black and pleasant, her nose a little hooked, her lips narrow and her teeth black (a defect the English seem subject to, from their too great use of sugar).

A German visitor's description of Queen Elizabeth I

The gentility commonly provide themselves sufficiently of wheat for their own tables whilst their household and poor neighbours in some shires are forced to content themselves with rye or barley.

William Harrison's account of the preference of Elizabethan gentry for white bread

I could speak in praise of the root, what a good and profitable thing it is and might be to a Commonwealth, could it be generally experienced.

Robert Boyle, informing the Royal Society of the virtues of the potato

It is not to be expected that milk should ever form a considerable part of the diet of labourers in the South of England.

Sir Frederic Eden, 1797

The British Diet, 1935

In 1935 the distinguished nutritionist John Boyd Orr, whose work has been referred to previously, carried out a study of the British diet and the way it had changed in the previous hundred years. He began by collecting information concerning the budgets of a sample of 2,640 families and divided them into six groups according to the average income per head for each family. He then calculated the proportion of the family's income spent on food for each group. The results were as follows, one shilling being the equivalent of five pence:[1]

Group no.	Income per head per week	Average food spend per head per week	Est. total no. in group
1	under 10 shillings	4 shillings	4.5 million
2	10 to 15 shillings	6 shillings	9 million
3	15 to 20 shillings	8 shillings	9 million
4	20 to 30 shillings	10 shillings	9 million
5	30 to 45 shillings	12 shillings	9 million
6	over 45 shillings	14 shillings	4.5 million
Average	30 shillings	9 shillings	45 million

Food expenditure thus accounted for about 30 per cent of household income whereas a century earlier it was estimated that it accounted for a little less than half, a sign of rising prosperity and of a fall in the prices of some foods.[2] Boyd Orr concluded from his study that the families in group six (and possibly group five) enjoyed food that met every dietary requirement of a healthy lifestyle: protein, fat, carbohydrate, minerals and vitamins, while those in the other groups were deficient in at least one respect. The 10 per cent of the population that fell in group one had diets that were deficient in every respect, a fact reflected earlier in the century by the social historian George Sturt (1863–1927), writing under the name George Bourne. His book *Change in the Village* described the ways of life of labouring families living near Farnham, Surrey, in the late nineteenth century, fifty years before Boyd Orr's study. The fare for a family of husband, wife and six children consisted of 'A gallon of potatoes a day, a gallon of bread a day and a gallon of flour once a week for puddings',[3] a diet notably lacking in green vegetables and hence in vitamins. Boyd Orr showed that consumption of bread and potatoes was uniform throughout all groups but as incomes rose, so did consumption of milk, eggs, fruit, vegetables, meat and fish. The differences in diets between the groups explained another of Boyd Orr's findings: that the prosperous middle-class scholars of Christ's Hospital School, founded by Edward VI for the poor and destitute, were on average 2.4in (5cm) taller than boys at council schools at age thirteen; and almost 4in taller than employed males at age seventeen.[4] This chapter will examine the background of some of the principal constituents of the diets that Boyd Orr examined in 1935 and which, according to his own calculations, accounted for about two-thirds of the energy intake of the British population: sugar, bread, potatoes and milk.[5] To these commodities, which remain staple elements of the British diet in the twenty-first century, is added the most essential item of all: water.

Water

The world is well supplied with water but very little of it is available for human consumption; 97 per cent is held by the world's oceans and, unless expensively treated, cannot be drunk. Much of the rest is in the icy wastes of Siberia and the poles, where few people live. Moreover, the abundance of water in populated areas is no guarantee of its availability. Bangladesh, served by 230 rivers, is one of the world's wettest places but inadequate water treatment and sewage facilities ensure that few of its inhabitants have access to clean, drinkable water. The charity *WaterAid* estimates that one-sixth of the world's population has to travel at least one kilometre each day to collect water from wells and springs where purity is often open to doubt. Our ancestors suffered similar anxieties. Until well into the nineteenth century water was, for many, a precious commodity. Once obtained it would be used and re-used for cooking, washing clothes or, occasionally, washing oneself. Once drunk it was gone for good.

Many street names in towns and cities still bear the names of the water supplies that were once the reason for their existence. Conduit Street and Lamb's Conduit Street in London and Hobson's Conduit in Cambridge all record the fact that they were once the sites of water supplies provided by philanthropic citizens. London's *Clerk's Well* has given its name to a district, Clerkenwell, and Sadler's Wells was a fashionable spa long before it was a theatre. In the thirteenth century Gilbert de Sandford allowed water to be taken by lead pipes from springs on his land at Mary le Bourne (Marylebone) to the Great Conduit in Cheapside, which remained a conspicuous feature of the City landscape until the nineteenth century. Pipes of elm and lead took the water to

the homes of wealthy citizens, while others either collected the water
themselves in buckets, or bought it from water carriers who carried it
on yokes in 'tankards' with specified capacities that were checked by the
City authorities.

By the reign of Elizabeth I, London's existing water supplies, inherited
from the mediaeval city, were proving to be barely adequate, so a series
of entrepreneurs applied their ingenuity to extracting water from the
Thames by mechanical means. In 1582 a Dutchman called Peter Morice
leased from the City the first arch of London Bridge for £25 10s a year
for 500 years. Within it he installed a waterwheel that pumped water to
premises in the City and it remained in use until 1822, when the demoli-
tion of the old London Bridge removed its arch. In 1594 Bevis Bulmer, a
mining engineer, built London's first water tower, 120ft high, close to the
present site of the Millennium Bridge. It was supplied by a horse-drawn
chain pump.

At this time the Thames was a relatively clean river. Sewage was disposed of in cesspools and other waste was, officially, collected in huge
heaps known as 'laystalls'. The contents of both were collected from time
to time and carted to farms in places like Moorfields to be burned or sold
as fertiliser. Only surreptitiously were the sewers and rivers, including
the Thames, polluted by human waste so the level of contamination was
relatively low until the great epidemics of the nineteenth century when
waste flowed freely into the rivers. However, the topography of London
and other cities was such that the major rivers, which naturally flowed
at the lowest points of cities, were of limited value as water sources; the
great majority of citizens lived at some distance from their banks and at
heights above the rivers and were therefore beyond the capacity of water-
driven pumps.

The earliest response to this problem came in the form of the New
River, built by Sir Hugh Myddleton between 1609 and 1613. It drew
water from Amwell, near Ware in the Chiltern Hills, to New River
Head, adjacent to Sadler's Wells, a fall of 18ft over a distance of about
forty miles as the New River winds its way south. Throughout its length
the New River is about 10ft wide and 4ft deep. The river bed was 'pud-
dled' by clay which was trampled into the bed to make it impervious to
water, and at intervals filters were installed to trap detritus like leaves and
rubbish. For much of its length it runs parallel to the valley of the River
Lee from which it also draws water. One of its principal supporters was
King James I who, in an uncharacteristically shrewd gesture for that
financially improvident monarch, invested £9,262 9s 6d in a half share

in the enterprise[6] – an investment which continued to pay a dividend to the Crown until 1956.

The terminus of the river, New River Head, was opened on 29 September 1613 when, in the presence of the Lord Mayor, the sluices were opened and the water began to flow via elm pipes to those citizens who could afford the five shillings (25p) connection fee and the six shillings and eightpence (33p) quarterly charge, one of the earliest customers being the father of the poet John Milton. The position of the terminus, 80ft above the Thames, enabled the company to distribute water by gravity without the need for costly pumping machinery. The water-carriers, who had originally regarded the river as a competitor, soon embraced it as a supplier, filling their tankards from its cistern and advertising it with the cry 'Fresh and fair New River water! None of your pipe sludge!'[7] The New River continued to enjoy a reputation for water of good quality, free of pollution, despite the fact that many citizens illegally used it to wash their clothes. It also escaped the great scandals of the nineteenth century when some water companies were rightly arraigned for causing cholera epidemics. The New River continues to supply London with water, feeding into the London Ring Main at Stoke Newington. The pattern of supplying towns by gravity from surrounding hills, which the New River had adopted, was followed by many smaller towns in subsequent years. Liverpool adopted it in the nineteenth century[8] along with Manchester, supplied from the Pennines, and Glasgow, whose water came from Loch Katrine. In 1836 George Sturt's little town of Farnham in Surrey saw the creation of the Farnham Water Company, whose indenture recorded that:

> Whereas the Inhabitants of the Town of Farnham are not at present well or conveniently supplied with soft water and whereas there are several springs of soft water on a hill above and on the northern side of the said town, the Lord Bishop of Winchester has kindly consented and agreed to grant twenty acres thereof for the purpose of supplying the Inhabitants of the said Town with such water.[9]

In the years that followed, other water companies sprang up in London and other cities, all of them financed by private enterprise, a process that gathered pace and urgency in the nineteenth century as many rural dwellers migrated to towns and cities and as waterborne diseases like cholera and typhoid spread rapidly amongst the densely packed population. In 1827 a campaigner called John Wright published a pamphlet whose title tells its readers all they need to know about its arguments: *The Dolphin or Grand Junction Nuisance Proving that Several Thousand Families in Westminster and its*

Suburbs are Supplied with Water in a State Offensive to the Sight, Disgusting to the Imagination and Destructive to Health. It was an attack on the quality of the water supplied by one company, the Grand Junction Company, which was itself an offshoot of the canal company of the same name, but its arguments could have been applied to most of the other water companies that were supplying London and other cities. The ones who drew their water from the Thames were especially guilty since, from 1815, householders had been permitted to dispose of the contents of their cesspools via the public sewers and underground rivers into the Thames itself. Since orthodox medical opinion held that epidemics were caused by foul-smelling air rather than polluted water, this did not bother the authorities. The complacency of the water companies was reflected by Charles Dickens in an article in *Household Words* in 1850 following a visit to the Grand Junction Company's premises at Kew. He observed that the company drew its water from the Thames which, being a tidal river, would carry the sewage of the City and Westminster to the company's intakes upstream. The engineer assured him that more problems of water pollution were caused by dirt entering cisterns within people's houses. A spokesman enlisted by the company, Dr Pearson, had assured a Royal Commission that 'The impregnating ingredients of the Thames are as perfectly harmless as any spring water of the purest kind in common life: indeed, there is probably not a spring, with the exception of Malvern, and one or two more, which are as pure as Thames water'.[10] It was not only the water companies who supplied foul water. London's first medical officer, (later Sir) John Simon, applauded the parish council of St Bride's, Fleet Street, for closing a well whose contents had become impregnated by 'products of animal decomposition' from the adjoining graveyard.

Not all engineers were as complacent as that of the Grand Junction Company and two in particular made decisive contributions to the quality and reliability of the water supply. In 1823 James Simpson (1799–1869) was appointed engineer to the Chelsea and Lambeth Water Companies. In 1828 he built for the Chelsea Company the world's first 'slow sand filter bed'. It consisted of layers of sand, seashells, gravel and bricks through which the water percolated before entering the company's reservoir. Virtually all the pollutants were trapped in the top inch of the sand layer, which was removed from time to time and replaced by fresh sand. It was realised at the time that the filter acted as a physical barrier to pollutants, but later scientists like Sir Edward Frankland (1825–99) made advances in chemistry and biology that revealed that the bacteria attracted to the bed made it a biological filter as well. Such filter beds are still in use and

Simpson made a further contribution to the cause of clean water when he persuaded the companies he served to remove their reservoirs to Seething Wells, near Kingston upon Thames, beyond the tidal limit at Teddington and thus untainted by Metropolitan sewage.

Simpson's greatest rival as a water engineer was Thomas Hawksley (1807-93). He was born near Nottingham and educated at the local grammar school before being articled to a local architect in 1822. In 1830 he undertook to construct new waterworks for the rapidly growing town, building a pumping station adjacent to the river at Trent Bridge where the water was naturally filtered through beds of sand and gravel; a similar process to that adopted by James Simpson two years earlier though on this occasion nature provided the filter. Towards the end of his life he claimed to have been involved in the construction of 150 water supply schemes throughout Great Britain and abroad, including places as diverse as Denmark, Sweden, Austria, Poland and Brazil.

Hawksley's most notable contribution to Britain's water supply network was made at Liverpool. In 1846, the corporation invited Hawksley to propose methods by which the water supply to the town could be improved. Hawksley recommended bringing water by gravitation from five reservoirs at Rivington, where the foothills of the Pennines merge into the lowlands of Lancashire, thirty miles from Liverpool, thus offering a good 'fall' for the water to the city on the Mersey. The extensive correspondence on Hawksley's 'Rivington Pike scheme' in the Liverpool City archives is an indication of the controversy it aroused. James Simpson advocated bringing water from Lake Bala in Wales and others favoured the drilling of more artesian wells. After much argument the celebrated railway engineer Robert Stephenson was called in to arbitrate upon the rival schemes and adjudicated in favour of Hawksley's proposals, which were completed in 1857. In acknowledgement of Simpson's invention of the sand filter bed, four acres of sand filters were built to ensure the purity of the supply and the system remains in use in the twenty-first century.

A greater disagreement between Hawksley and Simpson concerned the issue of 'constant supply'. Hawksley maintained that pressurised water supplies should be available continuously. Simpson replied that this would be wasteful and that the inferior valves and taps then available would guarantee leakage. Hawksley insisted that in Nottingham, where he had provided constant supply, manufacturers of plumbing supplies had responded by providing equipment of superior quality and that the valuable lead and copper artefacts, which were often stolen when supplies were turned off at night, were less likely to be stolen if the thieves knew that they were due for a soaking. Hawksley's arguments prevailed and constant supply became the norm. To Simpson, Hawksley and their colleagues we owe the fact that, by the end of the nineteenth century, most town and city dwellers were supplied with piped water but, before it could be drunk with safety, it also had to be protected from sewage-borne disease.

The End of Water-Borne Disease

In the 1850s the London doctor John Snow[11] had concluded that cholera was spread by polluted water. He had initially arrived at this conclusion by observing that people collecting water from a pump near his surgery in Broad Street (now Broadwick Street), Soho, contracted the disease whereas employees of the local brewery who quenched their thirst with its beer did not. Further studies of the incidence of cholera in South London confirmed it. Orthodox medical opinion clung for some years to the 'miasmatic' theory that cholera and other diseases could only be spread by foul air, though the final epidemic to strike London, in 1866, produced convincing evidence that it was the water of the East London Water Company, not the air of London, that was the underlying cause. In 1883 the German scientist Robert Koch (1843–1910) identified the cholera bacillus and demonstrated to the satisfaction of all but a few sceptics that it was carried in water. In 1892 cholera stuck Hamburg, causing great anxiety in Britain since cholera epidemics had always arrived from the continental seaports with which Britain traded. 8,605 people died in a city one-seventh the size of London, so if comparable mortality had occurred in Britain the epidemic would have been of unprecedented ferocity. So great was the alarm in Britain as the deaths mounted that the *Illustrated London News* devoted three successive issues to the epidemic which was daily expected to reach the capital.[12] There was no epidemic in Britain because in the latter part of the nineteenth century engineers like Sir Joseph Bazalgette (1819–91) had created sewerage systems for cities like London that intercepted sewage and conducted it to treatment works, where it presented no threat to the quality of the drinking water. About 135 deaths occurred from a 'disease reputed to be of the nature of cholera' which spread across sixty-four towns, with seventeen fatalities occurring in London, mostly amongst people returning from abroad.

Sir Joseph Bazalgette (1819–91) was appointed chief engineer to the Metropolitan Board of Works, London's first metropolitan government, on its creation in 1856 and held the job until the board was replaced by the London County Council in 1889. Prior to his appointment London's sewage was discharged into the Thames which thus became an open sewer and a source from which much of London's drinking water was vulnerable to pollution, cholera alone accounting for some 40,000 deaths in London in four great epidemics. Bazalgette drew up a plan for intercepting sewers which, running parallel to the Thames, intercepted waste and conducted it to treatment works at Barking, on the north bank and Crossness on the south. His plans were delayed for two years by political wrangling over design and cost but The Great Stink of 1858, when the stench from the Thames caused discomfort and anxiety to MPs at Westminster, resolved the matter and Bazalgette's system was completed by 1875. It remains in use today, as do other systems he designed for communities like Norwich and Cambridge. An account of Bazalgette's life and work is to be found in Stephen Halliday, *The Great Stink of London: Sir Joseph Bazalgette and the Cleansing of the Victorian Metropolis*, Sutton, 2001.

In 1897 on the occasion of Queen Victoria's Diamond Jubilee, a special edition of the journal *Public Health*, which recorded the activities and views of Public Health Inspectors and Medical Officers of Health, observed that, 'Of all the achievements of the Victorian era history will find none worthier of record than the efforts made to ameliorate the lives of the poor, to curb the ravages of disease and to secure for all pure air, food and water'.[13] This was claiming too much. By 1897 the water supplies of the great majority of British towns were protected from contamination by sewage and thus from waterborne disease, but even at that date many poorer households were not connected to a regular water supply, especially in rural areas. It would require the establishment of public bodies like the Metropolitan Water Board (1902) to ensure a regular, constant supply to poorer citizens, but the days of the great scourges of water-borne epidemics like cholera, typhoid and dysentery were in the past.

Sugar

Prominent amongst Boyd Orr's categories of foods whose price had fallen absolutely, as well as in real terms, was sugar. In 1835 the average British citizen consumed 20lb of sugar each year (in all forms, including confectionery) at a cost of sixpence a pound at a time when a bricklayer or other skilled workman would earn about 4s a day. By 1934 consumption had risen to 94lb a year, the price had fallen to threepence a pound and wages had increased about forty-fold.[14] A product which, even in the nineteenth century, had been a mark of some affluence amongst working families had become something between a sign of prosperity and a necessity, albeit one whose nutritional value was at least doubtful.

The great majority of Europeans managed perfectly well without sugar until well into the sixteenth century. Sugar cane was cultivated in India before the time of Christ and made its way to the Middle East where it was found by crusaders in the early thirteenth century and brought to Europe. Sugar cane needs a tropical climate to thrive and the product remained an exotic luxury in Europe until the sixteenth century when Christopher Columbus introduced the product to America and the Portuguese began to cultivate it in Brazil. In the following century it was appearing on the islands in the Caribbean.

It appears that human taste buds are naturally susceptible to seduction by sugar since it fulfils no important nutritional purpose. Essential sugars can be synthesised by humans from starch, leaving sugar to fill us with kilocalories, moderate the taste of unpleasant substances like medicines and damage our teeth. One writer has described sugar cane and sugar beet as 'probably the two most wasteful and unnecessary crops grown'.[15] It was becoming established in England by the late sixteenth century, though only amongst the wealthiest citizens, by which time its seductive power had already been noticed by Thomas Cogan, physician and one of the first masters of Manchester Grammar School. In his authoritative *Haven of Health* he commented that 'Sugar agreeth with all ages and all complexions'.[16] In 1587 William Harrison recorded that sugar cost 2s 6d (12½ pence) a pound and was a luxury well beyond the means of all but the most wealthy.[17] The German visitor Paul Hentzner visited Queen Elizabeth I's court at Greenwich ten years later and described the queen thus: 'Her face oblong, fair but wrinkled, her eyes small, yet black and pleasant, her nose a little hooked, her lips narrow and her teeth black (a defect the English seem subject to, from their too great use of sugar).'[18] At this time dental decay was largely the preserve of the upper classes and teeth blackened by sugar was a sign of affluence. These conditions were rarely encountered amongst poorer citizens.

In the centuries that followed, sugar's relentless progress through the diets of the population was not without controversy. Francis Bacon (1561–1626) complained that sugar was supplanting honey as a sweetener and that 'Sugar hath put down the use of honey insomuch that we have lost those observations and preparations of honey which the ancients had when it was more in price'.[19] Some writers drew attention to the fact that it appeared to contribute to tooth decay, including the distinguished physician Thomas Willis (1621–75), friend of Robert Boyle, Christopher Wren and John Locke, who also wrote of sugar: 'I do esteem the Invention and immoderate Use of it in this present Age to have contributed very much to the vast increase of the Scurvy'. This was an incorrect diagnosis but it prompted a riposte from Frederick Slare (1646/7–1727). Slare, German by birth, a distinguished scientist in his own right and early Fellow of the Royal Society, was a contemporary of Isaac Newton whose library contained a copy of Slare's essay, *A Vindication of Sugars against the Charge of Doctor Willis*.[20] Some of his arguments in favour of sugar make strange reading today. Thus he observed that 'Children who do love Sugar are often upbraided for spoiling their Teeth by the Use of it', whereas Slare claimed to have rubbed his gums and teeth with it for a week, 'and made my Gums better and Teeth whiter'. The Duke of Beaufort who, according to Slare, ate a pound of sugar a day, died at the age of sixty-nine with fine teeth and his internal organs intact, while Slare's grandfather, who was devoted to the product, lived to 100 and had supposedly grown a fresh set of teeth at the age of eighty. These doubtful examples of health and fitness led Slare to refer to sugar's role in preserving fruit as evidence of its 'healthy and salubrious Quality', claiming that:

> That which preserves Apples and Plumbs
> Will also preserve Liver and Lungs.

Slare added that, in the opinion of the physician to the fleet, the prevalence of consumption amongst the inhabitants of Lisbon 'proceedeth from some Venereal Cause, for he thought they rather did eat too little sugar'. The logic behind this claim is elusive but did not deter Slare from making further claims that the product could be used 'to cure sore Eyes, to preserve the Gums, or cure them when sore or Scorbutic' (the last being a reference to scurvy).[21] Slare was not alone in promoting the virtues of sugar. One of the earliest advocates of a vegetarian diet, Thomas Tryon (1934–1703), applauded the product on the grounds that it had enhanced the popularity of such nourishing vegetarian dishes as apricots, gooseberries and plums as well as beverages like tea, coffee and cocoa, whose rise in consumption went side by side with that of sugar.[22]

The growth in the popularity of sugar in the European diet is inescapably linked with the development of the slave economies of the Caribbean and South America. The first large sugar cane plantation was established in Barbados in about 1650 and the first labourers were not slaves but prisoners of the English Civil War, together with some criminals who were sent by Oliver Cromwell's government as indentured servants to the plantation owners.[23] However, the slaves quickly followed. In 1629 twenty-nine Africans were recorded on the island but a census in 1683 recorded a population of 46,602 negro slaves against a free population of 17,187, together with 2,381 indentured servants.[24] In 1663 7,400 tons of sugar was imported to Great Britain from the Caribbean. By 1775 this had grown to over 90,000 tons and the growth in supply was mirrored by a fall in price.[25] By the time that Francis Bacon made his complaint about the growing popularity of sugar its price had fallen from the 2s 6d/lb recorded by Harrison in 1587 to 1s 6d, and by 1700 to 6d, a price at which it settled for over a century. This represented a fall of 80 per cent since Harrison's time[26] and the taste for sugar had spread to all classes.

By this time it was understood that sugar could be made from an alternative crop, sugar beet, that would grow in Europe, but given the cheapness of Caribbean sugar there was no motive for European farmers to cultivate it. A French botanist, Olivier de Serres, had shown as early as 1590 that it was possible to extract sucrose from beet but the process remained a scientific curiosity rather than an economical prospect until the early nineteenth century. The Prussian scientist Franz Achard, who had won the esteem of King Frederick William II by demonstrating how tobacco and sugar beet could be cultivated in Prussia, opened a sugar beet factory in Silesia in 1801, but a greater impetus to the cultivation of sugar beet was provided by the Royal Navy. Following the battle of Trafalgar in 1805 the Royal Navy blockaded French ports, preventing the importation from the Caribbean of the sugar that had become an increasingly important constituent of the European diet. Napoleon therefore encouraged the use of beet as an alternative source of sugar and the challenge was met by Benjamin Delessert, descendant of a French Protestant family who spent much of his life in England (where he died in 1847). He developed a process by which sucrose could be extracted economically from beet and was presented with the award of the Legion d'Honneur by Napoleon in 1812. By the end of the Napoleonic Wars over 300 beet sugar mills were in use in Europe, providing a further source of the increasingly popular crop.

As human beings have become more affluent their consumption of sugar has increased, and not only in western societies. A product that was once regarded as a luxury for the few who could afford it has now become seen as a menace to human health. It can cause dental decay, obesity and heart disease and our weakness for sweeteners has been reflected in the amount we consume not only in confectionery, but also in staple items of diet. Thus between 1978 and 2007 the amount of sugar in a can of tomato soup more than doubled and increases were reported in breakfast cereals, bread (including wholemeal bread) and prepared meals. More surprisingly, the sugar content of 'natural foods' like bananas, pears and even carrots has risen as supermarket buyers have chosen to purchase sweeter varieties to reflect the growing appetite of their customers for sweeter products.[27] In the twenty-first century the average British citizen consumes about 105 grams of 'neat' sugar each week, in addition to the quantities consumed in other foodstuffs like cereals, confectionery, cakes and biscuits.[28] Moreover, the pattern of consumption varies, the quantities eaten increasing as one moves north, and the peak levels being reached in Scotland where tooth decay is at its worst.

Bread

The craft of the baker is probably as old as urban dwelling, if not older. In the book of Genesis, Pharaoh is recorded as having hanged his baker for some nameless offence, the unfortunate man's fate having been the subject of one of Joseph's early works in the interpretation of dreams, while oxen-drawn millstones may be seen depicted in Egyptian stonework. In the second century Christian bakers in Rome were accorded the status of freedmen; other trades were mostly conducted by slaves and the College of Bakers (*Collegium Pistorum*) was entitled to send a representative to the Senate. The ruins of Pompeii include an hour-glass shaped milling mechanism to be turned by slaves or animals and the development of early waterwheel technology by the Romans owes much to the need to mill wheat.[29] The Worshipful Company of Bakers is one of London's oldest livery companies, having paid a gold mark to the royal exchequer from 1155. About 150 years after this date the bakers split into two factions which mirrored controversies about the nutritional qualities of bread that continued into the twentieth century. The bakers of brown bread formed their own separate guild, producing a coarser (but more nutritious) bread from rye, barley or from buckwheat (now sometimes used in pancakes but not related to wheat at all). The bakers of white bread produced loaves from more refined wheat flour which, though containing fewer nutrients, was even at that date preferred by those who could afford it. The Brown-Bakers maintained their independence until 1645 when declining trade obliged them to reunite with the White-Bakers into the Worshipful

Company of Bakers which, in the twenty-first century, takes its place in
the Lord Mayor's procession and in the government of the City of London.
The company was given a role in controlling entry to the profession and
in ensuring that quality standards were enforced upon its members, a particular concern being the practice of adding sand to wheat in order to
increase the weight of the loaf.

The significance of bread in the English diet may be deduced from the
fact that it shares with ale the distinction of being the subject of one of
the first statutes in English law that was designed to set standards of quality, quantity and price. This was the *Assize of Bread and Ale* which passed
into law in 1266 in the reign of Henry III. It laid down the relationship
between the price of wheat and the 'farthing loaf', a farthing being the
lowest unit of currency and a quarter of an old (pre-decimal) penny. The
calculation was an elaborate one and reflects the importance of the loaf
in the lives of citizens. Shortly after Michaelmas each year, magistrates
would determine the price of corn in the locality, which could vary enor-
mously from place to place and from year to year.[30] In London this task
would be performed by 'four discreet men chosen and sworn thereunto'
who would purchase samples from markets at Cheapside, Billingsgate and
Queenhithe.[31] The price of the farthing loaf would then be set by the
magistrates (or in London's case the Mayor and City Corporation). As the
price of wheat rose so the farthing loaf diminished and each baker was
required to 'seal' the loaves he baked with his own distinctive trademark
so that the authorities could trace underweight or inferior bread to its
source and, where this occurred, impose punishments involving fines, the
pillory, gaol or suspension from the trade. Nine different kinds of bread
were identified, ranging from the superior 'Ranger Bread', made from
white sieved flour, to the cheaper 'Bread of Common Wheat', which
appears to have been less refined, to have contained more roughage and,
at half the price, was probably healthier. Each type of bread was regulated in its own way and each baker was told which type of bread he was
allowed to bake.[32]

Bailiffs or 'ale-conners' were appointed by manorial courts to check the
quality of both bread and ale, this task being carried out at least monthly
in the City and at least every quarter elsewhere. In London they were
appointed by the mayor and the City Corporation, a role recorded in the
Liber Albus ('White Book') compiled by the Clerk to the Corporation,
John Carpenter, in 1419 at the behest of Richard Whittington as he served
his third and last term as Mayor of London. Bread from Southwark and
other places outside the City could not be sold within the City walls

since the City Corporation had no jurisdiction over its quality. This could be regarded as a means of protecting the interests of local bakers and this usage was certainly recorded by William Harrison in his *Description of England*, written in 1587, when he observed that magistrates used the *Assize* to protect their own community's bakers from others who might offer bread of superior quality.[33] The assize remained on the statute book until 1815.

> **Richard Whittington (*c.*1359–1423)** was, in fact as well as legend, Mayor of London three times, in 1397, 1406 and 1419 (the title Lord Mayor did not come into use until the sixteenth century). The connection with the cat is more elusive despite the fact that early portraits commonly include one, as did an early statue at Newgate Prison which was substantially rebuilt from the proceeds of his will. He probably came from the hamlet of Pauntley, Gloucestershire, and, from modest beginnings, became a very wealthy mercer (cloth merchant). He advanced substantial loans to Henry IV and Henry V and so earned the confidence of the latter that Henry entrusted him with funds to rebuild Westminster Abbey and decreed that no building was to be demolished in the city without the authority of Whittington and two other prominent citizens. He paid from his own pocket for improvements to the city's sewerage and water supply and, besides the rebuilding of Newgate, his will provided for repairs to St Bartholomew's Hospital, the restoration and enlargement of the Guildhall and a hospital for 'thirteen poor men' which, after vicissitudes at the hands of Henry VIII, moved first to Highgate Hill (a place imperishably if improbably associated with the legend) and later to East Grinstead in Surrey in 1970, where dwellings for forty-five people are still maintained by the Mercers Company.

In the centuries that followed, the loaf of bread became a kind of totem of English life which reflected the state of the economy and, particularly, the condition of the poor: a substitute for the Retail Prices Index of a more sophisticated age. During the later stages of the reign of Elizabeth I, as the ageing queen did battle with her Parliaments over the raising of taxes, an indignant Member of Parliament listened as a list of proposed patents and monopolies was read out. A contemporary recorded the exchange that followed:

> Mr Hakewill of Lincoln's Inn stood up and asked thus: 'Is not Bread there?' 'Bread', quoth one. 'Bread', quoth another … 'This voice seems strange', quoth a third. 'No,' quoth Mr Hakewill, 'if order be not taken for these, Bread will be there before the next Parliament'.[34]

Until the sixteenth century villages would frequently have communal ovens which were administered by the Lord of the Manor. Those who attempted to bake their own bread in their own ovens could be fined but this system broke down with the invention of small domestic ovens, patents for three such devices being lodged in the early seventeenth century. As ovens became more widespread amongst prosperous households so there developed a taste for 'biskets', a recipe for 'bisket bread' featuring in a book of 1598. 'Biskets' were originally viewed as an effective method of preserving the product and were adopted on military campaigns and long sea voyages, but by the early seventeenth century sweetened biscuits were being consumed as delicacies.[35]

At this time there became evident a preference for white bread which for four centuries would bedevil the efforts of nutritionists to improve the British diet. The *Description of England* penned by William Harrison (1534–93) explained that 'the gentility commonly provide themselves sufficiently of wheat for their own tables whilst their household and poor neighbours in some shires are forced to content themselves with rye or barley'. Harrison went on to explain that 'The next sort is named brown bread, of which we have two sorts, one baked up as it cometh from the mill so that neither the bran nor the flour are in any way diminished ... this putteth it in the second place of nourishment'.[36] His contemporary Thomas Cogan was more emphatic and adduced medical reasons for preferring white bread, advising his readers: 'It followeth that bread to be best which is made of pure flour of good wheat ... Brown bread, made of the coarsest of wheat flour, having in it much bran, filleth the belly with excrements and shortly descendeth from the stomach'.[37] This preference for bread made from refined, white flour was to remain a characteristic of English households and survives in many quarters in the twenty-first century. In the eighteenth century Jonas Hanway (1712–86), who was rarely short of an opinion on anything, especially food, recorded that white bread was being replaced by other varieties, commenting: 'White bread is at present *out of fashion* [Hanway's italics] with great numbers of the superior ranks, and every kind of invention is introduced, by some bakers, to please customers and amuse them'. This tendency aroused Hanway's disapproval. There followed a discussion of the merits for children of puddings (advocated by *puddinists*) and bread (promoted by *anti-puddinists*), the outcome of which was: 'victory decided for bread', and he added a warning that 'half the children who die in England have a lump of indigested [sic] flour-pudding in their bodies: this is so much unfermented bread'.[38] If Hanway was correct in his observations (a rare event) then the disdain for white bread did not last long.

Later in the century the wheaten loaf was the central feature of the much criticised *Speenhamland System* of poor relief, which was prompted by the disastrously poor harvest of 1795. The magistrates of Speenhamland on the outskirts of Newbury, Berkshire, decreed in 1795 that the wages of the industrious poor would be topped up from the rates in relation to the price of a gallon loaf. The gallon loaf weighed almost four kilos and when this cost 1s (5p) then a working man was guaranteed a weekly wage of 3s for himself and his wife and a further 1s 6d for each child. This humane measure did nothing to encourage employers such as farmers to pay their workers a living wage, especially since the employers and other landowners paid the rates that subsidised the wages. The system, nevertheless, was widely adopted and remained in use until replaced by the workhouses of the Victorian era following the Poor Law Amendment Act of 1834. In the meantime, as noted in pages which follow, it had some impact upon the cultivation of a still unfamiliar product, the humble potato.

White or Brown

On several occasions during the second half of the eighteenth century, at times of wheat shortages caused by war or by poor harvests, Parliament passed laws authorising the production of 'Standard Bread', stamped with the letter 'S', containing, rye, barley, oats and more bran than the standard wheat loaf. It cost one (old) penny a loaf less than the wheat loaf but was never a success, being viewed as a mark of poverty. This obstinate preference, even amongst the poorest classes, for white bread made from refined wheaten flour, was to trouble nutritionists for centuries. It had been misguidedly endorsed by no less an authority than Adam Smith who in his *Wealth of Nations* remarked of his fellow Scotsmen that 'The common people of Scotland, who are fed with oatmeal [bread] are in general neither so strong nor so handsome as the same rank of people in England who are fed with wheaten bread'.[39] The misguided preference for white bread also helped to account for the adulteration of the product by the addition of harmful chemicals which imparted whiteness along with toxicity. Chief amongst these was alum, which was the subject of correspondence in *The Lancet* from the early days of that celebrated medical journal, founded in 1823. In 1829 a correspondent signing himself *Panis* argued that heavy fines should be imposed both on bakers who used alum and on chemists who supplied it.[40] This attracted a good deal of support in the correspondence that followed, though one writer placed the blame on 'the public whose foolish taste it is to prefer the bread that is whitest'.[41] The controversy rumbled on for decades and reached a climax in 1857 with a letter from the redoubtable Dr John Snow, who is more often associated with the discovery that cholera is a water-borne infection, but who had also turned his extraordinary powers of observation on to the subject of rickets.

> **Dr John Snow (1813–58)** was born in York and apprenticed to a surgeon in Newcastle. He became both a vegetarian and a total abstainer from alcohol while a student – unusual even in those more abstemious days. He was one of the first to use chloroform as an anaesthetic, administering it to Queen Victoria for the birth of Prince Leopold in 1853 and thereby putting to flight the clergymen and doctors who argued that the reduction of pain in childbirth was contrary to scripture (being woman's punishment for Eve's misbehaviour with the apple). He is best remembered for his observation that citizens who used a pump near his surgery in Broad Street (now Broadwick Street), Soho, contracted cholera whereas employees of the nearby brewery who drank only its beer were free of the disease. This led to his seminal studies of the cholera epidemics which killed almost forty thousand Londoners in the mid-nineteenth century but which was believed by orthodox practitioners to be caused by foul air rather than polluted water. The significance of his studies was recognised only after his early death at the age of forty-five. The site of the pump which prompted his observations is marked by a granite kerbstone, adjacent to a public house which bears the name and picture of the teetotal doctor.

In 1857, the year before his death, John Snow wrote a letter to the *The Lancet* which was headlined 'The Adulteration of Bread as a Cause of Rickets'. Snow had come to practise medicine in London in 1839 and had observed that rickets, a disease now known to be associated with a shortage of vitamin D and calcium in the diet, was more common in London and the south than in the north of England where he had practised in his early days.[42] He further observed that rickets was more common amongst wealthy families: 'I noticed that the most healthy-looking and best nourished children often suffered most from curvature of the bones of the legs, owing to their greater weight'. These were the children of families who purchased 'high-priced bread sold in the fashionable areas to the West of Regent Street' (i.e. Mayfair) where expensive white bread was more commonly eaten than it was in the poorer areas of London. And finally he recorded that, having analysed samples of flour purchased from millers and other samples from bakers, he had discovered that bakers' flour *always* contained alum to make their bread white whereas millers' flour *never* contained it. Since families in the north of England normally baked their own bread, whereas those in London and the south purchased it from bakers, this would, Snow suggested, explain why northern bread was more nutritious than southern and further explain the prevalence of rickets in London and the south. Snow was much more familiar than most of his fellow practitioners would have been with contemporary science and quoted Justus von Liebig in support of his views: 'Liebig has ascertained that alum decomposes the phosphate of lime of wheat', and that hence the addition of alum to bread would reduce its ability to contribute to the development of healthy bones. Moreover, it 'may perhaps explain the indigestibility of the London bakers' bread which strikes all foreigners'.

The scientific reasoning behind Snow's arguments was unsound since at this stage the existence of vitamins and their role in promoting human health was unknown, but he was correct in identifying the preference for whiteness as a quality in bread as harmful to the diet. This battle was to be joined by many others in the nineteenth and twentieth centuries. One of them was the Scottish economist and journalist John Ramsay McCulloch (1789–1864), a severe exponent of the 'classical' theory of economics in the tradition of Adam Smith which maintained that free trade and fierce competition would bring the greatest prosperity to all. In his *Statistical Account of the British Empire*, published in 1837, he expounded a strong and at times chauvinistic account of the merits of free trade as exemplified by Britain and its colonies and triumphantly cited the decline in the use of rye to make bread, in favour of wheat, as evidence of the prosperity of those who conformed to the British government's *laissez-faire* economic policies.[43] The benighted continentals, behind their protective tariff walls, were compelled to eat more rye bread and it was to be another century and a half before this product (condescendingly known as 'black bread') was to become a popular and premium-priced product amongst the English middle classes.

It would take two world wars to shake the British from their addiction to white bread. In 1911 Sir Oswald Moseley (1874–1928), father of the later Fascist leader, tried to promote the wholemeal loaf as a means of mitigating the nutritional deficiencies which had been revealed in volunteers for service in the Boer War.[44] He gained the support of the *Daily Mail* for his cause and also that of Hovis, who re-launched *Smith's Old Patent Germ Bread*, a product originating in the 1880s, but it failed to arouse the enthusiasm of the public and it was soon withdrawn. During the

First World War, as Britain became dependent for its food upon Atlantic convoys threatened by German U-boats, the supplies of wheat diminished and millers were obliged to increase the extraction rate of their flour from 70 per cent to 76 per cent and then to 85 per cent,[45] thereby including fibres ('roughage') which would have been removed when supplies were more abundant in peacetime. As a temporary measure, sufferers from the inflammatory bowel disease colitis were allowed to obtain low extraction white flour on a doctor's prescription, but as events unfolded it became clear that the consumption of 'dark bread' had no effect on the disease and the concession was withdrawn, amongst much protest.

Nevertheless, the end of the war marked a swift return to the white bread favoured by the populace, a pattern followed also in the United States. In 1921 the Ward Baking Company launched a nutritious brown bread with the encouragement of Harvey Washington Wiley, whose pioneering work within the US Department of Agriculture in identifying harmful additives is noted elsewhere.[46] Within four years the product was withdrawn, a financial failure. In 1936 a League of Nations Report noted that 'White Flour in the Process of Milling is deprived of important nutritive elements. Its use should be decreased'.[47] So, as the Second World War began, the British government proposed a compromise whereby two types of loaf would be made available. Bread made with low extraction flour, in which about 30 per cent of the grain would be discarded (along with many nutrients), would be fortified by the addition of calcium carbonate (chalk) and vitamin B1. This caused alarm: 'from many directions, including members of the medical profession, came accounts of the harmful effects that had already been caused'. Reports of arterio-seclerosis and high blood pressure were particularly prominent. In reality, 'the truth was that, owing to supply difficulties, the calcium carbonate had not then been added to the flour'.[48]

The alternative 'National Wheatmeal' or 'British Loaf' would discard only about 15 per cent of the grain, thus including much of the bran and nutrient content in the resulting loaf and requiring no fortification. The dark 'National Wheatmeal' loaf, though cheaper, failed to earn the confidence of the British public and accounted for no more than 5 per cent of total sales. Fortunately, Hitler came to the rescue. In the spring of 1942 losses of shipping to U-boat attacks were such that a serious shortage of grain occurred, so the Ministry of Food ordered that the extraction rate be raised to an unprecedented 85 per cent, thus effectively imposing the 'British Loaf' on a reluctant public. This had a beneficial effect on the nation's health and upon medical and scientific opinion, which 'deduced from this wartime experience that long-extraction flours, and bran particularly, had been blamed in the past for much that was not in fact attributable to them'.[49] Neither the millers nor the public were so easily persuaded. A post-war conference was followed by a White Paper in November 1945 in which the millers successfully argued that the extraction rate be gradually reduced to 70 per cent, though they did agree to the enrichment of the white bread that resulted with calcium and vitamin B. Bread remains a staple, though slowly declining, element of the British diet, approximately 720g being consumed by each of us each week,[50] though nutritionists may take comfort from the fact that the British aversion to wholemeal bread is in decline.

The Potato

The potato which, according to Boyd Orr's calculations, accounted for a greater proportion of the British diet than any other single element in the 1930s, was a comparatively late addition to the European diet. As observed in chapter three,[51] one of the earliest forms of food preservation involved the creation of *Chuno*, made from potatoes by natives of the high Andes where the potato tuber originated, and this was in use long before the advent of Europeans. Representations of potatoes on South American pottery may be found as early as 200 AD. It appears to have arrived in Spain in about 1570 though the Spaniards long regarded it as fit only for native South Americans. The introduction of the potato to England is traditionally associated with Sir Walter Raleigh, but the connection is an elusive one and may have involved the even more redoubtable Sir Francis Drake. Drake himself certainly knew of the potato because during his voyage round the world he put into port in Chile on 28 November 1577 and recorded that 'the people came down to us to the waterside with shew of great curtesie to bring to us potatoes, rootes and two very fat sheepe'.[52] The potato is first recorded in England in 1596 when John Gerard, a member of the company of Barber-Surgeons and gardener to Elizabeth I's minister Lord Burghley, included the potato in a catalogue of plants in his garden at Holborn on the present site of the north end of Fetter Lane.

In the following century the President of the Royal Society, Sir Robert Southwell, informed the august body that 'his grandfather brought potatoes into Ireland, who had them from Sir Walter Raleigh after his return from Virginia'. Raleigh in fact never visited Virginia, though he did finance a rather unsuccessful attempt to found a colony there. Gerard's Holborn catalogue referred to the plant as 'Potatoes of America or Virginia' and implied that they had been brought to England by Francis Drake when Drake brought back to England some English settlers who had tried and failed to establish a colony in Virginia (which had been financed by Sir Walter Raleigh). This is the closest one can come to linking the potato with Raleigh. The Germans credited Drake with bringing the potato to Europe and erected a statue in the town of Offenburg, Baden-Wurttemburg, dedicated to 'Sir Francis Drake, who spread the use of the potato in Europe, A.D. 1580'. The statue was removed by the Nazis.

In its early days the potato was regarded in England as a luxury product to be served to princes. In 1590 there is a record of 2lb of potatoes being purchased for Queen Elizabeth I at a cost of 2s 6d/lb. By 1607, when the Merchant Taylors' Company gave a feast for King James I, the price had fallen to 10d/lb for 60lb of potatoes, but the price was still well beyond all but the wealthiest classes at a time when a skilled worker like a carpenter would earn about a shilling a day, and it long retained the reputation of being costly to cultivate and expensive to buy.[53] In 1626 in his work *Sylva Sylvarum*, Francis Bacon recommended the new vegetable as a constituent of 'nourishing meals' and in 1662 Henry Oldenburg (c.1615–1677), the first Secretary of the Royal Society, set up a committee of the society to examine the potential use of the potato as a remedy against famine. The committee's members included the celebrated scientist Robert Boyle (1627–91) who informed his fellows, 'I could speak in praise of the root, what a good and profitable thing it is and might be to a Commonwealth, could it be generally experienced',[54] but despite such an authoritative endorsement and the examples set by monarchs, the new vegetable was slow to gain acceptance.

This was partly because of the 'Open Fields' system of agriculture, which continued to prevail in much of Britain into the nineteenth century. By this ancient arrangement a community's agricultural land would be divided normally into three fields within which each farmer would have 'strips' of land, usually a furlong in length, scattered amongst those of his neighbours. This was designed to ensure that the richer and poorer soils were more or less equally shared between the tenants. Two of the three fields would be cultivated each year and the third left fallow. The system encouraged a conservative approach to cultivation since there was a natural tendency for a farmer to cultivate the same familiar crops from year to year and to look with some unease upon the introduction of new, untried crops to strips adjacent to his own. At Deddington, Oxfordshire, potatoes were first grown on the open field fallow in 1809, and at Laxton, Nottinghamshire, where the system still survives, potatoes were not introduced until 1904. It is no coincidence that the first county in which the cultivation of potatoes was firmly established was Lancashire, where smallholdings had long prevailed over the open fields, and where the first potato market was established, in Wigan, in 1680.

By the eighteenth century in England the potato was coming to be more widely endorsed as a staple food, though still largely confined to the north of England. In 1724 Richard Bradley, professor of botany at Cambridge, wrote that 'potatoes and Jerusalem artichokes are roots of less note than any I have yet mentioned', but four years later in his *Botanical Dictionary*[55] he recorded that 'it is a root of great use, serving very well in place of bread in some countries'. By the end of the century they were available in London at less than a halfpenny a pound, though in southern rural areas they were still regarded as a luxury. Thus in 1770, when the mother of Jane Austen advised a tenant at Steventon, Hampshire, to cultivate them, she received the alarmed response: 'No, no, they are all very well for you gentry but they must be terribly costly to rear'.[56] East Anglia, with its rich fenland fields, was slow to adopt potatoes as a crop, a fact which Arthur Young, in his *Farmer's Tour Through the East of England* in 1771 attributed to the fact that 'the common objection to cultivating them in large quantities is the want of a market ... the object in cultivating potatoes is not Covent Garden but the food of cattle'.[57] Yet within twenty-five years of Young's judgment, Sir Frederic Eden, in his book on *The State of the Poor,* was writing that 'the very general use which is made of Potatoes in these Kingdoms as food for man is convincing proof that the prejudices of a nation with regard to diet, however deeply rooted, are by no means unconquerable'.[58] In *Wealth of Nations,* Adam Smith attributed much of the vegetable's popularity to the fact that the price of potatoes had fallen by half in the previous thirty years, but added his own endorsement to the product. Writing of 'porters, coalheavers and prostitutes', he observed of them that 'the strongest men and the most beautiful women perhaps in the British dominions are said to be the greater part of them from the lowest rank of people in Ireland, who are generally fed with this root. No food can afford a more decisive proof of its nourishing quality, or of its being peculiarly suitable to the health of the human constitution'.[59] He went on to explain that the nutritional qualities of potatoes were such that, if pasture and corn fields were devoted instead to the cultivation of the humble root, population would increase, profits would rise and economic growth would follow. Praise indeed from such a source!

By 1775 about 50,000 acres were devoted to the cultivation of potatoes, nearly all in the north of England. Twenty years later this acreage had doubled, 1795 proving to be a significant year for several reasons. As noted above,[60] the harvest of that year was particularly poor and followed several disappointing ones which began in 1792, a situation made worse by the fact that the Revolutionary Wars with France made it harder to import grain from Europe and elsewhere. The Board of Agriculture, faced with a starving and impoverished population, produced a report which gave encouragement and guidance on the cultivation of potatoes but had to face the prejudice that the product was fit only for animal food. Thomas Ruggles (*c.*1737–1813), who wrote extensively on the Poor Law, reported that 'the poor will not eat potatoes if they can get anything else', so the Board of Agriculture set about promoting the product as human food. In July 1795 *The Times* advocated a diet of mixed grained bread and porridge made from potatoes and oatmeal, and the following November the newspaper informed its readers that no less a person than the Prime Minister himself, William Pitt, recommended the use of potato flour in loaves. Potatoes received a further endorsement from Thomas Malthus, whose *Essay on the Principle of Population* (1798), with its gloomy forecast that only war, famine and disease could halt the ever-upward surge of population, included an endorsement of Adam Smith's praise of potatoes in his *Wealth of Nations,* since:

> if potatoes were to become the favourite vegetable food of the common people and if the same quantity of land was employed in their culture as is now employed in the culture of corn the country would be able to support a much greater population.[61]

From the 1790s onwards, the advance of the product was relentless so that by the middle of the nineteenth century over half a million acres were devoted to the crop which had spread to all parts of England and much of Wales and Scotland.[62] It had the additional advantage that it was not affected by the fall in agricultural prices which occurred in the latter half of the century, as free trade policies opened up British markets to cheaper grain and meat from the empire and the New World.

There were still battles to be fought in surprising quarters before potatoes assumed their place in the diets of the population as a whole. William Cobbett (1762–1835) may have been a radical in his political views, but his views on agriculture were far from progressive. He particularly disapproved of the newfangled potato crops recording, for example, in his tour of Hertfordshire in June 1822 that 'I have the very great pleasure to add, that I do not think I saw three acres of *potatoes* in this whole tract of fine country, from St Albans to Redbourn, from Redbourn to [Hemel] Hempstead, and from Hempstead to Chesham'.[63] However, even the disapproval of William Cobbett could not prevail in the face of the determined gentlemen of the Poor Law Overseers who, between 1819 and 1832, promoted a series of Acts which enabled them to create allotments and cottage gardens for the cultivation of kitchen produce by labourers, thereby reducing their dependence upon the public purse. By the time of the 1851 census 77,000 acres had been allocated to allotments, mostly devoted to the cultivation of potatoes and producing, between them, sufficient output to supply each agricultural labourer's family with the daily equivalent of 1lb of potatoes per head each day.[64] In much of the country, especially the rural areas, a food which had been rather despised at the beginning of the century had replaced bread and cheese as a staple item of the diet of working-class families.

On the Continent the product was accepted even more reluctantly. In its early days it was associated with leprosy, probably because of the contemporary prevalence within medicine of the *doctrine of signatures* which held that plants which resembled parts of the human body were in some way associated with their health. The doctrine is associated with the Swiss physician Paracelsus (1493–1541), whose well-deserved reputation for arrogance is reflected in the fact that the word 'bombastic' is derived from his real name (Theophrastus Bombastus von Hohenheim). Nevertheless, his influence on medical thinking was substantial in the sixteenth and seventeenth centuries and was reflected in the writings of the Nepalese scholar Giambattista della Porta (*c.*1535–1615) who in 1588, in his work *Phytognomonica*, compared the white, nodular tubers of the potato with the deformed hands and feet of the leper. The following century the English writer Lovell, in his *Complete Herbal*, informed his readers that they should be cautious in their use of potatoes because 'if too frequently eaten they are thought to cause leprosie'.[65] Such advice did nothing to promote the sale of potatoes and such prejudices survived for at least another century. In 1774 Frederick the Great sent some seed potatoes to the town of Kolberg (now Kolobrzeg in Polish Pomerania) which had recently suffered a famine. Frederick's hope was that the cultivation of the new crop would make the citizens less vulnerable to the failure of their traditional cereal crops, but the ungrateful subjects declared: 'These things have neither smell nor taste; not even the dogs will eat them so what use are they to us?'[66]

In the twentieth century the demands of war further strengthened the humble potato as a dominant element in the British diet. Since it was easily cultivated as a year-round crop in the soil and climate of Britain, Asquith's government encouraged its cultivation in the First World War to reduce the nation's dependence upon vulnerable Atlantic convoys so that, by 1918, production had increased by almost 60 per cent over its pre-war level to more than 5lb per head per week for every man, woman and child. In the Second World War, with an even greater threat to Britain's food supply, the government designated potatoes as a principal source of kilocalories in place of bread, setting up a 'Department of Potatoes and Carrots' within the Ministry of Food to encourage wider cultivation and the adoption of new varieties to give reliable supplies throughout the year. By the last year of the war, a peak of 1.4 million acres were under cultivation, including a new variety called Golden Wonder which later lent its name to a brand of potato crisp,[67] though by 2006 this had fallen by 75 per cent to 350,000 acres as potatoes were imported from increasingly distant destinations, often by air.[68] Potatoes remain one of Britain's favourite foods. Each of us consumes on average 707g per week of fresh potatoes (almost as much as bread). In addition each of us consumes on average about 258g of potato-based snacks such as crisps, for which we pay significantly more than we do for the fresh potatoes, the market for such snacks amounting to approximately £1.3 billion per year.[69]

Milk

The extent to which milk was consumed as a staple item of diet in the British population before about 1800 is far from clear. Its benefits to health were proclaimed by Thomas Cogan in his book *The Haven of Health,* published in 1584, though the science on which he based his assertions was questionable. He explained that 'Milk is made of blood twice concocted ... until it come to the paps, or udder, it is plain blood; but afterward by the proper nature of the paps it is turned into milk'. He added that it was especially good for those who were of melancholy humour, 'which is a common calamity of students', though not for other young men, who were by nature choleric. Women's milk was best, followed by asses' milk – a true claim since asses' milk is low in fat and thus easily digested by babies. He also claimed that the adult Earl of Cumberland had been cured of consumption by consuming breast milk, an assertion which, though mistaken, reflects the contemporary belief in the healing powers of

breast milk.[70] Dr John Caius (1510–73) re-founder of Gonville and Caius
College, Cambridge, was similarly suckled in his final years to mitigate his
'peevishness', though no record has been kept of the effectiveness of the
treatment.[71] Jonas Hanway, as so often, had an opinion on the subject that
was far from re-assuring. He was persuaded that vicious habits could be
imparted to innocent babies by wet nurses of bad character and, despairing
of the prospects of improving the behaviour of the wet nurses, he wrote
that: 'This author expects no speedy reformation and therefore recommends the feeding of infants with the milk of animals',[72] whose moral
character, one assumes, he preferred.

In 1587 William Harrison, in his *Description of England*, wrote that milk,
butter and cheese, which were 'wont to be accounted one of the chief
stays throughout the island are now reputed as food appertinent only to
the inferior sort', since the gentry, prosperous artisans and husbandmen
preferred a diet consisting mostly of meat.[73] In fact within a few years
cheese had been taken up by the more prosperous classes as a pleasant and
nutritious food, thereby increasing the quantities of its by-product, whey,
which farmers were in the habit of giving to the poor. The cause of cheese
was also advanced by the advent of the Civil War in 1642, since it was a
nutritious food which could easily be carried by armies on the march
and did not deteriorate. Moreover, in the latter part of the seventeenth
century products based on milk started to enter the diet, notably custard
and blancmange, using milk, eggs, flour and almonds to give a palatable
and nutritious food.[74] Two hundred years after Harrison, Sir Frederic Eden
(1766–1809), prompted by the suffering caused by the poor harvests of the
early 1790s, undertook a tour of Great Britain in which he recorded the
living conditions of labouring people throughout the land. He published
his findings in 1797 as *The State of the Poor*.[75] He wrote of the consumption
of milk that:

> It is not to be expected that milk should ever form a considerable part of the
> diet of labourers in the South of England until the practice of keeping cows
> becomes more general among cottagers than it is at present … In the vicinity of
> large towns the value of grassland is much too high to enable labourers to rent it
> to advantage … The usual diet of labourers is bread, butter, cheese, pickled pork
> and a little butcher's meat … milk is very scarce.

According to Eden, milk, like potatoes, was more commonly available in
the north of England than in the south, possibly because a larger proportion of the population were country dwellers and because the enclosure

movement had not taken such a firm grip there as in parts of the south.
London was a particular problem because its size made it more difficult
to reach all the population with a perishable product using rudimentary
means of transport. Farmers preferred to turn the milk into cheese which
would keep for a long time and bear the cost and time involved in transporting it to the Metropolis. London did, however, have a few of its own
dairies. The Nell Gwynn Dairy had been established in New Exchange
Court, off the Strand, as early as 1666 and there was a 'Milk House' in Hyde
Park at about the same time, Samuel Pepys recording his pleasure at drinking a tankard of milk fresh from the cow.[76] By 1700 there were enough
milkmaids in London for them to have a celebration of their own on May
Day, so some kind of market and distribution system for milk had clearly
been established by that date.[77] It was estimated that in 1798 there were
about 8,500 cows kept in London, many of them in squalid conditions like
those in Golden Square, Soho, while a fortunate few were to be found in
St James's Park to supply 'luxury' milk to the children of the wealthy as late
as 1885. Eden commented that the shortage of milk in London accounted
for its high price, three pence halfpenny a quart in London against a penny
a quart in rural Lancashire.[78] However in some parts of the country farmers were already beginning to show great enterprise in meeting the needs
of local markets. A notable example is to be found in the village of Over,
north-west of Cambridge. The farmers would time their purchase, sale
and calving of cattle in such a way as to ensure a supply of milk throughout the year for milk, butter and cheese for the nearby university and its
colleges, which were a sure market. In later centuries this would become
common practice.[79]

During the nineteenth century milk wholesalers would collect the
product from the London dairies, often adding to it from the 'black cow'
or water pump available in many dairies and thereby diluting the product
by about two parts of water to five parts milk. One enterprising whole-
saler gained a contract to supply a workhouse with milk by charging a
price twopence a gallon less than he paid, the difference being made up
by the addition of water.[80] There was no guarantee of the purity of the
milk or the water and since the milk was usually delivered to customers
in open buckets, any passing debris from smoke smuts and street dirt to
bird droppings was liable to enrich the product on its journey through
the streets. Such arrangements continued until well into the nineteenth
century. George Sturt recorded the activities of Mr Lovelock, Farnham's
milkman, in the latter part of the century:

He carried the milk on a yoke across his shoulders – carried it in two shining
pails hanging one of each side ... He came regularly every afternoon; perhaps
every morning; and I think he had no holiday for years.[81]

Dilution and street dirt were not the only hazards to affect the milk supply.
From 1840 Foot and Mouth Disease was present in some cattle and from
1865–66 an outbreak of Rinderpest prompted the passing of the Cattle
Diseases Prevention Act (1866) which prescribed the slaughter of infected
animals. It was not until 1862 that Louis Pasteur (1822–95) devised the technique of 'pasteurisation' to destroy harmful microbes in wine and it was not
applied to milk, with which it is most often associated, until the 1880s.

There were also some strange views to be found amongst the medical
profession on the qualities of milk. A lecture by a Dr Garrod was published
in *The Lancet*[82] in 1848 in which Garrod quoted the work of a French
doctor, l'Heritier, who had discovered by experiment that 'in the milk of a
brunette, when compared with that from females of fair complexion, there
existed a greater amount of solid matter'. He went on to add that 'milk is
stated by some to be influenced greatly by mental emotions and even
the sudden death of the infant has been asserted to have arisen from such
alterations'. Other authorities asserted that bottle feeding was even more
hazardous, 197 out of 244 infants at a hospital in Tours, France, having
died after being bottle-fed cows' milk.[83] The cause of cows' milk was not
helped by its association with tuberculosis (TB), the biggest single cause of
death in Britain and France in the nineteenth century. In Manchester in
the 1890s a survey revealed that almost one-fifth of that city's milk supply
was affected by TB[84] and this led to a public health campaign designed to
improve hygiene in dairies and to encourage citizens to boil milk. These
measures, combined with the introduction of pasteurisation, brought
about a gradual reduction in the incidence of the disease, though Sir John
Simon's attempts to have the disease made notifiable in the Infectious
Diseases Notification Act of 1889 was unsuccessful and TB did not achieve
this status until 1912. In the circumstances it is reassuring to note that the
Paediatrician Walter Cheadle, in a series of lectures on infant feeding at
Great Ormond Street Hospital in the 1880s, advised his audience: 'all milk
to be boiled immediately upon arrival', even though he acknowledged
that children did not like the taste of boiled milk.[85]

Entrepreneurs were not slow to take advantage of the shortages or supposed deficiencies of milk. In 1824 *The Family Oracle of Health* informed
its readers that by boiling garden snails, pearl barley, arrowroot and various other vegetables in water and adding the resulting broth to an equal

quantity of cow's milk they could produce a substance which was as nutritious as asses' milk. The ever-resourceful Justus von Liebig, whose activities are discussed elsewhere,[86] established Liebig's Concentrated Milk Company in Regent Street in 1867, consisting of a mixture of cows' milk, malt flour and potassium bicarbonate. Many others swiftly followed as the fashion for breast feeding declined in the Victorian era, many of the proprietary products consisting mostly of starch and being deficient in protein, fat and the (as yet undiscovered) vitamins and minerals which were necessary for infant health. It was not until the 1890s that legislation required the manufacturers to declare on their labels that these products were not suitable for children.

Despite these forbidding developments, milk consumption in towns increased during the second half of the century, the growth owing much to the coming of the railways. Farmers learned that they could earn more by selling fresh liquid milk to towns than by converting it to cheese. The London and North-Western Railway alone carried 1.2 million gallons of milk to London in 1866 from farms along its route to Birmingham, and this traffic was matched by the other railway companies at this time, thereby gradually replacing the output of dairies based in the Metropolis itself and reducing the price to one closer to that which prevailed in the countryside. In 1868 it was estimated that the average consumption of milk per head was about one-fifth of a pint (115ml), and thereafter it gradually increased.[87] To put this figure into context, the equivalent figure in 2006 was about 300ml.[88]

The relationship between health and milk, with particular reference to TB, was illustrated by the activities of the Liverpool Corporation, whose acute public health problems in the middle of the nineteenth century had prompted it to appoint Britain's first Medical Officer of Health as early as 1847. It took the lead in promoting the use of nutritious, sterilised milk for infants whose mothers were unable to breastfeed them. In 1901 it set up Infant Welfare Centres where 'a preparation of pure cows' milk is made to resemble human milk as closely as possible'.[89] In the first fifteen years of the scheme, 32,742 infants were supplied from the centres, of whom 1,815 died, though of these only 262 were reasonably healthy when first brought to the centres. It also instituted a rigorous system of bacteriological examinations of milk samples and of cows. These revealed that, between 1901 and 1915, 502 cases of tubercular milk were identified from a total of 9,350 samples – a great improvement on the condition of Manchester's milk in the 1890s when one-fifth was found to be infected. Other cities followed Liverpool's lead.

In the twentieth century the cause of milk as a health-giving product was helped by the advocacy of the Russian microbiologist Ilya Mechnikov who, in 1908, won the Nobel Prize for Medicine. Born in the Ukraine in 1845, he was educated there and at Justus von Liebig's University of Giessen. Mechnikov was an early continental champion of Darwin's *Origins of the Species* but of uncertain temperament, attempting twice to commit suicide following the deaths from illness of his two wives. He earned his Nobel Prize for his work on the immune system but he also developed a theory that lactic acid would prolong life, and he consumed sour milk or yoghurt every day in support of this theory. His death in 1916 at the then advanced age of seventy-one seemed to make the point and inspired the Japanese scientist Minoru Shirota to begin research which led to the production of the Yakult health drink.

School Milk

In the 1920s an experiment was conducted involving 1,400 schoolchildren aged five to fourteen in schools in Scotland and Belfast. Children receiving milk each day gained in height and weight by 20 per cent compared with those who received no milk supplement. The experiment was written up in *The Lancet* by John Boyd Orr[90] and led to the 1934 Milk Act by which one-third of a pint of milk was made available to schoolchildren via local authorities with a subsidy from the government, the milk being free to 'necessitous children' and otherwise costing one (old) penny. In 1946, inspired by the work of John Boyd Orr which opened this chapter, the Labour government, led by Clement Attlee and with Ellen Wilkinson as Education Minister, introduced free milk for all schoolchildren. Those who attended school in the forties, fifties and sixties can remember the specially produced one-third pint bottles which were dispensed during the morning break or dinner hour and consumed, sometimes unwillingly, under the sharp eyes of the class teacher. They undoubtedly benefited many children, especially those from poorer families. In 1971 the new Education Minister, Margaret Thatcher, took away the entitlement to free school milk for children aged seven and over. Some local authorities threatened to rebel by increasing the rates to replace the government subsidy which had been removed as an economy measure. The rebellion petered out and Margaret Thatcher, before becoming 'The Iron Lady', earned herself the name 'Thatcher, Milk Snatcher'.

The British Diet, 2007

The 'staffs of life', which were examined by Sir John Boyd Orr in 1935 and which accounted for about two-thirds of calorie consumption – sugar, bread, potatoes and milk – continue to be prominent features of the British diet in 2007, but many foods are now commonplace that were rare or unknown in 1935. These include not only new fresh products like avocados and star fruit, but processed foods such as prepared meals which are designed to support the more frantic lifestyles of the twenty-first century. However, the most remarkable transformation in our eating habits has been in the consumption of food from restaurants and hotels – 'eating out', including takeaways. In 1935 this was such a modest feature of the British diet that Boyd Orr did not feel the need to examine it, but in 2006, expenditure on this 'catering' sector exceeds 80 per cent of the expenditure on food bought for preparation and consumption in the home.[91] The implications of these changes in our diet are examined in chapter seven.

3

'Man's War against Nature'

All the produce of the kitchen garden
> William Cadogan's advice to the Coram Foundation on the most nutritious
>> diets for their orphans

Man has lost the capacity to foresee and to forestall. He will end up by destroying the earth.

> Albert Schweitzer

The Food and Drug Administration has acted as an official sponsor of processing and marketing practices that have transformed the defrauding of consumers into a competitive advantage.

> Ralph Nader

'All the Produce of the Kitchen Garden'

In 1769 the governors of the Foundling Hospital consulted the distinguished army physician William Cadogan (1711–97) about the best ways to feed their orphaned charges. The Foundling Hospital, one of the most remarkable charities ever created, was the brainchild of Thomas Coram (c. 1668–1751), a sea captain from Lyme Regis in Dorset who was a pioneer in the development of trade between Great Britain and its early colonies in North America. He retired with a modest fortune and devoted his life to raising money to provide a home for abandoned children whose bodies he had seen rotting in the streets near his home in Rotherhithe. He spent eighteen years (1721–39) lobbying and gained the support of both men and women from the aristocracy. Finally, on 17 October 1739, George II granted a charter for 'an Hospital for the Reception, Maintenance and Proper Education of such cast-off Children and Foundlings as may be brought to it'.

From its earliest days the Foundling Hospital attracted the support of many prominent citizens including painters who donated works to raise funds like William Hogarth, Thomas Gainsborough and Joshua Reynolds, while Handel gave an annual performance of *The Messiah* for the same purpose. The inveterate campaigner Jonas Hanway, in the time that he could spare from campaigning in favour of eating vegetables and against the drinking of tea, became a governor of the hospital, wrote an account of its early history, and compared it with similar institutions on the Continent which, according to Hanway, were built 'to conceal the amours of the Popish Clergy'.[1] In 1756 the governors presented a petition to Parliament, drawing attention to the inability of the hospital to accommodate all the children who were being brought to its doors. It is an indication of the esteem in which the foundation was held that Parliament, at a time when charitable works were normally consigned to private philanthropists, voted £10,000 for the support of the hospital, on condition that it accepted all children offered to it below a certain age.

The hospital acquired premises in Coram Fields, Holborn, close to the site of the later Great Ormond Street Hospital, where mothers could leave their unwanted children in a basket. The hospital moved to Berkhamsted, Hertfordshire, in 1935 and remained in use until 1951 when the practice of fostering replaced the need for such a home, though the Coram Foundation remains active in child welfare work. The original Holborn site is the home of the Foundling Museum and Coram Fields, a public park which may only be visited by an adult in the company of a child. The governors of the hospital, from the earliest times, showed an unusually enlightened interest in the dietary needs of their young charges, hence the request to William Cadogan for his advice.

William Cadogan (1711–97) had been educated at Oriel College, Oxford, and qualified as MD at the University of Leiden, in the Low Countries, then the acknowledged centre of medical education in Europe. The thesis for his doctorate, entitled *De Nutritione,* had examined the effects of nutrition on the human body and he retained his interest in the subject after returning to England and setting up as a physician in Bristol. His 1748 *Essay Upon Nursing and the Management of Children,* which he wrote in response to the Foundling Hospital's approach, became, in the words of a later writer, 'the textbook of the Foundling Hospital'.[2] In his opening remarks on children's diets Cadogan remarked: 'In my opinion this business has been too long fatally left to the management of women who cannot be supposed to have prior knowledge to fit them for such a task'.[3] However, after this unpromising start his treatise set the nutritional standards not only for the Holborn hospital itself but also for the six branch hospitals which the charity established for infants aged less than one year in towns like Aylesbury and Shrewsbury. The food was greatly superior to that which most of their contemporaries would have received. The menus of the time make reference not only to copious amounts of bread, butter and cheese but also to boiled mutton, roast beef, vegetables and broth (for the boys) and rice pudding (for the girls). One of the skills which the boys were taught was husbandry in the kitchen garden, which existed within the precincts of the hospital and no doubt helps to account for Cadogan's advice that 'a Child may be allowed any kind of mellow fruit, either raw, stewed or baked; roots of all sorts and all the produce of the kitchen garden'[4] within the diets – a generous supply of fresh fruits and vegetables which would have been beyond the means of most town dwellers of the time. Cadogan added: 'As we are partly carnivorous Animals a child ought not to be fed wholly upon Vegetables'. The hospital enjoyed a well-deserved reputation for its happy, well-educated and healthy children. In March 1853 in his journal *Household Words* Dickens wrote: 'this home of the blank [i.e. nameless] children is by no means a blank place … the Governors of this charity are a model to all others'.

Fall from Innocence

The fresh fruit and vegetables and 'all the produce of the kitchen garden' enjoyed by Coram's foundlings were luxuries to which few citizens of London could aspire in the eighteenth century when methods of transporting produce and keeping it fresh were primitive. In the centuries that followed, mankind's 'war against nature', from which this chapter takes its title,[5] was devoted to ensuring that foods could be brought from distant farms, and later distant lands, in a condition which was safe and appetising. As well as being fit to eat it should taste good, look good and even, more recently, sound good.[6] 'Modern' methods of producing and preserving food are not always as modern as we assume. In the middle of the seventeenth century, a century before Cadogan's advice to the Foundling

Hospital, Sir Kenelm Digby (1603–65) visited a farm producing chickens and noted three features of its operations. First, the chickens were fed a mixture of barley and milk because this caused them to gain weight rapidly. Secondly, the chickens were crowded and confined in small coops so that they could not move around, lack of exercise meaning they did not lose the weight they gained from the feed. Finally, a candle was left burning in their quarters at night to keep them awake, and feeding. Such conditions would be recognised by a modern battery hen.[7] In other respects nature prevailed for a little longer. In the middle of the same century a country-woman brought a bag of peas to London, the first of the season, and turned down the substantial sum of 5s offered by a cook in The Strand in the hope of obtaining a better price from Joan Cromwell, wife of the Lord Protector (she was disappointed, being offered only half the sum by the thrifty Joan). This reflected the fact that, amongst the prosperous classes, the ability to serve seasonal fruits and vegetables before one's friends and neighbours was a sign that one was well-connected. In the centuries that followed the innocent days when Thomas Coram's children could be fed in part from the fresh produce of their own hands, great ingenuity has been applied to ensuring a steady supply of processed foods supported by methods of pres-ervation which, together with the development of air freight which can transfer foods cheaply between hemispheres, has gone a long way towards abolishing the seasons.

Moreover, additives have imparted to fruits and vegetables seductive colours unknown to nature, and flavour enhancers tempt every palate. As a result many people believe that human beings, especially children, are in many cases less well nourished than were Coram's orphans and, in some cases, are actually harmed by the food they consume. It is well understood that certain substances, like saturated fats, can cause people to put on weight and raise their cholesterol levels; that chemicals like lead and mercury are poisonous; and that substances like cannabis and heroin affect the mind. But controversy surrounds other less familiar additions to our foods. In the latter half of the twentieth century, as the science of food technology has advanced and has been harnessed to the marketing of branded foods, concerns have been raised about the effects of these proc-esses upon human health and behaviour. Given the speed of that advance, to a point where the global market for food and drink additives is worth about £12.5 billion, it would be surprising if none of the substances had an adverse effect upon human well-being. But the size of the industry and the huge profits that are made from its activities by large corporations ensure that it is well able to defend itself against its critics.

Conditions ranging from migraine and epilepsy to adolescent misbehaviour and under-achievement in schools have been attributed to the consumption of additives by some authorities, while others have argued that chemicals as natural as salt or as unnatural as aspartame are innocent of the charges levied against them. Moreover, some foods which were previously beyond suspicion have been cited as possible causes of illness, while measures taken by well-intentioned public authorities to improve our health have felt the full force of the law. Thus in 1984 an article in *The Lancet* suggested that breast milk, usually regarded as the most innocent nutrient of infants, seemed to be associated with an increase in childhood eczema on the grounds that 'constituents such as processed foods might not easily be rendered harmless in the maternal digestive system and may be absorbed relatively intact to cross as allergens in breast milk'.[8] The previous year *The Lancet* had reported a ruling in the Scottish Court of Sessions that it was beyond the power of local authorities to add fluoride to water supplies to strengthen children's teeth and reduce dental decay, a programme supported by the British Dental Association.[9] So how sinister are the methods by which foods are preserved?

The Preservation of Food

The most effective way to preserve food in a condition fit for consumption is, of course, to leave fruit and vegetables in the fields (until they ripen) and to keep animals alive. The latter method was adopted by enterprising fishermen from the fenlands of East Anglia in the eighteenth century. They put their catches in water-filled barrels and made their way to London, replacing the water each evening until they reached the capital where there was a ready market for their fish.[10] In 1797 Sir Frederick Eden recorded an experience which, likewise, eliminated the need for preservative methods involving a visit to a Scottish Highland croft. When an unexpected visitor called, the hostess cut, threshed, winnowed and ground some barley from her fields; added it to a continually boiling pot containing kale; and served it with flat, round cakes called bannocks made from oatmeal. In Eden's words: 'Thus, in less than half an hour, an excellent repast was smoking on the table'.[11] All other attempts to preserve food from decay and keep it in a condition fit for human consumption are, essentially, a war against nature. In the natural order of things all foodstuffs – meat, fruit, vegetables, dairy products, cereals and others – will decay with the passage of time unless some steps are taken to prevent them from doing so. These preservative processes therefore aim to create unnatural conditions by depriving bacteria of the water, air and temperatures that they need to thrive. The practice of 'salting' meat and fish was known to the Romans and worked by drawing moisture out of the product and thereby creating an environment inhospitable to bacteria. In the eighteenth century, Oxbridge colleges and the Inns of Court preserved meat by laying it in brine for two days and then rubbing it with salt. This process would keep it edible for a month. Similarly bacon was dried and smoked while pork and vegetables were pickled in vinegar, the vinegar using acid to prevent the growth of moulds and to create sauerkraut and similar products.[12] Sugar fulfils a similar purpose in the preservation of fruits and the preparation of jams and other preserves. Unnatural conditions can also be created by such measures as bottling or canning to deprive the bacteria of air; dehydrating the foods to deprive bacteria of water; freezing to deny them the ambient temperature they need; or by adding artificial chemical preservatives more sophisticated than sugar or salt. In some cases foods are heated to kill off bacteria before being canned in airless conditions, as in the case of soups and meat dishes. In others the controlled growth of micro-organisms creates products with their own distinctive qualities such as yoghurt and cheese. Some processes are designed to kill particularly harmful bacteria while preserving others in order to leave the product with a palatable taste. Thus pasteurisation, which was originally developed by Louis Pasteur (1822–95) to prevent microbiological attacks on wines, is now more often associated with milk. The milk is heated to 72°C for about fifteen seconds and then rapidly cooled, leaving the flavour intact while killing disease-causing bacteria. Less harmful bacteria survive so the milk will still become sour unless ultra-heat treatment (UHT) is used, applying a much higher temperature to kill all bacteria and giving a long shelf life at the expense of some change in flavour.

'Portable Soup'

In the eighteenth century 'portable soup' was developed as a means of victualling the Royal Navy during long voyages. Recipes for it (also known as *pocket soup* or *veal glue*) are included in one of the earliest and most popular cookbooks, *The Art of Cookery*, written by Hannah Glasse (1708–70) in 1747 and in the work of Mrs Beeton (1836–65). It may be regarded as the ancestor of the modern bouillon cube and was produced by creating a broth of lean meat (the fat being removed to prevent rancidity), bones, vegetables and plenty of salt which acted as a preservative. The liquid would be repeatedly boiled and strained for hours, until it had been reduced to a jelly- or glue-like substance which would be cut into slabs measuring a few inches square. When the slabs were immersed in water and boiled they were re-constituted as a reasonably nourishing broth, though deficient in vitamins – not something that would have worried the seafarers of the time who were not aware of the existence of such things. Portable soup was routinely carried in ships of the Royal Navy from about 1750. Captain James Cook (1728–79) took some portable soup on his exploration of the South Seas though, as explained in a later chapter, the sauerkraut he also took with him was of greater benefit to his crews in protecting them from scurvy once they had overcome their reluctance to eat the strange and unfamiliar food.

Preservation by Canning

An early method of 'canning' was described by the scientist Robert Boyle who proposed that meat could be preserved (for example, to be used on sea voyages) by roasting and slicing it, packing it tightly in casks, and pouring melted butter over it to fill any cavities and drive out any remaining air. The cask would then be tightly sealed. This is the basis of the modern canning process.

Robert Boyle (1627–91) was born in Lismore Castle, Ireland, son of the Earl of Cork, a wealthy aristocrat. Educated at Eton and via the Grand Tour of Europe he settled first at a family property in Dorset and, in 1655 at Oxford where he joined a group of 'experimental philosophers' (whom we would now call scientists), forming the core of what, in 1660, became the Royal Society of which Robert Boyle was a founding member. He devoted the rest of his life to the 'experimental' approach to science earlier advocated by Francis Bacon in opposition to the 'Aristotelian' method, which simply built upon the beliefs of ancient philosophers. His first major scientific work, 'The Sceptical Chemist' published in 1661, questioned the ancient doctrines of 'elements' and 'humours' and his experiments led eventually to his construction of an air pump which created a vacuum chamber – something previously believed to be impossible because contrary to nature. His experiments in physics also led eventually to the formulation of Boyle's Law which made the connection between pressure, volume and temperature when applied to air. He enjoyed an international reputation and became known in Europe as 'the English Philosopher', a title all the

more remarkable because, as a contemporary of Newton, Hooke and others, he
was not without competition in the field.

It is not known whether Boyle's system was ever put to practical use but
a further step was taken when Napoleon, concerned about the feeding
of his armies, announced a prize of 12,000 francs for anyone who could
devise a method of preserving food for armies on the march. In 1809 the
prize was awarded to Nicolas Appert, a Parisian confectioner, who put
fruit, vegetables and meat in glass jars, firmly sealed the mouths with corks,
and immersed the vessels in boiling water, thus destroying bacteria which
could have attacked the food. Since the science of bacteriology had not
yet emerged, Appert cannot have known *why* his system worked, only that
it *did* work. The method was briefly known, in his honour, as *appertisation*.

There were, however, disadvantages to the method. Some bottles cracked
in the boiling water while others were broken in storage or transit, so a
merchant trading in London called Peter Durand (who may himself have
been French since he was also known as Pierre Durand) devised a method
of substituting metal canisters for Appert's glass bottles, a process which
he patented in 1810 though he appears not to have used the system itself.
Instead he sold the patent rights to a man called Bryan Donkin (1768–
1855), a serial inventor who had two patents to his credit in the field of
paper making and printing. He set up the first canning factory (which
they called a 'preservatory') in Bermondsey with a fellow paper maker,
John Hall. Donkin and Hall became suppliers of tinned food to the Army
and by 1830 tinned produce was being sold, on a small scale, in shops.
The following year the Admiralty ordered that all its ships should carry
tinned meats as 'medical comforts' and large contracts for the products
were awarded.[13]

The results were not always as planned. Experiments with large canisters
weighing 20lb or more produced serious quality problems as bacteria in
the centre of the can were not always killed by the heating process, so cans
were limited to 10, and eventually 6lb. In 1845 a Royal Navy expedition
consisting of two ships led by Rear Admiral Sir John Franklin (1786–1847)
set out in search of the elusive North-West Passage, which was long
believed (wrongly) to provide a commercially viable link between the
Atlantic and the Pacific via the Arctic. The expedition was lost and its fate
remained a mystery until the 1980s when some human and other remains
of the expedition were found on King William Island, off the northern
coast of Canada. Amongst the artefacts found were large quantities of
canned meat which had become tainted by contact with the lead seals of

the cans and, if eaten, would have caused lead poisoning. It is possible that this contributed to the fate of the expedition, none of whose members survived.

It is certainly the case that, seven years later, *The Lancet* reported serious problems with provisions at the Royal Navy's victualling store at Gosport, near Portsmouth.[14] Under the heading *Putrid 'Preserved' Meat*, it reported that, of 2,707 ten-pound canisters of preserved meat, only 197 were fit for human consumption, the remainder being putrid to a greater or lesser degree. The 197 sound canisters were given to the local poor while the remainder was dumped in the sea off Spithead. The meat was reported as having been imported from Moldavia and packed in Great Britain. This scandal led to a further investigation which, later the same year, discovered that another supplier had provided 387,795lb of unfit meat.[15] Some years later a ghoulish element was added to the tinned meat when it began to be referred to, by members of the armed forces, as 'Sweet Fanny Adams', a reference to the murder and mutilation of an eight-year-old child of that name in Alton, Hampshire, in 1867. As late as 1889 the Public Health Laboratory in north-west London reported that almost one-fifth of meats that they had randomly checked were found to be contaminated.[16] Canned foods were quickly adopted in the United States, where the first can opener was patented in 1858, bayonets and even bullets having previously been used to open the tough and sometimes obstinate canisters.

Refrigeration

The collection and use of snow and ice to preserve food was known and practised in ancient times as far apart as Greece, Persia and China. The first recorded experiment with food preservation by this means is usually credited to Francis Bacon (1561–1626) and may have cost him his life. His career as an Elizabethan courtier and a rather corrupt Lord Chancellor has been overshadowed by his status as a pioneer of the scientific revolution that underpinned the enlightenment of the seventeenth and eighteenth centuries through his insistence on observation and experiment as the pathway to truth and understanding. In 1626 he stuffed a chicken carcass with snow in a test of his hypothesis that this would prevent it from decomposing. He did not live long enough to learn the results of his experiment since he died shortly afterwards of pneumonia, quite possibly contracted during the experiment. The lesson was not lost, however, because in his diary Samuel Pepys recorded a conversation in a London coffee house in December

1663: 'Fowl killed in December (Alderman Barker said) he did buy and, putting them into the box under his sledge, did forget to take them out to eat till April next and were through the frost as sweet and fresh to eat as at first killed'.[17]

In 1748, William Cullen used a pump to create a partial vacuum in a chamber containing ethyl ether which then boiled, absorbing heat from the surrounding air and creating a small quantity of ice. In the century that followed, others, including Michael Faraday, demonstrated some of the principles by which a combination of physics and chemistry could be used to create artificially low temperatures. By the 1840s refrigerated railway wagons were in use in the United States, cooled by ice tanks at the end of each wagon and ventilators through which air would pass, via the ice, to the produce within.

Between 1866 and 1871, as Britain's free-trade policies encouraged imports from low-cost producers, meat exports from Australia to Britain grew from 16,000lb per annum to 22,000,000lb. At first, canning was the only available method of preservation, but this would soon change. A Scottish émigré to Australia, James Harrison, had introduced refrigeration to meat packers in his new home by the early 1860s, an ice-making machine being installed at Darling Harbour, Sydney, in 1861.[18] In 1873, amidst much celebration, the steam ship *Norfolk* sailed for London with twenty tons of mutton and beef, frozen and in tanks cooled with ice and salt. The outcome was a fiasco. The ice melted as the ship sailed through tropical waters, most of the rotting cargo was dumped overboard and that small portion of it which reached England was unfit for human consumption. Seven years later, on 2 February 1880, the SS *Strathleven* entered London with forty tons of beef and mutton which arrived in good condition. It was sold at Smithfield a few days later for fivepence halfpenny a pound, compared with the twopence a pound it would have fetched in Melbourne. Henceforward refrigerated meat would be shipped regularly from Australia and New Zealand to the British market. Alternative methods of preservation were suggested, but without success. An English professor of physiology and Fellow of the Royal Society, Arthur Gamgee (1841–1909), suggested that oxygen was the agent of putrefaction (a widely held belief at the time) and devised a method of asphyxiating animals with carbon dioxide, thereby, it was supposed, expelling the offending agent from their carcasses and ensuring their preservation.[19] As far as is known, the method was never tested and would certainly not have worked.

In America a Civil War veteran, Thaddeus Lowe, invented a 'Compression Ice Machine' which he installed in a ship to ferry meat and fruit between Texas and New York. The venture was a commercial failure but a signal for the future. By the early twentieth century all of America's major meat packers like Armour and Swift were using refrigeration in their processing plants, storage facilities and railway wagons. Road vehicles followed in the middle of the twentieth century.

Clarence Birdseye

Clarence Birdseye (1886–1956) has a special place in the history of preservation by freezing. His father was a Brooklyn lawyer and his mother the daughter of a successful inventor, whose genes Clarence presumably inherited because during his life he filed 300 patents, the last being for a process for turning sugar cane pulp into paper. As a young man he acquired a taste for hunting and in 1912 travelled to Labrador to acquire furs for sale in the rapidly growing American market. While in Canada he observed that the Inuit had developed a method of quick-freezing caribou meat to preserve its flavour. In 1922 he went into the wholesale fish business and applied the freezing techniques he had observed amongst the Inuit. In his words: 'My contribution was to take Eskimo knowledge and the scientists' theories and adapt them to quantity production'. An early venture of his own ended in bankruptcy but in 1924, with financial backing, he founded the General Seafood Corporation in Gloucester, Massachusetts. His technique was to pack the fish in waxed cardboard boxes, ready for sale to consumers, before freezing it so rapidly that its cellular structure was preserved. In the first few years the sales were to other businesses including catering outlets, but in 1930 twenty-six products went on sale in retail outlets in Springfield, Massachusetts. They included meat, fish, fruits and vegetables including the famous frozen peas. This may be regarded as the birth of the retail frozen food business which spread rapidly within the United States and abroad as manufacturers of refrigeration equipment recognised the opportunity represented by the new market and began to manufacture inexpensive units for use in retail stores. In 1933, 513 retail outlets were selling frozen foods in the USA and by 1948, despite the interruptions of war, this had risen to 60,000. At the outbreak of the Second World War, one-third of the US strawberry crop was being frozen despite the fact that the cellular structure of strawberries made them rather unsuitable for the process. By this time the company had been sold to the Postum company (later General Foods) whose founder, Charles Post, will be observed making use of the ideas of the Kellogg brothers at Battle Creek, Michigan, and thus earns another place in the history of 'man's war against nature'. Thanks to Clarence Birdseye and Charles Post, 'seasonal' products like peas would hence be available all the year round to people with refrigerators. This occurred long before the controversial practice developed of air freighting fruit and vegetables (notably strawberries) off-season to affluent western consumers.

Frozen foods arrived a little later in Great Britain. Unilever introduced the Birds Eye products to Britain in 1933 but it was not until after the Second World War that the market benefited from the impetus given to it by entrepreneurs such as Carl Ross (1901–86), owner of a Grimsby trawler fleet. In 1947 he persuaded the Ministry of Agriculture, Fisheries and Food (MAFF), which was still issuing ration quotas for fish, that by freezing catches it would be possible to iron out the peaks and troughs in supply, caused by such uncontrollable influences as weather. He built a frozen food business that included shellfish, vegetables and poultry as well as white fish and persuaded the first television chef Philip Harben to feature 'frozen nephrops tails' in a recipe, thereby launching scampi into the British kitchen.[20]

Drying

The third attack on nature's tendency to promote the decomposition of foods, after canning and refrigeration, occurred in the form of drying, in effect removing from meat, fruit and vegetables the water which bacteria need to survive and do their work. The process of drying foods by exposing them to hot sunshine has been established for centuries. The Icelandic saga of Einer Sokkason records that this twelfth-century Icelandic hero, having annoyed the inhabitants of Greenland, made good his escape from them while purloining some of the Greenlanders' stores of dried fish.[21] In the following century the *Journal of Friar William Rubruck* records his journey to the land of the Tartars in 1253–55 where he observed the Tartar people drying curds so that they became 'as hard as iron' for re-hydration in winter when milk was in short supply. Long before the arrival of Spanish invaders in the sixteenth century the native inhabitants of Peru produced *Chuno* by spreading potatoes on the ground high in the Andes overnight where they froze and where the low pressure at those altitudes encouraged the ice crystals to vaporise. The potatoes would then be trodden with bare feet to expel water, a process which would continue for four or five days to produce dehydrated potato and, with a slightly modified procedure, a snowy-white potato flour.[22] At the time of the Spanish settlement of South America, Hakluyt's *Voyages*, published from 1589, recorded the practice of drying the flesh of oysters by the people of the South Seas.

In the early years of the settlement of North America cooked maize was preserved by drying it which, with salted fish, constituted the first export business of Massachusetts. The native Indians of the plains dried Buffalo meat by cutting it into thin strips and hanging it in the sun while those of the Yukon and Alaska introduced the additional refinement of smoking the meat, giving it a characteristic flavour. In California the drying of peaches and grapes was practised in the nineteenth century. In the 1860s in Australia, where the developments in refrigeration were gaining pace, mutton or beef was dried on steam-heated plates and ground into powder for use on long voyages, where the addition of water would make a nourishing broth and the use of flour would make biscuits.

Battle Creek Toasted Cornflakes

Other developments in the preservation and packaging of food were occurring in the American Mid-West, some of them prompted by a co-founder of the Christian Seventh Day Adventist sect, Ellen G. White. This remarkable lady wrote extensively on religious subjects and on vegetarianism, her works having been more widely translated than those of any other American author. In 1866 Ellen and her husband, James White, founded a Health Reform Institute at Battle Creek, Michigan, to promote their religious, vegetarian and other dietary ideas and in 1875 they appointed as Medical Superintendent one of their protégés, a newly qualified young doctor called John Harvey Kellogg whose younger brother, William Keith Kellogg, became the bookkeeper of the Battle Creek Sanitarium [sic]. At John's death in 1943, at the age of ninety-one, he held more than thirty patents, most of them for new food products and processes. Amongst these were *granose*, dehydrated flakes of wheat, barley, oats and maize, which would keep for long periods, meet the requirements of the strictest vegetarians and, it was hoped, prevent constipation. Kellogg also advocated the then fashionable hydrotherapy involving cold showers and ice baths, as well as vibrating chairs and a 2,000 calorie per day diet. The present recommended levels for a workforce that is less physically active are 2,500 for a man and 2,000 for a woman.[23]

The bookkeeping brother, William Keith Kellogg (1860–1951), had different ambitions. One of the products the brothers devised in a laboratory at the Battle Creek Sanitarium was the first flaked cereal. William saw the potential of the product as a breakfast food for the poor who could not afford meat and wanted a change from porridge. He wanted to patent the process, but John Harvey disagreed and allowed residents of the Sanitarium to witness the manufacturing process. One of these was Charles Post, who took advantage of the opportunity to make his own product under the name Post Cereals, which eventually became General Foods. William Keith Kellogg therefore founded the Battle Creek Toasted Corn Flake Company whose products were marketed as healthy breakfast food and is now, of course, known as Kellogg's, still based in Battle Creek.

During the American Civil War, troops were supplied with dried vegetables, fruits and soups in the belief that they would protect the troops from scurvy – a mistaken view since much of the ascorbic acid which combats the disease is lost in the process of dehydration.[24] They were also found in the ration packs of those who fought in the Boer War[25], and dehydrated products left over from the war were still available and fit for use by the Army which went to war in 1914. This process, while it preserved the foods, also rendered them rather unpalatable as did a later, similar method which involved placing them in hot air dryers. Vegetables like carrots, for example, would have to be soaked in water for one to two hours before they were ready for cooking and even then a rubbery texture was likely to result. In 1933 the explorer St John Philby recorded in his account of his Arabian travels, *The Empty Quarter*, that nomadic tribes would cut meat into thin, wide slices and hang them over thickets whereupon, 'For a while, the stench in and around our camp was appalling', and after which the putrefying meat would be disposed of and the remainder stored for future use.

These problems were overcome by the method known as Accelerated Freeze Drying. The Swiss had long known that, if clothing is hung out to dry on a very cold day it will freeze but, when it has thawed out, the clothing will be dry. Perhaps it is no coincidence that one of the first companies to market freeze-dried products on a large scale, Knorr, was founded in Switzerland. Commercial freeze drying essentially follows this pattern. Food is frozen very rapidly, and placed in a vacuum which enables the frozen crystals to vaporise without passing through an intermediate liquid phase. It works most effectively with relatively thin pieces of food and has been successfully applied to fruit, vegetable, meat and fish, though it fails with products which have very high moisture content like water melon and lettuce. The products are easily re-constituted by the addition of water and can be cooked in a few minutes. It has the advantage that the products are effectively preserved over an almost indefinite period, even in tropical climates, and food is easily packaged and light and easy to transport. For these reasons, they are favoured for use by troops in combat conditions.

The technique was first developed at the Low Temperature Research Station in Cambridge from 1929 on behalf of the Agricultural Research Council.[26] One of its earliest applications was in the preservation of human blood plasma for transfusions and of early penicillin samples during the Second World War, events which also encouraged the rapid development of freeze-drying techniques to supply troops with light, palatable and safe foodstuffs. Further improvements in techniques after the war led to the rapid growth of the consumer markets for freeze-dried products, with multinational corporations like Unilever, Corn Products and Nestlé competing with one another in a very profitable market. The early use of science to frustrate the normal processes of nature was thus viewed as respectable and harmless, but as the twentieth century advanced and science became more complex and sophisticated, it was seen as less benign and, in certain hands, as positively sinister.

Making it Look Nice

Colours which occur naturally in foodstuffs are frequently 'fugitive' – that is to say, they are lost when exposed to food processing or sunlight, though the loss of colour rarely involves any loss of nutritional value. However, if peas lose their naturally pale green colour through storage or processing, and if consumers prefer their peas bright green, it is hard to blame food processors for adding back the colours lost through the use of harmless chemicals – provided of course that they are harmless. The use of colourings for nefarious purposes has a long history. In earlier centuries red lead was commonly used in cheeses like Gloucester to enhance their colour, and was added to mustard for the same reasons. Chalk was added to milk to make it whiter and to flour in order to make it whiter and bulkier, thereby enhancing the grocer's profits. The law of the times was so inadequate that it is doubtful whether some of these practices were illegal until the passage of the Adulteration of Food, Drink and Drugs Act in 1872.

In 1867 the French Emperor Napoleon III announced a competition to produce a cheaper substitute for butter suitable for the less wealthy and especially those who lived in towns with limited access to the product of the dairy farm. In 1869 his countryman Hippolyte Mege-Mouris invented and patented a process for making margarine from a mixture of animal fat and skimmed milk. The word itself appears to have been an American construct and first appears in a US patent application in 1873, four years after Mege-Mouris's discovery.[27] The product was an unattractive dull grey colour so when Mege-Mouris sold the patent to Anton Jurgens (1805–80) the enterprising Dutchman added a yellow dye which made the product resemble butter. This caused alarm in circles with large dairy interests and in 1886 the Margarine Act forbade the use of yellow dye in the United States, a prohibition which remained in force in the dairy heartland of Wisconsin until 1967. In France, for similar reasons, the advertising of margarine was restricted until the 1980s. Nevertheless, the product quickly became popular and the addition of artificial flavourings meant that margarine was, for many years, marketed as tasting like butter. It is one of the great paradoxes of food marketing that margarine has long been much more profitable to its producers than butter has been to farmers, despite the fact that margarine based its claims to the consumer's loyalty on its supposed resemblance to the natural product. Margarine has now grown up and is marketed on the basis that its vegetable oil content makes it a healthy product. Yet this is only one of many examples of processed foods being much more profitable than their natural originals. Crisps, for example, of which £1.3 billion worth are consumed each year in Great Britain, mostly by children, earn far higher profits for food processors than do potatoes for farmers, despite the fact that crisps, with their amazing collection of colourings, flavourings and salt, are regarded by most nutritionists as having no place in a healthy diet.

Some colouring methods are harmless. Thus it has long been known that, for reasons known only to psychologists, most people prefer brown eggs to white, though the nutritional values are exactly the same. Since the colour of the egg is determined by the breed of chicken laying it, egg producers have tended to favour chickens that lay brown eggs or have, in some cases, varied the chickens' diet to determine the egg colour.[28] This may be an odd reflection upon human behaviour, but no one has suggested that it is damaging to health. A similar situation applies to sausages. People like their sausages brown, so some sausage casings (skins) are treated with colourant based on caramel to give them the desired appearance and a similar approach has been taken with kippers. The production of pink salmon is more controversial. Most salmon eaten by humans is now farmed and pink dye, whose chemical name is canthaxanthin, is applied to ensure that the flesh is the pink colour that consumers expect from salmon, even if it achieves a pinkness unknown to nature. It is not so clear that this dye is harmless, though it is accepted that farmed salmon contains more fat than wild salmon.

Governments have not been indifferent to the issue of food additives. As early as 1954 the British government's Food Standards Committee reported:'We have found the whole subject of food colours clouded with uncertainty' and recommended that their use be limited and that any found faintly harmful to animals be excluded from the human food chain. Of those submitted for judgement, twelve were found to be harmless; for thirty-two,'the available evidence is deficient or conflicting'; while thirty-five 'have been shown or are suspected to have harmful effects'.[29] Thirty dyes were eventually authorised for use in human foods. In 1987 an experiment was carried out amongst the residents of High Wycombe in Buckinghamshire, 30,000 of whom received a questionnaire which invited them to declare whether they thought they suffered allergic reactions to additives. Eighty-one said they did (responses to such enquiries are notoriously low) and, when the eighty-one respondents were subjected to a series of tests involving colours, preservatives, anti-oxidants and aspirin, three showed some reactions. This cannot be regarded as a truly scientific test, rather as an illustration of the misunderstandings that surrounded the subject of additives as late as 1987.[30]

Three decades later, in 1983, the situation was thrown into further confusion when three employees of Industrial Bio-Test, a supposedly independent testing institute in Chicago, were convicted of fraud, having evidently faked the results of toxicity tests on certain colourants submitted to them by manufacturers.[31] Some of these had been approved by the British Food Additives and Contaminants Committee. In 1983 it was combined with the Food Advisory Committee but during its existence it did some valuable work in excluding certain colourings, notably from baby foods. In 1973 and again in 1979 the Ministry of Agriculture declared that'a case of need has not been demonstrated for the use of added colouring matter in these [baby] foods'.[32] Nevertheless, it was revealed during a Parliamentary debate on 24 May 1985 that the Japanese and Greek governments had banned the use of certain colourants that were permitted in Britain. Conal Gregory, MP for York, whose constituency contained the Rowntree factories, added to the debate his own concerns about products added to foodstuffs for other purposes. He complained that chocolate sold in the United Kingdom 'would be considered imitation chocolate in Belgium and the Netherlands because it does not contain the required amount of cocoa solids. The West Germans say that a minimum of twenty-five per cent cocoa solids should be used before a product can be called chocolate'. Some may feel that the Belgians, Dutch and Germans had a point and that in this case the European Union performed a useful service in raising standards.

Making it Look *and Sound* Nice

Appearance is about more than colour. French winemakers had long used
bull's blood to clarify wines of VDQS quality (Vins Delimites de Qualité
Supérieure) thus helping to distinguish them from the cheaper table wines,
but the BSE panic of the 1990s put a stop to this practice in 1997, despite
the remoteness of the connection between the condition caused by BSE
(Creutzfeldt-Jacob Disease), the blood and the wine. There were no complaints from wine drinkers. A more recent controversy concerns the use of
chemicals like carbon dioxide and nitrogen to produce foamy 'cappuccino'
toppings from products as varied as Parmesan cheese, tuna, mango and
ginger. Heston Blumenthal, proprietor of The Fat Duck at Bray, Berkshire,
voted 'The World's Best Restaurant' by those who concern themselves
with such things, was reported as offering oyster foam as a feature of a dish
called 'The Sound of the Sea'. Diners were invited to listen on an iPod to
the sound of breaking waves while consuming the oyster foam which represented 'mist above the waves'. This kind of activity may be regarded as, at
worst, harmless nonsense for those with more money than sense, but other
manifestations of food technology have been presented as more sinister by
some well-qualified sources.

Not Just Additives

Thus in 1979 *The Lancet* published an article alarmingly headed
'Epidemic of Breast Enlargement in an Italian School',[33] which studied
1,647 boys and 476 girls attending schools in Milan. Fifty-eight per cent
of the boys aged six to ten and sixty-seven per cent of the girls aged six
to seven were recorded as having larger breasts than would have been
expected for children of that age and, in the words of *The Lancet,* 'an
uncontrolled supply of poultry and beef was suspected as being the cause
of this outbreak'. The unproven implication was that female hormones
in the feed supplied to the beef and chickens was responsible for the
breast enlargement. The process of rearing chickens has been blamed for
much else. The separation of hatchlings from their mothers has been
blamed for depriving the chicks of protective bacteria in their mothers
and to this, in turn, has been attributed the high incidence of salmonella
in the eggs later produced by the chicks.[34] Further criticism has been
levelled at the practice of feeding hatchling produce which is rich in
protein and hormones so that they grow fully in six weeks instead of the

normal twenty weeks – a practice which may help to explain the effects upon small Italian children.

The 1980s saw a number of studies of the effects of certain foods, untouched by additives, on medical conditions. In 1982 a study at Addenbrookes Hospital, Cambridge, showed that the distressing condition irritable bowel syndrome could be affected by diet, with wheat, bananas, corn (maize) and potatoes provoking the condition in different patients.[35] Three years later, in 1985, another study at Addenbrookes identified a similar effect in Crohn's Disease, the culprits this time being cereals and dairy products.[36] In the same year *The Lancet* also reported a study at Great Ormond Street Hospital for Children designed to ascertain whether a migraine was caused by food allergy.[37] Eighty-eight children suffering from migraines were subjected to an *oligoantigenic* diet, which formidable expression refers to a diet based on long-established products which were believed to be harmless and free of additives. They included lamb, chicken, rice, potatoes, bananas, apples, brassica and some vitamin supplements. Eighty-two of the children were judged to have shown significant improvements but the article concluded, rather gloomily, that 'so many foods can provoke attacks that any food or combination of foods can be the cause'. Not much progress there then. A further study was reported in the *Journal of Paediatrics* in January 1989,[38] involving forty-five children aged two to sixteen who suffered epilepsy, migraines and behavioural problems and who had been referred to the hospital's department of neurology. Again they were subjected to an oligoantigenic diet and forty of the forty-five showed improvements in their conditions. Foods which were suspected of being the causes of their troubles were then gradually re-introduced to their diets and the effects recorded. Milk and cheese from cows and citrus fruits were recorded as triggering symptoms in more than half the cases, while at the other end of the scale, bananas and apples provoked adverse reactions in 9 per cent and 6 per cent of cases respectively. This would appear to confirm the findings of *The Lancet* reports that the most innocuous foods, even without the help of additives, can trigger adverse reactions in some subjects.

Not everyone was convinced. In the same decade, salt came under suspicion as being injurious to health. A number of studies had suggested that salt, long accepted not only as a flavour enhancer but also as an early and essential preservative agent for foods like meat and fish, could have an adverse effect upon blood pressure and heart conditions. However, in 1984 a letter signed by thirteen doctors from six universities in four countries questioned this, asserting that:

> Difficulties arise when the need to present clear-cut, authoritative guidance for the 'healthy diet' results in dogmatic advice for which there is no scientific evidence ... The idea (or likelihood) that salt in the diet has some positive value is totally ignored. Instead some are even suggesting that this basic substance is a general poison like alcohol or tobacco.[39]

It is now widely accepted that excess salt in the diet can raise blood pressure and that many prepared foods do contain more salt than they might, though the precise meaning of the term *excess* is still debated.

Confused Science

Additives which are authorised by the European Union for use in foods are given 'E-numbers', which are the usual nomenclature by which they are designated on food packaging. Some 400 substances are numbered in this way, for flavouring, colouring, preserving, emulsifying and similar purposes. The issuing of an E-number is no guarantee that the substance is permissible in every EU country, since regulations vary between states and the situation is further complicated by the fact that regulations governing the labelling of medicines vary from those concerning foods. Labels of some medicines, for example, refer to the effects of E-numbers on allergic conditions, while such information may be omitted from food labels. Moreover, the testing procedures which lead to the issuing of an E-number, and thereby the approval of the EU authorities, is no guarantee that the substance is removed from controversy. A recent example concerns sodium benzoate (E-211) which has for many years been used as a preservative in fizzy drinks, an industry with global sales of over £70 billion, with a strong following amongst children. Research by Professor Peter Piper of the University of Sheffield suggested that earlier tests to ascertain the safety of the additive had overlooked the effect of long-term consumption upon DNA, with possibly harmful effects including Parkinson's disease. Other research suggested that, when drunk in combination with vitamin C, a common element in fruit-based soft drinks, it could produce benzene which could itself promote cancerous growths. As a result of this discovery, four fizzy drinks were withdrawn from sale in the EU. Thus an additive approved after tests by the EU, the US Food and Drug Administration (FDA) and the World Health Organisation may be responsible for producing long-term cell damage with serious outcomes.[40]

Another additive which has attracted critical attention for a number of reasons is taurine, an acid which is a natural and necessary constituent of bile and was first isolated by two Austrian scientists in the 1820s who extracted it from the bile of oxen – hence its name, based on the Latin word *Taurus,* meaning bull. There is no truth in the popular legend that it is extracted from bulls' testicles, though this myth helps to encourage the naïve view that it gives power and energy to those who consume it. Many other claims have been made for taurine, most of them unproven by recognised scientific processes. Taurine supplements fed to mice supposedly prevented them from becoming overweight on a high fat diet, while some believe that it is a treatment for bipolar disorder (manic depression). It is also claimed that it reduces muscle fatigue and is therefore promoted in energy drinks, notably *Red Bull,* whose name is a reference to the ingredient itself. Other less reassuring claims have associated taurine with various adverse effects on the heart and brain, but no investigation has ever confirmed these. It became a cult drink amongst students in America in the 1990s because of its supposedly energy-giving properties, though a study whose findings were published in 2003, *Debunking the Effects of Taurine in Red Bull Energy Drink*, and whose title tells the reader all he needs to know, suggested that such effects as were conferred by Red Bull were produced by the high concentration of caffeine in the drink.[41] The sale of Red Bull is banned in some countries, notably France, because of its association with taurine, though the latter is permitted in certain infant foods since premature babies may be deficient in taurine. Thus a substance which is necessary to human health, naturally occurring and has been in use for decades as an additive in popular drinks, is variously described as an energy-giving, ineffective, positively harmful and necessary substance for infants. Confused?

Sweet or Sour?

Some of the most ferocious controversies over food additives have concerned sweetening substitutes for sugar. Aspartame, which is marketed as Nutrisweet, is based on aspartic acid and was licensed for use in human foods and drinks by the US Food and Drug Administration in 1981. The president of its manufacturer, G.D. Searle and Co., was Donald Rumsfeld, supporter at the time of the President, Ronald Reagan, and later Secretary of Defence under President George W. Bush. Rumsfeld was never far from public controversy and his connection with the company may have attracted more critical comment than would have been the case with a less prominent figure.[42] The product is widely used as a sweetening agent by corporations like Coca Cola, Pepsi Cola, Nestlé and Monsanto, but from the year of its authorisation it was controversial. The FDA reported in 1995 that, in the previous fourteen years, 75 per cent of reports of adverse reactions to substances in the food supply involved aspartame.[43] It was suggested that aspartame was linked to a variety of harmful and sometimes fatal conditions, a particular concern being brain tumours, whose incidence had increased in the years since 1981 (though some suggested that this owed more to diagnosis than to a real increase in numbers).

A series of studies of the effects of the product were conducted in laboratories in many locations. Dr John Olney, assisted by the activist lawyer James Turner, claimed in the 1970s, before aspartame was authorised for use, that aspartic acid, its principal component, damaged the brains of infant mice. In 2005 a study conducted in Bologna, Italy, found no link between aspartame and such conditions as brain tumours, leukaemia and lymphoma when it was fed to rats, but it did suggest that it could cause damage to kidneys and nerves.[44] In April 2006 the US National Cancer Institute published the results of a study of over half a million men and women, which showed no link between aspartame and brain tumours, leukaemia or lymphoma, but such studies on human volunteers were clouded by a suggestion that the form in which the aspartame was administered – slow-dissolving capsules – failed to replicate the effects of the product when it was ingested in drinks, the normal method of consumption. Further controversy arose when the European Food Safety Authority (EFSA) became involved. EFSA was established in 2002 to set and monitor safe levels of consumption of additives throughout the European Union. Having considered the results of the Italian and other studies, EFSA declared that there was no reason to modify existing advice on the recommended safe levels of consumption of the product. It was then alleged that the chairman of the panel which had advised EFSA also worked for an organisation partly funded by users of the sweetener.

Further controversy surrounds some of the fructose syrups that are derived by processing maize, some of them six times as sweet as sugar and thus attractive to people who wish to reduce their intake of that tooth-decaying, calorie-inducing substance in soft drinks and similar products. Some of these fructose products, however, are claimed to have caused obesity in mice and humans and to be associated with cardiovascular disease and raised levels of cholesterol.

Silent Spring

One of the first and seminal works which questioned the uses to which science was being put was Rachel Carson's book *Silent Spring*, first published in 1962. It was Rachel Carson who first described the activities of the farming and food industries as 'Man's war against nature'[45] (though the 'war' had in fact been respectably waged for decades, as observed earlier). She observed that, during the twentieth century, the burgeoning chemical industry had created hundreds of substances to exterminate insects, weeds, rodents and other living things which had come to be regarded as harmful or inconvenient to man and his activities. She drew attention to the insecticide DDT which, in 1948, had earned Swiss chemist Paul Muller the Nobel Prize for Medicine following his discovery of it nine years earlier. It had been very effective in killing mosquitoes which spread malaria and was regarded as a great benefit to mankind, but Rachel Carson drew attention to its harmful effects. It was routinely sprayed on alfalfa as an insecticide and the alfalfa was then fed to chickens, making its way into their eggs which were, in turn, consumed by humans. In the same way, its use on crops for animal feed entered the human food chain via the milk of cows. She suggested that it could cause cancer in humans and had the additional effect of causing birds' eggs to have thinner shells, with implications for the survival of some species. As a result the agricultural use of DDT was banned in the United States and, subsequently, in other countries. She also demonstrated how very small concentrations of chemicals low down the food chain (for example in water) could increase in intensity as they made their way up the chain via insects, plankton, birds and fish until, by the time they were eaten by humans, the concentration could increase 600 fold.[46] Moreover, she observed that many bacteria are essential to the cycle of nature – for example, by causing the decay which creates humus, essential to the fertility of soil. An unintended consequence of the artificial destruction of bacteria could be a reduction in the fertility of the soil.

She drew attention to other harmful effects of the use of chemicals and proposed some alternatives. In the 1950s a programme of spraying was undertaken in the United States to kill beetles that caused Dutch Elm Disease. This led to the deaths of many birds without saving the Elms. In Canada, salmon had been virtually eliminated from some rivers through the use of sprays against insects that were attacking evergreen trees while others, used on hardwoods, eventually entered the human food chain via contaminated milk.[47] She proposed the use of natural predators to control pests; in effect, enlisting other species to help man in his war against nature. Thus in the 1920s moths had been imported to Australia from South America to control prickly pear cactus which was spreading too rapidly in parts of the outback. In the 1880s the Vedalia Beetle was taken from Australia to California to destroy insects causing cottony cushion scale which had devastated the Californian citrus industry. Within two years the beetles had done their work and the fortunes of the industry were restored, but the introduction, from the 1940s, of pesticides to destroy other insects had the effect of killing the beetles.[48] At the time that *Silent Spring* was written, the potential menace of species introduced to places where they have few natural predators was not appreciated. In 1935, 102 cane toads were imported to Australia from Hawaii. Cane toads were recognised as effective agents against certain pests, especially against cane beetles on sugar plantations. By 2006 their number had increased to over 200 *million*, and they were spreading from their original habitat, Queensland, at the rate of forty kilometres a year and had reached New South Wales and the Northern Territory. They are believed to be responsible for the drastic decline in numbers of a range of native species including some marsupials and lizards. 'Natural' control is not always as natural as it seems and scientists are now much more hesitant about using introduced species in this way. The tendency of science to outstrip humanity's understanding of its long-term consequences had been highlighted by the great humanitarian Albert Schweitzer, who declared: 'Man has lost the capacity to foresee and to forestall. He will end up by destroying the earth'.[49]

Others have observed that additives have moved on from their earlier role as methods of preserving food from decay (as in the case of salt) or of making food look attractive and have, in some cases, been used merely to enhance profits. Thus meat can be treated with chemicals called polyphosphates to increase its capacity for retaining water and thus making processed meats heavier. This quality was most flagrantly exposed in a trade journal in 1975 under the headline, *Why sell meat when you can sell water?*[50] Examples are also cited of products that are so dominated by additives that they bear little resemblance to what they are supposed to be, notably a vegetable soup that is evidently uncontaminated by any recognisable vegetable.[51]

On the other hand the application of science to agriculture has a role in helping to feed the rapidly growing population of the planet. According to the United Nations in 1950 the global population was 2.5 billion and by 1999 it had reached 6 billion, much of this growth occurring in India and China where, as a result of their rapidly growing economies and rising standard of living, the demand for food is expected to increase disproportionately.

In 1968 famine was endemic in India and the country was regarded in some quarters as a hopeless case, but in the next forty years its annual production of wheat, for example, increased more than sevenfold from 10 million to 73 million tons annually. But in 2007, for the first time in forty years, India had to import wheat from Australia. In the nineteenth century, more food was produced by extending the area of cultivated land in the prairies of America and the farms of Australia and New Zealand. In the twentieth century, further increases have been achieved by the application of science to agriculture. We cannot do without it, but we must control it.

'The Defrauding of Consumers'

In the 1970s further questions were asked, particularly in the United States, about ethical issues in the production and marketing of food, sometimes from a viewpoint that was extremely hostile to corporate America. The developments should be seen in the context of the American consumer movement whose birth may be traced to the publication, in 1965, of Ralph Nader's book, *Unsafe at Any Speed: the Designed-in Dangers of the American Automobile.* The book was highly critical of the US motor industry and its attitude towards safety and made Ralph Nader a national, if controversial, celebrity. He even emerged as a presidential candidate in the 2000 election and, by drawing liberal votes from Al Gore, probably contributed to the election of George W. Bush, with all the consequences that followed. In the 1960s and early 1970s a number of his followers turned their attention to the US food industry in terms which were far more critical than those associated with the British Consumers' Association, whose publication, *Which*, while often critical of individual products, was not overtly hostile to corporations in general. I (the author) once discussed some food industry issues with one of Ralph Nader's most active followers and was informed that he would 'not sit down' with any representative of an American corporation because he did not trust them. This was disconcerting, not least because I (unknown to my interlocutor) was myself an employee of the British affiliate of such a corporation. More to the point, it was hard to see how progress could be made in resolving problems without some discussion taking place. Nader himself wrote of the US government's agency charged with the oversight of food policy: 'The Food and Drug Administration has acted as an official sponsor of processing and marketing practices that have transformed the defrauding of consumers into a competitive advantage'.[52]

The United States already had in place laws to regulate the safety of foods, thanks largely to a Civil War veteran called Harvey Washington Wiley (1844–1930) who, having qualified as a chemist, was appointed chief chemist to the US Department of Agriculture. Wiley began a campaign to identify and eliminate from the diet additives and preservatives shown to be dangerous. His work had alarming aspects, not least his recruitment from amongst Department of Agriculture employees of a group quickly nicknamed 'the poison squad' because they volunteered to eat foods which were known to contain high levels of substances which Wiley regarded with suspicion. As far as is known, they all survived, but Wiley's relentless work resulted in the passing of the Pure Food and Drug Act, 1906, which set up an inspection regime to detect defective meat and, besides requiring better labelling of foods, also outlawed certain ingredients in foodstuffs and patent medicines. It had the odd effect of allowing Coca Cola to continue to add small quantities of cocaine to its drink (hence the *Coca* part of the name) while prosecuting the company for adding too much caffeine. The caffeine was reduced and the cocaine soon eliminated. The Act also led to the establishment of the Food and Drug Administration with responsibility for ensuring that foods and medicines were as safe as they could be. The Act was not perfect and attempts to strengthen it were not always well received by corporations. In the 1930s President Roosevelt's Under-Secretary for Agriculture, Rexford G. Tugwell, proposed to introduce clearer food labelling and to reduce the quantities of pesticides allowed on fruit. This prompted a telegram from the Associated Grocery Manufacturers of America to the Washington correspondents of leading newspapers, reminding them of their responsibilities: 'May we respectfully call your attention to revised Tugwell-Copeland Bill as a measure that may seriously affect future newspaper advertising volume'. Similar assaults were mounted by the advertising business and the Bill died.

The controversy over the sweetener aspartame has been noted above and another sweetener, cyclamates, aroused an equally bitter controversy and became one of the principal points of attack on the Food and Drug Administration (FDA) and on the industries it regulated.[53] In 1950 Abbot Laboratories had filed an application to the US Food and Drug Administration concerning a cyclamate product, sucaryl sodium, 'for use in foods and beverages by diabetics and by others who must restrict their intake of sugar'. It had been discovered, by chance, by Michael Sveda while he was working as a graduate student at the University of Illinois, the patent being purchased by Abbott. The product was duly licensed by the FDA but its use was gradually extended to products intended to produce weight loss as well as those used for clear medical reasons in diabetic foods. As the years passed, conflicting studies endorsed or criticised the product. Some studies suggested that it might be the cause of tumours in rats; others questioned the methodology and conclusions of these studies. In 1959 cyclamates were added to the 'GRAS' ('Generally Recognised as Safe') list of products which also contained such familiar names as salt and vinegar. Products on the list could be added to almost any foods including confectionery, jam, preserved fruits and soft drinks, many of them commonly consumed by children.

In 1966 some Japanese scientists announced the results of tests which demonstrated that, in some people, cyclamates could produce a reaction which produced more harmful chemicals which, in turn, had produced deformities in chickens similar to those caused by thalidomide (itself a cause of considerable controversy at this time). A further study in 1969 showed that a mixture of cyclamates and saccharin caused bladder cancer in rats. It appeared that eight rats, from a sample of 240, had developed tumours when fed a mixture of saccharine and cyclamates at a rate equivalent to the consumption, by a human being, of 350 cans of diet soda per day.[54] The Lancet's comment on the fury which followed was that 'Never have so many pathologists been summoned to opine on so few lessons from so humble a species as the laboratory rat', and the equally eminent journal Nature wrote that the evidence against cyclamates was 'as solid as candy floss'. Nevertheless, in October 1969 the US Secretary of Health, Education and Welfare announced: 'I am today ordering that the artificial sweetener cyclamate be removed from the list of substances generally recognised as safe [the GRAS list] for use in foods'. The announcement appears to have been prompted by a degree of panic since three weeks later the ban was modified. Cyclamates could not be used in drinks but were permitted in foods provided they were listed on the label. A proposal to test the safety of cyclamates by including them, in generous quantities, in the diets of prisoners, was dropped, one hopes on humanitarian grounds.[55] Britain banned the product the following year.

Cyclamates remain controversial. The highly regarded United States National Academy of Sciences has declared that 'the totality of evidence from studies in animals does not indicate that cyclamate is carcinogenic'. No one has suggested that the National Academy is a creature of the food or chemical industries and fifty-five nations (including Canada) now allow the use of cyclamates in human foods. Abbott Laboratories continue to lobby for the restoration of the product to the US register but the controversy is such that it gets in the way of the science. The saccharin

which featured in the original test along with the cyclamates has escaped
most of the censure and suspicion which the test spawned, despite the fact
that high doses of saccharin have produced tumours in mice.[56] The case of
cyclamates illustrates the difficulties that surround the production and marketing of healthy foodstuffs, particularly when the dreaded word 'cancer' is
invoked. In 1983, in the journal *Science*, the highly respected Bruce Ames,
professor at the University of California, Berkeley, drew attention to the
fact that carcinogens occur naturally in a wide variety of foods, including
black pepper and some mushrooms and cooking oils. Michael Sveda, the
discoverer of cyclamates, died in 1999, believing that the sugar industry
had played a significant part in the campaign against cyclamates. In the
words of his obituarist:

> Sveda was among a little-appreciated group of scientists who dramatically
> improved the world's quality of life. Sadly, in his lifetime, he saw his contribu-
> tions vilified and rejected as a result of anti-scientific, technophobic witch-hunts
> that caused chemicals to be banned at the drop of a rat.[57]

James S. Turner's book *The Chemical Feast*, published in 1970, drew attention to other controversial issues within the food and drink industry, some
of them occurring within the industries themselves. The market for fruit
juices, especially orange juice, within the USA is huge, its two principal
centres of production being Florida and California. For reasons of climate
and soil, juice from California is naturally darker than that of Florida and,
because Americans prefer their juice dark, the Florida growers argued the
case for colourants to give their juice a darker hue, while the Californians
set themselves up as champions of purity. Shiftier practices were at work
elsewhere in the industry. The FDA prosecuted a well-known producer
of branded fruit juice for diluting its 'pure' juice with water. The fine of
$6,000 was, it was suggested, a fraction of the additional profits made from
the adulteration.

Reference is made in a later chapter to the effects upon mental well-
being of diets which are over-dependent on 'junk' foods (however
defined), these being cited as reasons for poor behaviour in schools and for
scholastic under-achievement. From the 1970s, some authorities and interest groups advanced similar arguments in respect of some additives. Much
of the evidence was anecdotal, though it was given some weight by an
American paediatrician called Ben Feingold (1899–1982) who, in a book
called *Why Your Child is Hyperactive,* suggested that certain artificial flavourings and colourants affected the behaviour of children. In September 2007

there appeared the results of a controlled trial carried out by Southampton University on 153 three-year-old children and 144 eight- to nine-year-olds. The children were chosen to be representative of the age groups as a whole and were not confined to those suffering from Attention Deficit Hyperactivity Disorder (ADHD), although in the period 1991 to 2006 the number of prescriptions written for children with ADHD had risen from 2 to 456,909.[58] The children were fed mixes of additives in different drinks, the substances involved including a range of artificial colourants and sodium benzoate (E-211), which is used as a preservative in fizzy drinks like Diet Coke, Irn Bru and Orangina (which would otherwise have to be stored, once opened, in a refrigerator). The diet was chosen to represent one that many children could reasonably be expected to consume routinely. The experiment, which was carried out at the behest of the Food Safety Agency (FSA), revealed marked changes in hyperactivity, and in particular a deterioration in levels of concentration, among many, though not all, the children. The results were given added authority by a highly respected headteacher, Dame Anna Hassan, head of Millfields School in Hackney, who reported an improvement in behaviour when she changed the menu in her school in favour of organic foods.[59] There were immediate calls for the substances to be banned from human foods, especially those aimed at children, but the Food Safety Agency declined to do this preferring, instead, to advise parents to check drink labels for the presence of additives. Whether parents could be expected to do this, or to know which E-numbers they were looking for, was left open to question. Moreover, the FSA passed the results of the experiment to the European Food Safety Agency (EFSA) for its consideration, which some saw as a further delaying tactic.

'Man's war against nature' in the food industry thus has two faces. On the one hand it has ensured that a wide variety of palatable foods is available throughout the year through such techniques as canning, drying and refrigeration. It has also ensured that low-cost producers in thinly inhabited areas like Australia can send their produce to distant and heavily populated continents like Europe. However it has also resulted in some more ambiguous achievements. The doctoring of hens' food to promote the production of brown eggs, preferred by consumers for reasons buried in the human psyche, is probably harmless. The fact that processed foods, like flavoured potato crisps, are much more profitable to their suppliers, and more popular as children's snacks, than the potatoes themselves is probably not harmless since the excessive consumption of such products causes obesity. And there seems little doubt that some of the techniques and chemicals used to flavour, colour or preserve food are harmful – but there is little agreement on which ones.

Postscript

At the same time another front has opened in 'man's war against nature' – that of genetically modified crops. Will they enhance our ability to grow more healthy foods for the world's increasing population, without the need for chemical products to repel weeds, pests and drought? Or will they release monstrous hybrids which will destroy the environment? One commentator has suggested that the technology associated with genetic modification could be used for extremely sinister purposes by terrorists: 'The research methods used to transmit desired genes into plants could easily be adapted for nefarious purposes: creating pathogenic bacteria resistant to multiple antibiotics or able to synthesis lethal toxins'.[60] The view taken of these developments is more benign in the United States than in Europe, which has been unconvinced that the new techniques will do more good than harm. This argument has a long way to run.

4

Diseases of Deficiency

Hardly able to let drop an anchor
An account of the effects of scurvy on crews of Captain James Lancaster's
expedition to the East Indies in 1601

I had some of it dressed every day for the officers' cabin table and left it to the
option of the men to take as much as they pleased or none at all ... before a
week I found it necessary to put everyone on board to an allowance.
Captain James Cook's remedy for scurvy – sauerkraut

Flexible like wax that is rather liquid, so that the flabby and toneless legs scarcely
sustain the weight of the superimposed body, so that the tibiae yield to the
weight of the fabric pressing down on them from above and become bent.
Daniel Whistler's description of the newly discovered disease of rickets, 1645

'The Fattening House'

In 1585 William Cecil (1520–98), Elizabeth I's Lord Treasurer and principal
counsellor, reflected upon the fortunate fact that, since the queen's acces-
sion in 1558, there had been no harvest failures. This unusual sequence of
good harvests helped to account for the comparative domestic tranquillity
of the early years of her reign, but it was not to last. The following year the
harvest failed, an occurrence repeated twice in the following decade and at
intervals of about seven years in the period 1600–1640. Since contemporary

methods of storing and preserving foods and of transporting them to areas
of need were primitive, harvest failure could mean famine, discontent and
rebellion, not least because ineffective methods of transport made it difficult to move bulky supplies from areas of comparative plenty to those of
privation. It is no coincidence that the years leading up to the Civil War in
England and to the French Revolution were frequently afflicted by poor
harvests. By the late eighteenth century the improvement in agricultural
methods and the development of something like an effective system of
inland waterways had helped to reduce the incidence and effects of serious
food shortages in Britain. The process was helped by the practice of growing pulse vegetables in fallow fields since they could be preserved more
easily than brassicas and they contained a lot of protein – a fact not fully
appreciated until the twentieth century. However, it did not follow that the
population was well nourished.

Shortly after it was opened in 1821, the Millbank Prison, situated on
the present sight of Tate Britain, became known as 'The Fattening House'
because of the generous diet received by its prisoners, amounting to the
equivalent of about 3,000 kilocalories daily and including quantities of
meat beyond the purses of honest working-class families. Public dissat-
isfaction was such that the diet was reduced to about 2,600 kilocalories
per day.[1] Early in the twentieth century the Quaker philanthropist Joseph
Rowntree (1834–1925) conducted a study of the physical condition of
thirteen-year-old boys in the city of York where his company had its
chocolate factory. He demonstrated that the middle-class boys were on
average 3½in taller and 11¼lb heavier than the children of the labouring
classes. Joseph's son Benjamin (1871–1924) calculated that, to maintain
a minimum level of 'physical efficiency' consistent with the work they
did, a labouring-class family in York needed a weekly income of 21s 8d,
whereas almost 7 per cent of York's labouring families had incomes below
this level. At about the same period the American writer Jack London
(1876–1916) commented that the English population were, on average,
shorter than Scandinavians and Americans. When he encountered an
unusually tall Englishman, Jack London commented humorously that the
man would be suitable for the horseguards, only to learn that the man
was, indeed, of that regiment.[2] It has been estimated that, in 1900, the
average daily intake of the labouring classes was a little over 2,000 kilocalories at a time when they were required to undertake hard, physical
work. To put the figures into context, the recommended levels in 2007
for a less physically active workforce are about 2,500 for men and 2,000
for women, figures similar to the Millbank diet of 1821.[3]

An inadequate intake of kilocalories was bad enough, but even amongst relatively prosperous families the absence of essential vitamins and minerals from an otherwise adequate diet could have harmful consequences. Death from malnutrition due to starvation was a grim and familiar reality during mediaeval times and it was well into the nineteenth century before the development of new agricultural methods was supplemented by the availability of food from the farms of America and Australasia and, together, banished starvation from the tables of all but the poorest citizens of Britain. The idea that disease could be caused by the absence of essential nutrients from an otherwise plentiful diet was alien to most medical practitioners until well into the twentieth century, when vitamins were identified and their significance grasped. Paradoxically, domestic improvements in agricultural productivity in the eighteenth and early nineteenth centuries may have contributed to vitamin deficiencies amongst the poor. In her trilogy *Lark Rise to Candleford*,[4] published between 1939 and 1945, Flora Thompson (1876–1947) applauded the fact that, in her native Oxfordshire villages, many rural households had small allotments on which they grew nourishing vegetables and fruits, rich in vitamins, which supplemented their otherwise plain diets. Yet these were the lucky ones. The enclosure movements of the nineteenth century had led to the creation of larger, more efficient farms but at the expense of depriving many poorer citizens of their grazing rights on the now enclosed common land. George Sturt (1863–1927), in his account of rural communities around Farnham, Surrey, published in 1912,[5] reminded his readers that this had the effect of reducing access to fuel and fresh milk for small householders, whose modest incomes had to be spent buying produce which would previously have been available to them without payment. The abolition of the Corn Laws in 1846 and the subsequent embrace of free-trade policies by Victorian administrations had reduced the price of staple commodities like corn and meat, but the loss of common land and the move of rural populations to large cities far from their smallholdings meant that many poorer families had diets which were lacking in fresh vegetables and fruits and the vitamins and minerals they contained.

It was relatively easy to believe that deaths brought by the great pestilences like the Black Death were a punishment sent by God; or that epidemics like those of cholera that swept through Europe in waves in the nineteenth century were caused by bad air or 'miasma', that pervasive explanation of disease that occupied the minds of all but the most radical medical authorities of the time. It was much more difficult to believe that sailors, who were fed plenty of salted beef, fish and ship's biscuits, were dying because there was something missing from their diet: something as simple as lemon juice or watercress.

Nevertheless, some of the earliest writers on medicine showed awareness of connections between diet and medical conditions. The German egyptologist Georg Ebers (1837–98) purchased the papyrus that bears his name in Luxor in 1874. It dates from about 1550 BC and is now in the University of Leipzig. It recommends liver as a remedy against night blindness, a condition caused by a deficiency in vitamin A of which liver is, indeed, an abundant source. A thousand years later Hippocrates was following the author of the Ebers papyrus in prescribing ox liver and honey for the same condition, as did the missionary Dr David Livingstone (1813-73) in Africa in the nineteenth century. During the First World War, when the existence and role of vitamins was barely understood, an increase in eye diseases associated with 'night blindness', poor vision in failing light, was recorded in Denmark. It was traced to the fact that, during the war, Denmark exported a larger than normal proportion of its butter, a product rich in vitamin A (carotene) which is a remedy for the condition.[6] Hippocrates' contemporary, the Greek historian Herodotus, writing of the wars between the Greeks and Persians, observed that Persian casualties had thinner skulls than those of the Greeks and Egyptians. He attributed this characteristic to the fact that the Persians wore turbans whereas the Greeks and Egyptian went bareheaded. There may even have been some truth in his belief since the thin Persian skulls could have been a sign of rickets, a condition relieved by exposure to the sun, a source of vitamin D.

The Science of Vitamins

The modern science of vitamins (and minerals) may be said to date from about the turn of the nineteenth/twentieth centuries when a group of scientists, many in Britain and the Netherlands, came to understand that plentiful diets which were lacking in mysterious and unidentified 'accessory food factors' could produce harmful and sometimes deadly conditions. In 1905 the Dutch scientist Cornelius Pekelharing (1848–1922) observed that mice which were fed a generous quantity of protein, carbohydrate and lard died unless they were also given milk which, he deduced, contained 'an unknown substance' (numerous vitamins in fact) which were essential to life. He published his findings in a Dutch journal where they were overlooked.[7] Eight years earlier, in 1897, his countryman Christiaan Eijkmann had investigated the cause of beri beri, characterised by wasting, paralysis and death, amongst natives of Indonesia which was then part of the Dutch overseas empire. He established that a diet of polished rice was a common factor in those who contracted the disease. In 1911 a Polish researcher working in England called Casimir Funk ascertained that those eating whole rice did not contract beri beri and he later identified a substance present in whole rice which cured the disease, vitamin B1 or thiamin. He also identified a number of other conditions associated with deficient diets and published his findings in 1912, explaining:

> It is now known that all these diseases, with the exception of pellagra, can be prevented and cured by the addition of certain preventive substances; the deficient substances, which are of the nature of organic bases, we will call *vitamines*.[8]

This is the first recorded use of the word *vitamines*. At this time it was believed that thiamin was the only B-group vitamin and another quarter century passed before another, niacin, was identified as a factor in preventing pellagra.[9]

In 1906 the biochemist Frederick Gowland Hopkins (1861–1947) wrote an article entitled 'The analyst and the medical man',[10] which drew attention to the existence of essential dietary factors for the prevention of certain diseases like scurvy and rickets, while acknowledging his ignorance of what they were or how they worked:

> In diseases such as rickets, and particularly in scurvy, we have had for long years knowledge of a dietetic factor; but though we know how to benefit these conditions empirically the real errors in the diet are to this day quite obscure.[11]

Six years later, in 1912, Hopkins published in the *Journal of Physiology* an article entitled 'Feeding Experiments Illustrating the Importance of Accessory Food factors in Normal Dietaries', whose forbidding title should not conceal its significance since it demonstrated that a diet, however plentiful, that lacked what he still called 'accessory food factors' would not be adequate for human health. As noted elsewhere, in 1929 he won the Nobel Prize for Medicine which he shared with Eijkmann. This was one of many Nobel prizes associated with the discovery of vitamins which followed during the twentieth century, a fact which underlines their rapid acceptance by the medical and scientific community as elements essential to human health. Funk had to make do with the satisfaction that he introduced the word *vitamine* to the English language (it later lost its 'e' at the suggestion of Jack Drummond). Many vitamins had yet to be identified but, after Hopkins, Eijkmann and Funk, scientists at least knew what they were looking for and why vitamins were important.

Scurvy

Of all the diseases associated with poor diet, scurvy is the most celebrated as well as being 'probably the nutritional deficiency disease that has caused most suffering in recorded history'.[12] It was known to the Romans as *Purpura Nautica*, and associated even in those times with long sea voyages, though Pliny the Elder, who died in 79 AD, described a condition closely resembling scurvy affecting one of the Roman Army's disastrous expeditions to Germany fifty years earlier. Until the nineteenth century it accounted for far more deaths amongst sailors and explorers than war. The word derives from the Icelandic 'skyrbjugr' meaning 'cut swellings' suffered by their seafarers on long voyages and was described in graphic terms by a doctor of the Royal Navy, who carried out one of the first systematic attempts to find a cure:

> Swelled legs, putrid gums, extraordinary lassitude of the whole body, ulcers of the worst kind, attended with rotten bones and such a luxuriancy of fungous flesh as yielded no remedy.[13]

It is also characterised by bloody patches beneath the skin, acute constipation, swelling and bleeding of gums, leading to an inability to chew and eventually to an unpleasant death. One of the most celebrated explorers, Vasco da Gama, commented upon the condition and stumbled upon the remedy, though without realising that he had done so. After rounding the Cape of Good Hope in 1498 he commented that 'many of our men fell ill here, their feet and hands swelling and their gums growing over their teeth so that they could not eat'.[14] A few days later he bought some oranges from some Moorish traders which were consumed by his grateful crew and within a week all had recovered, a fact he mistakenly attributed to the atmosphere of Mombasa, 'for the air of this place is very good'. The belief that fresh air was a remedy for scurvy would endure for centuries.

The French explorer Jacques Cartier suffered similarly during his expedition to Quebec and Montreal in 1535–36, but during his voyage round the world in 1577–79, Francis Drake saw his company recover from the condition when refreshed by herbs and lemons.[15] In 1593 Richard Hawkins (1562–1622), son of the better-known slave trader John Hawkins, saw his crew make an apparently miraculous recovery from scurvy after trading cloth for oranges and lemons in Santos, Brazil. He commented:

> Many, with the sight of the oranges and lemons, seemed to recover heart. This is a wonderful secret of the power and wisdom of God that hath hidden so great and unknown virtue in this fruit, to be a certain remedy for this infirmity.[16]

It is hard to imagine a clearer endorsement from a more authoritative source, but two further centuries had to pass before it was widely accepted that citrus fruits, especially lemons, were a sovereign remedy against scurvy and a further century before the vitamin C they contained was identified. So why did it take so long for eminent, intelligent and well-intentioned men to accept the evidence of Hawkins and others? Their reluctance may owe something to the fact that, until well into the seventeenth century, scurvy was often confused with syphilis with which it shares some symptoms, and syphilis is *not* remedied by vitamin C. Tobias Smollett (1721–71), who had himself worked as a ship's surgeon's assistant, in his 1772 novel *The Expedition of Humphrey Clinker* bracketed scurvy, scrofula, cancer and syphilis as conditions which could all be caught by taking the waters at the fashionable spa at Bath. The views of the authorities are also easier to understand if they are considered in the context of the medical orthodoxy of their times and help to explain why so many quack remedies were on offer for this common condition. Although the 'humoral' doctrines concerning the causes and cures of disease propagated by Hippocrates and Galen had been challenged,[17] there was little to put in their place. According to Galen, a disease like scurvy, characterised by its bloody swellings, was a condition of the blood, hence associated with 'hot and moist' qualities and should therefore be treated by 'cold and dry' remedies which would have ruled out lemon juice, especially as Galen so disapproved of fruit.[18] The attention of Jonas Hanway was drawn to the effects of scurvy upon the teeth and gums and he managed to combine some useful insight into the value of citrus fruits with a further diatribe against tea, the drinking of which he regarded as the root of many evils, writing in 1757 in his *Essay on Tea*:

> If we drank less tea and used gentle acids for the gums and teeth, particularly sour oranges, though we had a less number of French dentists, I fancy this essential part of beauty would be much better preserved.[19]

Other diagnoses and remedies were less sympathetic and much less attractive. In 1736 a physician to the fleet, William Cockburn (1669–1739), attributed scurvy to idleness, writing that 'the boatswain's favourites' suffered most from the condition since arduous work would counteract the harmful effects of a diet of salt pork and salt beef to which he attributed the condition:'I think I have said enough to explain how this sickness is produced with us and to show that 'tis a necessary consequence of an idle life and of feeding on Salt Beef and Pork'.[20] In another publication he suggested that dysentery was an effective cure for scurvy![21] On the other hand Thomas Lowndes (1692–1748), founder of a prestigious chair in astronomy at Cambridge, tried to persuade the admiralty that consumption of salt from his mines in Cheshire would overcome scurvy, while Admiral Sir Thomas Pasley (1734–1808) fed his crew the earth in which he had grown vegetables and declared that their condition had improved. His remedy was not widely adopted.

Some of the earliest authorities on the subject were Dutch, this being no doubt a reflection of the fact that the Dutch were a seafaring nation whose crews were regularly attacked by scurvy. The Dutch physician Hermann Boerhaave (1668–1738) followed Galen in believing that scurvy was a disease of the blood exacerbated by the damp climate of the Netherlands, but he could not altogether ignore the mounting evidence in favour of lemons and prescribed those as well as vinegar, crab apples and Moselle wines as a remedy. His compatriot, the scientist and Lutheran theologian Johann Bachstrom[22] (c.1688–1742), went further and, in a treatise of 1734, *Observationes circa Scorbutum*, wrote:

> Causam veram et primarium Scorbuti nullam aliam esse quam abstinentiam
> diuturniorum a quocumque genere recentium vegetabilium
> (The only real, principal cause of scurvy is a daily avoidance of every type of
> fresh vegetable)[23]

Theories about the efficacy of fresh vegetables in preventing and treating scurvy reached the ears of the English philosopher John Locke (1632–1704) while in exile in Holland in the 1680s, leading him to send some red cabbage seeds to his friend Edward Clarke to be cultivated for the purpose.[24] But despite the evidence and the conversion of authorities like Bachstrom, many years were to pass before such views became orthodox.

Nevertheless, some were prepared to act upon Hawkins's experience even though they did not understand its scientific basis. In 1601 the East India Company dispatched four ships on its first expedition to Sumatra. The fleet was commanded by Sir James Lancaster whose own crew were kept free of scurvy because 'he brought to sea with him certain bottles of the juice of lemons which he gave to each one as long as it would last, three spoonfuls every morning', while the crews of the other three ships succumbed and were, in his words, 'hardly able to let drop an anchor'.[25] The first surgeon-general of the East India Company, John Woodall, in his treatise *The Surgions* [sic] *Mate*, advised the company's surgeons that 'the use of the juice of lemons is a precious medicine and well tried'.[26] In 1607, therefore, the company's minutes resolved that, henceforth, 'lemon water' would accompany future expeditions.[27] When sailors resisted the bitter liquid the company replaced it with wine which may have made the crews a little happier for a while but was in the longer term detrimental to their well-being. The Dutch East India Company had arrived at a similar conclusion and by 1661 were growing a thousand citrus fruit trees at the Cape of Good Hope and even experimenting with small gardens on ships.

Scurvy was not confined to seafarers. Dr John Hall, whose chief claim to fame is that he married Shakespeare's daughter Susanna, kept notes of the more interesting cases that he treated which were published in 1657 as 'Selected Observations on English Bodies' and include twenty-two cases of scurvy. One of these was his own wife, who recovered when her husband prescribed watercress, which is exceptionally rich in vitamin C.[28] Shakespeare himself made very early use of the word 'scurvy' as a derogatory adjective as in 'scurvy fellow' (*Othello*, 1604) and 'scurvy politician' (*King Lear*, 1605), possibly influenced by his daughter's experience of the disease.[29]

The Royal Navy

By the late seventeenth century scurvy was a cause of sufficient concern to Britain's national interests to attract the attention of people more influential than Dutch writers or English doctors. The nation's growing interests in colonies in America and its expanding trade with the East Indies made the maintenance of an effective merchant and war fleet an essential element of national security and the mounting toll of deaths amongst seafarers arising from scurvy (far more than ever died in battle) aroused the interest of politicians and public servants as well as medical men. In 1696 Samuel Pepys, Secretary to the Navy, criticised navy victuallers for replacing raisins and currants with cheaper beef suet on vessels of the Royal Navy, 'since it's the parent of scurvy'.[30] Pepys was wrong, of course. It was not the suet that caused the scurvy, rather the absence of raisins, currants and fresh fruit, but he was moving in the right direction. The decisive event was the voyage of Commodore George Anson (1697–1762).

Anson had set off from Portsmouth in 1740 to attack Spain's Pacific possessions during a war between Spain and Britain. This he succeeded in doing and returned to Portsmouth after an heroic circumnavigation of the earth in 1744, laden with Spanish plunder. However, of the eight ships that set out in his squadron, only one, *The Centurion*, returned with him to Portsmouth and more than half of the crews had perished, almost all of them from scurvy.[31] Anson had observed that the ravages of the disease had subsided when, after stopping at the port of Juan Fernandez, his ships had taken on fresh vegetables. The significance of Anson's experience was not lost on the Scottish doctor, James Lind.

James Lind

James Lind (1716–94) was born in Edinburgh and was apprenticed to an Edinburgh surgeon where he attended lectures in the medical faculty of the university and learned of the work of Boerhaave, one of whose pupils was a fellow student.[32] In 1739 he joined the Royal Navy as a surgeon's mate and in 1746 was posted to the frigate HMS *Salisbury*, where he set about investigating the causes and cures of scurvy. He had observed that voyages beginning in spring suffered less from scurvy than those beginning in autumn or winter and hypothesised that this could be due to the greater availability of fresh vegetables in spring. He announced: 'I shall propose nothing from theory but shall confirm all by experience and facts' in his search for a cure or, in the words of the time, for 'anti-scorbutic' remedies.[33] This renunciation of the Hippocratic framework in favour of Newtonian scientific method was followed by the world's first clinical trial. When the crew began to go down with scurvy Lind chose twelve of the victims and divided them into six pairs. One pair were given a spoonful of orange and lemon juice and the others cider, seawater, horseradish, garlic or vinegar. The pair who received the citrus juices recovered within six days, while the others remained sick, though the pair receiving cider showed some signs of improvement. This is puzzling since the vitamin C content of apples is destroyed by the fermentation process. Perhaps it was really apple juice they were drinking. Lind concluded that 'oranges and lemons were the most effectual remedies for this distemper at sea'.[34]

In 1748 Lind retired from the Royal Navy, entered Edinburgh University and devoted himself to writing and research. In 1753 he published *A Treatise of the Scurvy*, the first work on the subject to be based on scientific experiment. It was dedicated to Anson, whose forthcoming appointment (in 1757) as First Lord of the Admiralty by William Pitt the Elder (1708–88) would ensure that a cure for scurvy remained a priority for the naval authorities. In the past their lordships had preferred to administer the poisonous chemical element antimony to sufferers in the form of Dr James's Fever Powder, probably because it was believed (wrongly) to be a cure for syphilis, with which scurvy was often confused. Despite the confidence and authority that Lind drew from his clinical trial, he was still enough of a 'miasmatist' to assign some responsibility for the condition to the air. He argued that a cold, wet climate, combined with moisture arising from sea air, would lead to clogged skin pores, trapping harmful substances within the body. Fruit and vegetables, he suggested, helped to clean the pores but this did not remove the need to ensure that the lower decks of ships were properly ventilated:'the principal and main predisposing cause to it [scurvy] is a manifest and obvious quality of the air, viz., its moisture', and he suggested that cold baths and good ventilation were therefore essential to a cure. New ships were particularly hazardous because of the 'vapour exhaling from the wood'. Where necessary, the decks should be fumigated with burning tar, but in general it would be sufficient to install hand or wind pumps of the kind devised by the Reverend Stephen Hales and installed by that enterprising cleric in Newgate Prison to prevent outbreaks of typhus in London's notorious gaol.[35] Many of these devices were duly installed. Lind also advocated that the citrus juices be converted to 'rob' or syrup by the addition of sugar, which would have the effect of destroying most of the vitamin C.

Dr Stephen Hales (1677–1761): born in Kent, Hales was a clergyman, botanist and biologist. He served as curate at Teddington, Middlesex. Like many clergymen of the age, including Gilbert White and George Crabbe, he devoted his considerable leisure time to the pursuit of science. He was a pioneer in botany, particularly in the study of the mechanisms by which plants use water and in demonstrating that plant sap flows upwards. He studied the effects of electrical impulses on the physiology of animals and devised a method of measuring blood pressure. He became a Fellow of the Royal Society in 1718 and in 1754 was a founder of the association that later became the Royal Society of Arts. He campaigned against the drinking of spirits and advocated the distillation of drinking water from seawater. In his honour an annual Stephen Hales prize is awarded by the American Society of Plant Biologists to one who has made a noteworthy contribution to that science.

Captain Cook

The voyages most often associated with the conquest of scurvy are those of Captain James Cook (1728–79). His initial experience was as a merchant seaman during which time he became familiar with the 'Whitby Colliers', sturdy, stable and capacious vessels whose qualities were ideally suited to long, arduous voyages in unpredictable seas with large quantities of stores. Moreover, their broad, flat bottoms enabled shallow waters to be navigated in safety. In 1755 he joined the Royal Navy and served in the Seven Years' War, during which he gained a reputation as a navigator and mapmaker when he charted the St Lawrence River for General Wolfe during the siege of Quebec. In 1768 he was chosen by the Admiralty to lead an expedition to the Southern Ocean in *The Endeavour*, a Whitby-built collier. The purpose of the expedition, which was promoted by the Royal Society, was to observe the transit of Venus across the face of the sun, since this would enable astronomers to calculate inter-planetary distances. Cook's three voyages had more momentous consequences: his discovery of New Zealand and Australia; the first crossing of the Antarctic Circle; and the mapping of much of the Pacific; but in this context the significance of his expeditions lies in the conquest of scurvy, a condition which would certainly have killed many of his crew on such a long voyage but for the precautions he took.

The Endeavour was victualled with quantities of sauerkraut (pickled cabbage, rich in vitamin C); 'portable soup' (offal, salt and vegetables evaporated into a kind of cake by a primitive dehydration process); malted barley; and 'rob' of orange and citrus juice from which vitamin C would have been virtually eliminated. *The Endeavour* also regularly took on fresh supplies of fruit and vegetables when it set into ports on its long voyage. Cook's *Journal* recorded that the seamen did not care for the sauerkraut so, to overcome their aversion:

> I had some of it dressed every day for the officers' cabin table and left it to the option of the men to take as much as they pleased or none at all … before a week I found it necessary to put everyone on board to an allowance.[36]

One of those who ate at the officers' table was Sir Joseph Banks (1743-1820) Fellow (and later President) of the Royal Society and celebrated botanist whose name is born by eighty species of plant, many of them gathered on Cook's first expedition. He recorded that he consumed sauerkraut and lemon juice to ward off scurvy and reported his experiences to his fellow scientists. Clearly the allure of feeding from the officers' fare had the desired effect because Cook's voyages suffered very little from scurvy, though some of the crew contracted the disease in the second voyage on *Resolution*, Cook's own observations suggesting that this was due to the fact that, during the ship's anchorage in New Zealand, some of the seamen had chosen to eat meat rather than vegetables. On his return from his second voyage, Cook's account of his journey was published in the Royal Society's *Transactions*, where he reported that:

> Sour Kraut, of which we had also a large provision, is not only a wholesome vegetable food but, in my judgement, highly antiscorbutic and spoils not by keeping.[37]

The portable soup, he thought, was 'the means of making the people eat a greater quantity of greens than they would have done otherwise', though he gave much of the credit for the health of the crew to the malted barley. Of the orange and lemon rob he commented: 'I have no great opinion of them alone'. This was not a bad evaluation of the evidence. The Vitamin C in the sauerkraut would have warded off scurvy, while the process of turning the orange and lemon juice into 'rob' by adding sugar would have rendered it ineffective. He was wrong about the malted barley and he may have been influenced in his flattering judgement about its virtues by the fact that the President of the Royal Society at the time, Sir John Pringle (1707–82), the leading authority of the age on military medicine, was an ardent advocate of the anti-scorbutic properties of 'sweet wort' made from malted barley. The Royal Society had, after all, been responsible for promoting Cook's original expedition.

Captain Cook was awarded the Royal Society's highest accolade, the Copley Medal:

> For his Paper, giving an account of the method he had taken to preserve the health of the crew of HM Ship *The Resolution*, during his late voyage round the world. Whose communication to the Society was of such importance to the public.[38]

The importance attached to Cook's paper may be judged by the company in which he stood as winner of the Copley medal. Other winners included Joseph Priestley, Charles Darwin, Louis Pasteur and Albert Einstein. The acceptance by the Royal Society, the world's most eminent scientific body by far, that scurvy was rooted in diet was a decisive influence upon

public policy. In 1780, the year after Cook's death, the Scot Gilbert Blane
(1749-1834) was appointed physician to the West Indies Fleet. Like James
Lind, he had studied at Edinburgh University and had then become physician to Admiral Rodney who took Blane with him to the West Indies to
care for his chronic gout. Blane instituted a regime of cleanliness and diet
that dramatically improved the health of the crews during the long campaigns at sea during the French Revolutionary wars. In 1776, at the outset
of the American War of Independence, one seaman fell sick for every 2.4
in the service; by the end of the Napoleonic Wars this had fallen by almost
80 per cent to one in 10.7.[39] In 1795 the carriage of citrus juice (usually
lime juice from the West Indies) on Royal Navy vessels became standard
practice. It was about this time that the word 'limeys' came to be applied
by Americans, first to British sailors and later to Britons in general on
account of their consumption of lime juice. Before the Battle of Trafalgar,
when Nelson was blockading the French port of Toulon, his munitions
included 30,000 gallons of lemon juice which ensured that his crews
remained in good health, none succumbing to the disease which, fifty
years earlier, would have made the blockade impossible to sustain. Nelson
also believed, with others, that too much salted food could cause scurvy
and he therefore minimised the amount of salted meat fed to his seamen.
The effects of the widespread adoption of citrus juice may be seen in the
number of cases of scurvy treated at the Haslar Naval Hospital, Gosport.
About 1,754 cases were treated in 1760; in 1806, there was only one.[40]

Scurvy in the Nineteenth and Twentieth Centuries

Scurvy did not disappear and even those activities which were spared
its ravages did not always appreciate the reasons. Between 1819 and 1825
Admiral Sir William Parry (1790–1855) undertook three voyages to the
Arctic in a vain search for the North-West Passage. These remained free of
scurvy but the credit was given, not to the lemon juice that they carried,
but to the novel canned meats supplied to the expedition by Donkin and
Hall's new factory in Bermondsey.[41] A later expedition to the Arctic led by
Admiral Sir George Nares (1831–1915) was struck by scurvy because they
had been supplied only with lime juice, which has a lower concentration
of vitamin C. In 1854 the Merchant Shipping Act had decreed that all sea
voyages lasting more than ten days must carry antiscorbutics, but these
could either be lemon and lime juice or sugar and vinegar. Only in 1894
did another Act specify that lemon and lime alone were acceptable and

that they must be administered at the rate of 10z daily – an adequate dose of vitamin C even for the lower-strength lime juice.

The most tragic cases of scurvy occurred in the Army. During the Crimean War many deaths were caused by scurvy although adequate supplies of lime juice had been shipped to Balaclava – and left there far from the troops. In 1916 the humiliating surrender of the British forces that were occupying Kut-al-Amara in modern Iraq was prompted in part by an outbreak of scurvy amongst the troops, many of whom died. Cases of scurvy are also found in modern accident and emergency units of hospitals, usually amongst alcoholics whose neglect of diet other than lager and vodka can cause the onset of the disease. Vitamin C remained in the news, not least because of its fervent advocacy by the American Linus Pauling (1901–94), double Nobel Laureate (1954 Chemistry, 1962 Peace), who believed it was a remedy for a wide variety of illnesses ranging from the common cold to cancer. His views on the efficacy of vitamin C in such cases remain controversial, unproven and widely doubted.[42]

Even in the twentieth century some eminent medical authorities sought the cause of scurvy elsewhere. Sir Almroth Wright (1861–1947) believed that it was caused by 'acidic blood' and therefore abhorred the use of fruits containing citric acid like lemons and oranges. As late as 1933 the *Oxford English Dictionary* claimed that scurvy was 'induced by exposure and by a too liberal diet of salted foods', a view that would have been endorsed by Nelson. It was not until the 1930s that the Hungarian scientist Albert Szent-Gyorgyi (1893–1986), who had worked with Hopkins at Cambridge, isolated vitamin C and identified it as ascorbic acid, for which he was awarded the Nobel Prize for Medicine in 1937.

Sir Almroth Wright (1861–1947) was born in Yorkshire and died in Buckinghamshire, a year after his retirement at the age of eighty-five. He was the son of an Irish clergyman and a Swedish mother and was educated at Trinity College, Dublin. His memory and energy were such that he studied both modern languages and medicine at the same time, graduating with high honours in both, and he claimed to have memorised more than a quarter of a million lines of poetry. He worked variously as a clerk in the Admiralty, as a demonstrator in the pathology department of Cambridge University and in a similar post at the new University of Sydney, Australia. Upon returning to England in 1891, he was appointed professor of pathology at the army medical school, Netley, Hants, where he undertook a series of experiments on the use of vaccines to combat disease. One such experiment in which he used himself as the guinea pig almost proved fatal. His experiments with an inoculation against typhoid were more successful, but the unpleasant side effects of the treatment caused the authorities to hesitate before administering it. As a result, troops serving in the Boer War were not inoculated, resulting in the deaths of over 9,000 men, while almost a quarter of the troops were incapacitated by the disease. In 1902 he was appointed pathologist and bacteriologist at St Mary's Hospital Medical School, Paddington, where he was soon joined by a number of other distinguished scientists, one of whom was Alexander Fleming. Wright was knighted in 1906.

Rickets

Scurvy may be the most infamous disease caused by nutritional deficiency but rickets has proved more enduring, especially in conditions where malnutrition prevails, notably in times of war and in developing countries. Weak and deformed bones are a common feature of the condition, leading to such conditions as bow legs and shortness of stature. It is caused by a shortage of vitamin D which prevents bones from developing properly, causing them to bend and fracture. It is most often associated with children, whose bones need a plentiful supply of vitamin D (and of calcium which vitamin D helps the body to process) if they are to grow as they should, but it is also found amongst adults. Calcium is readily available in milk and other foods commonly fed to small children, but not many foods naturally contain large quantities of vitamin D, the exceptions being oily fish like sardines, salmon and tuna, and of course cod liver oil. For this reason many foods are now fortified by the addition of vitamin D, notably margarine and some breakfast cereals. The vitamin is also absorbed from ultra-violet rays of the sun and, oddly, individuals who are intolerant of sunlight, such as red-haired, pale-skinned people, create vitamin D more rapidly from the sun and are less vulnerable to the condition. Conversely dark-skinned people need more sunlight to achieve the same effect. Some meats also contain small quantities of vitamin D that animals have themselves taken in from this source.

Cases of rickets are recorded in England from the 1640s when it was often referred to as 'the English disease'. It is not clear why it was scarcely mentioned before this time. A serious famine occurred in southern England as a result of poor harvests in the 1590s and another affected the north in 1623, events which might explain why mothers and young children showed symptoms of the condition from the early seventeenth century.[43] Moreover, the Tudor enclosure movements had been undertaken at the expense of less prosperous residents, who lost the ability to graze their cows on common land or smallholdings, thereby depriving them, and more importantly their growing children, of the calcium which is essential for developing strong bones. In the middle of the sixteenth century one of the principal commissioners charged with ascertaining the effects of enclosures, John Hales, had described the effects in stark terms:

> Towns, villages and parishes do daily decay in great numbers; houses of husbandry and poor men's habitations be utterly destroyed everywhere, and in no small number; husbandry and tillage, which is the very paunch of the commonwealth, greatly abated.[44]

It has already been observed that, in the following century, Sir Frederic Eden commented that milk, an essential source of calcium, was relatively scarce in towns[45] and it is likely that this trend was well established in the south of England by 1600, thus depriving children of poorer families of the calcium they needed for the development of strong bones. Certainly, in 1767 Jonas Hanway, during one of his journeys around England, observed that the people of Stevenage in Hertfordshire could not afford milk in their diets.[46]

Rickets was described by Daniel Whistler (1619–84), an English physician, in his doctoral thesis submitted to the University of Leiden in 1645. Whistler came from London, was educated at Trinity College, Oxford, and later became a fellow of Merton College, of which the celebrated physician William Harvey (1578–1657), discoverer of the circulation of the blood, was warden, and he was elected Fellow of the Royal Society in 1663. He described the bones of victims as being 'flexible like wax that is rather liquid, so that the flabby and toneless legs scarcely sustain the weight of the superimposed body, so that the tibiae yield to the weight of the fabric pressing down on them from above and become bent'.[47] He believed that the condition was caused by the consumption of too much alcohol by mothers during pregnancy. Whistler's PhD thesis, like most such publications, attracted little attention, but a more influential work on the subject was that of Francis Glisson (1597–1677), to whom is usually attributed the 'discovery' of rickets but whose own work on the subject did not appear until 1650, five years after Whistler's thesis. Glisson came from Dorset and studied at Caius College, Cambridge (William Harvey's undergraduate college), becoming professor of physic (i.e. medicine) at Cambridge in 1636. His treatise *De Rachitide* was translated into English and published as *A Treatise of the Rickets, being a disease common to Children* in 1651. Glisson commented: 'an absolutely new disease … became first known about thirty years since in the counties of Dorset [Glisson's home county] and Somerset', and it had spread to London.

He observed that children were not born with the disease, though the delivery of children was often made more difficult by the fact that the mother's pelvis was afflicted by the condition and this may account for the invention of primitive forceps at this time by the Chamberlens. He also observed that 'this disease doth more frequently invade the cradles of the rich than affect poor men's children', and speculated that it was caused, not by malnutrition, but by over-feeding leading to indigestion.

The Chamberlen family: Peter Chamberlen the elder was born to a Protestant family in Paris in 1560 and was brought to England as a child. A younger brother, also called Peter, was born in 1572, both brothers becoming surgeons and 'man-midwives'. They fell out with the College of Physicians when they proposed that midwives (who were mostly female) should be incorporated into a society with recognised skills. This was seen as a challenge to the authority (and incomes) of male physicians. The brothers were credited with the invention of a secret instrument to aid delivery. The instrument was kept in an ornate box and the labouring woman was blindfolded or otherwise prevented from seeing the device, though it may be assumed that she would have had other matters on her mind at the time. In 1813 some pairs of the mysterious instrument, obstetric forceps made of metal, were discovered beneath the floorboards of the family home at Woodham Mortimer, near Maldon in Essex. A third Peter Chamberlen, son of Peter the younger, was born in 1601 and also became a doctor midwife, attending Queen Henrietta Maria for the birth of Charles II.

In the eighteenth century the condition became steadily more prevalent. In 1773 Sir William Fordyce, in his *New Inquiry into the Causes of Fevers*, was as alarmed as Sir Frederic Eden about the situation in London, commenting particularly upon the prevalence of rickets: 'There must be very nearly twenty thousand children in London and Westminster attended with tun bellies, swelled wrists and crooked limbs owing to the impure air which they breathe, the improper food on which they live or the improper manner in which their fond parents or nurses rear them up'.[48] By this time theories were being advanced as to the cause of rickets. A French scientist called Bonhomme, writing in *Annales de Chimie* in August 1793, argued, correctly, that a lack of phosphorus in the diet inhibited the conversion of calcium into healthy bone tissue.[49] In this he was correct, but he was wrong in believing that excessive acid in the diet was the culprit. William

Cullen (1710–90),[50] doctor, chemist, inventor of the process of refrigeration, and unrivalled as a lecturer on clinical medicine at Edinburgh Royal Infirmary, published his lectures as *A Treatise of Materia Medica* and in it he wrote of rickets: 'There is no doubt that a certain diet may contribute to the same end, but what may be the most eligible I dare not determine. I cannot find any reason to believe that strong beer can ever be a proper remedy'. He was correct in the latter judgement.[51]

At the time Cullen was writing, residents of the Scottish Western Isles were already employing a folk remedy whose origins were lost to history: cod liver oil. This procedure came to the attention of Dr Kay who in 1782 administered it to patients at Manchester Infirmary, with beneficial results,[52] an experiment that made a greater impact at the time in Germany than in Britain. In 1841 an English doctor called John Hughes Bennett (1812–75) wrote *A Treatise on Cod-liver Oil as a Therapeutic Agent,* though unfortunately he regarded it mainly as a remedy for tuberculosis, which it is not. In the 1880s the English surgeon (later Sir) John Bland-Sutton (1855–1936), whose lifelong interest in zoology appears to have arisen from his father's business as a taxidermist, had eliminated rickets from lion cubs at London Zoo by introducing to their diet cod liver oil mixed with milk and crushed bones. This experiment was more widely publicised than that of Kay and influenced practice in the following century.

Rickets in the Nineteenth and Twentieth Centuries

In 1867 one-third of the children examined at Great Ormond Street Children's Hospital suffered from rickets while in 1884 *every* child examined at a Glasgow hospital showed signs of the condition – a problem which was to persist in Glasgow well into the twentieth century. Despite these appalling statistics it was not until the outbreaks of rickets that followed the First World War that any systematic attack upon the problem was mounted. A serious outbreak of rickets occurred in Vienna in 1919 following the Allied blockades which had caused severe malnutrition in Austria and Germany. A distinguished Austrian professor, Baron Clemens von Pirquet, believed that the condition was spread by a contagious microbe but (later Dame) Harriette Chick (1875–1977), who was sent by the Allies to deal with the crisis in the Austrian capital, had other ideas. Born in London to a prosperous family, Harriette Chick had studied science at University College, London, and later worked in Vienna and Munich. Despite opposition from hostile males she then obtained posts at the Lister Institute of Preventive Medicine in Chelsea and the Medical Research Committee (later Council) where she carried out pioneering work on 'accessory food factors' which became better known as vitamins. Upon arrival in Vienna she administered cod liver oil to those suffering from rickets, later publishing her findings as *Studies of Rickets in Vienna, 1919–22*. Clemens von Pirquet was persuaded that his microbial theory was wrong. However, Chick observed that sunlight could cure rickets as well as cod liver oil, a verdict that would have been endorsed by earlier 'miasmatists' like James Lind,[53] who believed that fresh air and sunshine were sovereign remedies for many of life's complaints. While Chick was at work in Vienna, the English doctor (later Sir) Edward Mellanby (1885–1955) was seeking ways of reducing the incidence of rickets in children, 80 per cent of those in schools run by the London County Council having been shown to suffer from the condition. Mellanby experimented on puppies, feeding them a diet of low-fat milk and bread. They developed rickets, which was later eliminated when they were fed cod liver oil, thus confirming the folk remedy adopted by Dr Kay in Manchester in 1782 and by John Bland-Sutton on his lions. Mellanby, while recognising the role of cod liver oil as an 'anti-rachitical factor' as revealed by his experiment, fortunately recognised the essential role of milk in the infant diet:

> Undoubtedly milk ought to remain the staple article of diet, not only until weaning but for some years after this time … It is probable that bread is the worst offender [in filling up children with inappropriate calories].

Mellanby concluded: 'Rickets is a deficiency disease which develops in consequence of the absence of some accessory food factor or factors.'[54]

At this stage it was well understood that certain substances were needed, often in minute quantities, to ensure human health and that cod liver oil and sunshine contained whatever was needed to cure rickets. The word 'vitamin' was already in use (though Harriette Chick and Edward Mellanby still preferred the non-committal 'accessory food factors'), but the chemical itself, vitamin D, had still not been identified. This task fell to a team led by the anti-Nazi German Dr Adolf Windhaus (1876–1959) who was awarded the Nobel Prize for Chemistry in 1928 for his discovery. Nine years later he identified a compound present in human and animal skin which, when exposed to ultra-violet light, could be converted into vitamin D. Windhaus survived the Second World War, despite his defence of Jewish scientists, his criticism of the Nazi regime and his refusal to undertake scientific research under the Third Reich, his status as a Nobel Prize winner protecting him from overt persecution.

The discovery that rickets could be eliminated by simple and inexpensive dietary measures led to its gradual decline in western societies in the twentieth century, but it remains a problem in some communities and regions. In 1979, by which time it was rare in England, it was found still to be common in Glasgow, particularly in the city's Asian community, a situation attributed to the poor diet and housing conditions which many of them endured. Tenement blocks and the streets which held them were often devoid of sunlight even in fine weather and, as previously observed, dark-skinned people do not convert ultra-violet rays to vitamin D as effectively as do those with pale skins. In 1979, therefore, the Greater Glasgow Health Authority began a campaign which involved the issuing of free vitamin D tablets to those of Asian descent aged under eighteen. At its peak, 3,300 doses were being issued each day, a slightly larger number than the total number of Asian children registered at Glasgow schools. This led to a rapid decline in cases of rickets and the campaign was then extended to Asian mothers, with comparable results.[55] In the twenty-first century rickets has reappeared amongst young Asian and Afro-Caribbean children in Britain whose lack of exposure to sunshine in Britain's winters is inadequately supplemented by vitamin D from dietary sources.

Pellagra: Mal de la Rosa

In 1735 the Spanish physician Gaspar Casal (1679–1759) identified a revolting skin disease amongst Spanish peasants which he called *mal de la rosa,* a reference to the unsightly rash and physical deformities which were its characteristics and which caused it to be mistaken for leprosy. Nor was it preferable to leprosy. In additional to the hideous appearance with which it burdened its victims, it also caused acute depression, diarrhoea, dementia and death. Although it was first identified in Spain, it was in the United States, a century later, that it attracted the serious attention of the medical authorities.

It was probably to be found in the southern states from the early nineteenth century, but it was not until the early years of the following century that it was conclusively identified there, South Carolina reporting 30,000 cases in 1912 with a mortality rate of 40 per cent. It was concentrated in institutions like orphanages, long-stay mental hospitals, prisons and in villages where employment was dominated by one cotton mill, especially in the more impoverished of those southern states. In the period leading up to the Second World War, some three million Americans contracted the disease, now known as *pellagra*, with deaths approaching 100,000. The task of combating the disease was entrusted by the US Congress to Joseph Goldberger (1874–1929), a Jewish immigrant from Hungary who had been brought to the United States in 1883, when he was nine years old.[56] He qualified as a doctor in 1895 and, after a spell in private practice, entered the service of the US government where he fought epidemic diseases, including yellow fever, dengue fever and typhus, all of which he himself contracted while combating outbreaks in the southern states of Louisiana and Mississippi and in Mexico. During the course of these misadventures the Jewish immigrant met and married Mary Farrar, the aristocratic, Protestant kinswoman of the former president of the Southern Confederacy, Jefferson Davis, contrary to the wishes of both families. Fortunately, husband and wife were equally devoted to the cause of science.

Goldberger observed that epidemics of pellagra in hospitals, prisons and orphanages were usually confined to the inmates, the staff normally being free of the disease whereas other epidemics, like those of typhus ('gaol fever') affected inmates and staff alike. From this he concluded that the orthodox view, which held that pellagra was transmitted by germs, was mistaken. Goldberger hypothesised that the origins of pellagra lay in diet, and he arranged for diets of fresh meat, milk and a variety of vegetables to be supplied to the residents of two orphanages in Mississippi and a hospital in Georgia. Normally they would have been fed on a diet consisting overwhelmingly of maize, biscuits and meat which would be lacking in essential vitamins. Dramatic results followed, with those receiving the new diet remaining free of pellagra while those on the normal corn-based diet succumbed. A further experiment on prisoners at a prison in Mississippi gave the same results.

Incensed at the reluctance of his critics to accept that pellagra was caused by the unhealthy diets of many poor and vulnerable southerners, Goldberger proceeded to demonstrate the falsity of the 'germ theory' of pellagra by injecting himself, a number of assistants and his wife with quantities of blood taken from pellagra patients. They followed this by swallowing wheat flour pills containing scabs taken from the skins of the patients combined with urine and even faeces; and they introduced to their own nostrils mucus from the noses of the patients. These dramatic manifestations of his confidence in his 'dietary' explanation of pellagra he called his 'filth parties', but opposition now became political. Many southerners still resented the outcome of the Civil War which had ended slavery half a century earlier and left the south feeling that it was the poor as well as the defeated neighbour. The implication that inferior diets accounted for the prevalence of pellagra in the south was a further blow to southern pride delivered by the Jewish Yankee immigrant working for the Federal Government. President Warren Harding's attempts to persuade the governments of southern states to improve the welfare and health care of their poorer citizens was met with indignation that the former Confederate States were being humiliated and vilified. A collapse in cotton prices in the 1920s caused a further drop in the southern standard of living, an even greater dependence on the maize diet and an increase in pellagra cases. But the collapse in prices, followed by the failure of many cotton crops as a result of insect infestation, led to a greater diversity of food crops being cultivated in the south, an improvement in diet and a decline in pellagra as the residents became less dependent on maize, a modest source of the missing 'accessory factor'.

Joseph Goldberger died in 1929, his ashes being scattered on the Potomac in Washington. He never discovered the precise nature of the dietary deficiency that caused pellagra. In 1937, within a few years of his death, niacin, a B-group vitamin, had been identified by his fellow American Conrad Elvehjem (1901–62) as the missing element. Its addition to bread in the years that followed eliminated pellagra from the United States. Like goitre, which vanished when iodine was added to salt, it virtually disappeared from doctors' consulting rooms.

The Celtic Disease

In the 1970s one baby in every hundred born in Ireland and Wales was affected by *spina bifida*, a condition in which the spine is not fully formed, resulting in such conditions as curvature of the spine and lack of control of the legs. It is one of a group of conditions called *neural tube defects.* Incontinence is another consequence sometimes found. The incidence in England was much lower, though in Scotland it was relatively high. It was also noticed that, in the United States, the condition was much more common amongst people of Irish descent than in other communities – hence the name 'The Celtic Disease'. An examination of the diets of the populations concerned indicated that the Celts ate less fresh green vegetables than the Anglo-Saxons who predominated in England and led some to conclude that the missing ingredient was folic acid, a B-group vitamin common in green-leaved vegetables, the word 'folic' deriving from the Latin for 'leaf'. An alternative explanation, based on folklore about the Irish addiction to potatoes, suggested that the condition was caused by excessive consumption of that blameless vegetable. However, an experiment at the University of Wisconsin, Madison, which involved feeding large quantities of potatoes to chimpanzees, produced only very happy, healthy baby chimpanzees, so the theory was discarded.[57]

In the late 1970s Professor Richard Smithells of the University of Leeds conducted a test involving expectant mothers 'who had previously given birth to one or more infants with a neural tube defect'[58] (spina bifida). Nearly 180 of them agreed to participate in his study and were given three tablets each day containing a variety of vitamins (including A-, D- and B-group vitamins) and iron during their pregnancies. Of these women, one gave birth to a baby with spina bifida. A 'control' group of 260 women who had also given birth to infants with spina bifida, but who either declined the tablets or whose pregnancy was detected too late for them to participate, gave birth to thirteen babies with the condition. Professor Smithells was not a man given to extravagant claims but in 1982, addressing a group of parents who had children with spina bifida, he reassured them that, in appropriate doses, vitamins could do no harm and almost certainly did some good.

In April 2006, it was announced that the Food Standards Agency (FSA), the government's watchdog charged with monitoring the quality of food, was recommending that folic acid, vitamin B9, should be added to flour and to certain common types of bread. They believed that this could cut by half the number of babies born each year (about 550) with neural tube defects and cut the number of abortions prompted by the condition. In May the FSA board agreed unanimously to press forward with the measure and in June 2007 the board instructed the agency's officials to implement the measure.[59] Spina bifida was never as widespread as scurvy or rickets, but its effects are very distressing to the sufferers and their families and there seems now to be a chance that this scourge, like the earlier ones, will begin to diminish in its effects on the population.

Diet, Brain and Behaviour

In the late twentieth century interest is also being shown in the effects of vitamin-deficient diets on the functioning of the brain. In 1986 the *British Medical Journal* published articles on the effects of iron deficiency on mental capacity, arguing that 'there is now substantial evidence that iron deficiency has an adverse effect on brain function'. The writer added that, whereas breast milk and artificially fortified cows' milk offered a relatively high uptake of iron in the infant diet, 'the early introduction of fresh [i.e. unfortified] cows' milk may lead to iron deficiency'.[60] Iron deficiency was particularly prevalent amongst Bangladeshi families. In 2002 the *British Journal of Psychiatry* reported on an experiment conducted amongst some young adult prisoners whose deficient diets, it was suspected, helped to account for their criminal, and especially for their violent, behaviour. Over 230 prisoners were fed a special diet containing vitamin and mineral supplements and were subsequently found to have committed 35 per cent fewer offences than a control group who received the normal prison diet.[61] In the 1970s Dr Benjamin Feingold, a paediatrician based in California, suggested that the increasingly common attention deficit hyperactivity disorder (ADHD) was related to children's diets and in particular to certain artificial flavourings and colourings used in their food. His book, *Why Your Child is Hyperactive*, was published in 1974 and created a small industry of its own amongst parents who were concerned about their children's behaviour. His arguments remain controversial but have spawned many similar movements who believe that there is a link between mental well-being, diet and, in particular, additives. Most recently the spotlight has been turned upon Omega 3 (alternatively Omega 6) fish oils, to which have been attributed the power to enhance reading ability, prevent heart disease and treat mental illnesses.[62]

Increasingly, interest in diet has been picked up by the mass media, notably television. In 2002 an alarming *World in Action* programme entitled 'The Threatened Generation' suggested that diets of 'junk food', heavy in kilocalories but light in essential vitamins, was making children vulnerable to obesity and heart disease and this, in turn, led the British Medical Association to publish a guide called *Diet, Nutrition and Health*. In 2006 the popular television chef Jamie Oliver led a campaign to improve school meals by replacing turkey twizzlers, crisps and fizzy drinks with pasta, fruit, green vegetables and fruit drinks, but the campaign, supported by extra funds from the Treasury, had unexpected consequences when the children, and their parents, voted with their purses and recorded a 30 per cent drop in take-up in the meals. Some parents even boasted of smuggling burgers and chips to their children during school hours. There were, however, some promising results. At Chineham Park primary school in Basingstoke, Hampshire, an intensive educational and dietary campaign led by a nutritionist and supported by a daily exercise regime, promoted healthy eating and recorded significant improvements in behaviour and motivation, with a marked decline in ADHD. The results of the schools' SATs assessments (scholastic aptitude tests) were very encouraging, showing marked improvements in English, Maths and Science as well as in behaviour and concentration.[63] A study by the School Food Trust, chaired by Prue Leith, veteran campaigner for improvements in our diets, was carried out in six primary schools in Sheffield. It made the interesting discovery that children who ate lunches rich in fruit and vegetables worked more effectively in the afternoons when lessons were firmly directed by teachers, but their greater alertness and energy could make them more easily distracted and boisterous when working loosely supervised in groups. It appears that the relationship between diet and concentration is more complex than some had assumed.[64] Other programmes swiftly followed, the BBC's rather gimmicky *Truth about Food* claiming that a high-calcium diet reduced pre-menstrual tension and that a diet including fruit and vegetable 'smoothie' drinks rich in the B-group vitamin folic acid, zinc and vitamin C could improve sperm counts in previously under-fertile males.[65]

Conclusion

The science of vitamins and minerals as elements of our diet and well-being is barely a century old, but the number of Nobel Prizes won by its practitioners testifies to the importance of these long mysterious and unknown elements to the human condition. As physical ailments like scurvy, rickets and pellagra have gradually been treated and their effects reduced, especially in the developed world, attention has been shifted to a new frontier – the effects of diet on human behaviour and mental well-being. It may perhaps be anticipated that the twenty-first century will see the same advances made in these spheres as the twentieth century witnessed in physical illness.

5

Nutrition or Just Calories?

Hospitals are filled with a thousand screaming victims; the palaces of luxury and the hovels of indigence resound alike with the bitter wailings of disease; idi- otism and madness grin and rave among us and all these complicated calamities result from the unnatural habits of life to which the human race has addicted itself during innumerable ages of mistake and misery.

> The poet Shelley advocating vegetarianism

The opening of the twentieth century saw malnutrition more rife in England than it had been since the great dearths of mediaeval and Tudor times.

> Sir Jack Drummond

Read the label, set a better table

> J. Walter Thompson's advertising campaign for nutrition labelling

One of the least likely among comparable countries to promote health and longevity

> A description of the British diet in *The Lancet*, August 1986

Numbers or Colours?

In 2006 there arose in Great Britain a divergence of opinion over meth- ods of conveying to consumers the nutritional values of processed foods: a divergence which revealed both the complexity of the subject and its controversial nature. Following a considerable period of consultation, which by some accounts went back to the 1980s, the Food Standards Agency (FSA), established by an Act of Parliament in 2000 to monitor the quality of the nation's food, recommended that a 'traffic light' system be used on food packaging to indicate the nutritional content of a prod- uct. Thus a prepared meal might have a red light for fat, indicating that its fat content was high; a green light for sugar, suggesting that there were no grounds for anxiety in that field; and a yellow light for salt, indicating caution. The FSA's own research had led it to conclude that the traffic light system was the clearest way of communicating such information to consumers who were easily baffled by often conflicting claims on such matters as kilocalories, vitamins, minerals, cholesterol and all the other components of the science of nutrition. Some may have believed that the traffic light system was all too clear since it could hardly fail to draw atten- tion to the fact that some products, notably confectionery and soft drinks, contained large quantities of such products as sugar. Several prominent manufacturers, including Cadbury's, Mars, Nestlé and Pepsi, announced that they would adopt a rival system in which Guideline Daily Amounts (GDAs) would be used as a reference point.

The GDAs were developed in 2003 by the Institute of Grocery Distribution (IGD) in collaboration with government and consumer groups to establish the daily quantities of certain nutrients that should be consumed under a number of categories: protein, carbohydrates, salts, sugars and fibre. The dissenting manufacturers announced that, instead of the traffic light scheme, they would express the nutrient content of their products as a percentage of the GDA, and the waters were further muddied when the largest British food retailer of all, Tesco, announced that it would also adopt GDAs in place of the traffic lights. Were the dissidents influ- enced by fears that their products would not look too good in the glare of red, yellow and green? Or was the difference simply a reflection of the fact that nutrition is a notoriously difficult concept to express in simple terms? The FSA was reported to be 'angered by the food industry's pre-emptive action'[1] and in 2008 the Health Secretary, Alan Johnson, called upon the industry to adopt a common system based upon the 'traffic lights'. The issue had certainly generated much controversy in earlier centuries and made some fortunes for peddlers of dietary theories, many of which do not bear close examination. The situation has been further complicated by the fact that the nutritional content (including calorific values) of food is often related to 'portion sizes' that bear no resemblance to the portions habitually chosen by consumers. This is particularly the case with breakfast cereals where the calorie content of a 'portion' is sometimes a fraction of that actually eaten. In 2008 an additional complication has entered the controversy over food labelling: the 'carbon footprint'. Estimates of the amount of carbon emitted by products in their passage from farms to consumers via factories, distribution depots and retailers are beginning to appear on packaging. How will the declaration that a packet of cheese and onion crisps has added 75g of carbon to the problem of global warming influence consumers, especially when read in conjunction with barely intelligible data on GDAs and traffic lights? Consumers can perhaps be forgiven for consigning such matters to the bottom of their list of priorities!

Red Meat

Reference was made in chapter one to the confidence placed in 'mighty Roast Beef' as the food best suited to Englishmen.[2] There is some evidence that the availability of meat in mediaeval England owed something to the Black Death which, between 1348 and 1350, killed between one-third and one-half of the population, leaving a shortage of labour to cultivate crops. As a result many fields and villages were abandoned while areas which had been devoted to arable cultivation were turned over to livestock, notably sheep, which required less labour and formed the foundation of the wool trade, bringing prosperity to the areas that adopted it. Consequently mutton was more readily available, as was the meat of dairy cattle and pigs.[3] Some writers regarded the meat of domesticated animals like sheep, cows and chickens as more nutritious than that of wild animals like venison and game birds, this view being expressed by William Harrison in his 1587 publication, *The Description of England*. Written from the comfort of his rectory near Saffron Walden, Essex, Harrison seems to have disapproved even of keeping deer and rabbits as domesticated animals, presumably on the grounds that this might give a false impression of their nutritional value.[4] The idea that red meat was a unique source of nutrition and strength long persisted. As late as 1866 a textbook called *Training in Theory and Practice* was published by a rowing coach called Archibald Maclaren in which he described the dietary practices of the Oxford and Cambridge boat race crews. He divided foodstuffs into three categories: *albumen*, found in egg whites, which nourished the tissues; *saccharine*, or sugars; and *oleaginous*, substances which provided heat (energy). He disapproved of hot drinks, especially at breakfast since 'there is nothing more injurious to the stomach than hot drinks of any kind', recommending instead 'uninebriating'

continental wines diluted with water as a 'morning beverage.'[5] Oxford's
crews trained on red meat, tea, beer and a little jelly and watercress. The
Cambridge diet included potatoes, green vegetables and fruit which were
excluded from the Oxford diet. Despite Maclaren's eccentric views on
diet, Oxford had a good record, winning every race between 1861 and
1869, reinforcing the belief that red meat was the source of strength and
that vegetables, as consumed by Cambridge, were of little value.

Vegetarianism

Some earlier writers were less devoted to the cause of meat, believing
that vegetables contained all that man needed and, in some cases, arguing
that a carnivorous diet promoted base and aggressive instincts. The word
vegetarian came into use in the middle of the nineteenth century,[6] but
ancient writers, including Pythagoras (c.572–c.490 BC) advocated the practice on the grounds that the soul migrates between living creatures and
that it was therefore immoral to eat any of them. His views were later
adopted by Socrates and Plato, though Aristotle's injunction, 'plants are
created for the sake of animals and animals for the sake of man',[7] appeared
to sanction human consumption of meat. In the Christian era there was
some controversy over Biblical authority on the nature of man's diet. The
book of Genesis (in chapter 1, verse 28) appeared to sanction a carnivorous
diet: 'replenish the earth and subdue it: and have dominion over the fish of
the sea and over the fowl of the air and over every living thing that moveth
upon the earth'. But in the very next verse we read: 'I have given you
every herb bearing seed, which is upon the face of all the earth, and every
tree, in the which is the fruit of a tree yielding seed; to you it shall be for
meat'. Some regarded this as promoting vegetarianism, but after the Great
Flood, God was recorded, again in Genesis, as having told Noah: 'Every
moving thing that liveth shall be meat for you',[8] which seemed to restore
a carnivorous diet. After the Reformation the practice ran into religious
obstacles, the Catholic Church teaching that all things had been made for
man's use and that to abstain from eating meat as a matter of principle
was a form of heresy.[9] On the other hand a number of Protestant groups
promoted vegetarianism as a return to a more innocent state such as had
existed before Adam took the apple from Eve. These were not always salu-
tary in every respect in the eyes of Puritans. Thus in the time of Cromwell's
Protectorate (1649–58), John Robins and his followers, known as 'Shakers'
or 'Ranters', advocated not only vegetarian diets but also free love and

nakedness. Robins was gaoled and his sect dissolved, but such events help to explain why vegetarianism has long attracted ridicule in some quarters.[10] In Graham Greene's chilling novel about Haiti under Papa Doc Duvalier, *The Comedians*, Mr Smith, the vegetarian candidate for the US presidency, is a sympathetic portrait but unmistakably absurd.

Nevertheless, vegetarianism continued to be strongly advocated by many Puritans who laid claim to a number of eminent supporters. Francis Bacon (1561–1626), whose experiments with frozen chicken are recorded elsewhere,[11] praised a vegetarian diet though he does not appear to have observed such a diet himself, while René Descartes (1596–1650) was a vegetarian from choice (though he regarded it as perfectly moral to eat meat). Thomas Hobbes (1588–1679) was claimed, doubtfully, as a vegetarian on account of the great age to which he lived and a similar claim was made for the even more eminent Isaac Newton (1642–1727), though the claim that Newton was a vegetarian appears to have owed more to the frugality of his diet than to its herbivorous content. Travellers to India in the sixteenth and seventeenth centuries discovered Hinduism and Jainism with their reverence for animals and frequently vegetarian habits, to which they attributed both their apparently peaceful existence and their less energetic and enterprising societies than those of Europe. On the other hand the French physician Francois Bernier, who visited India in the mid-seventeenth century, observed that the vegetarian diets observed by the armies of the Moghal emperors gave them a military advantage, since it was far easier to locate and transport vegetable products such as lentils or rice than barrels of salted beef.

Rousseau and Malthus

Jean-Jacques Rousseau (1712–88), in his search for the noble savage, thought he had discovered a scientific basis for man's non-carnivorous nature in the construction of the human breast, a part of the anatomy in which he showed a more than normal interest. He observed that carnivorous animals such as cats and dogs had many teats so that they could suckle large litters from the plentiful supply of milk which he attributed to their diet of meat. On the other hand humans had only two teats with which to suckle one (or occasionally two) infants since a much larger diet of herbivorous material was required to produce an adequate supply of milk. Rousseau thus concluded that this was evidence enough 'for removing Man from the class of carnivorous animals and placing him among the frugivorous species'.[12] Ten years after Rousseau's death Thomas Malthus (1766–1834) wrote his *Essay on the Principle of Population,* which drew attention to the propensity of human reproduction to outpace the growth of the food supply and suggested that war, disease and famine were necessary correctives to this tendency. Having observed that arable crops produced more nutrients per acre than did grazing, he commented that 'the only chance of success would be the ploughing up all the grazing countries and putting an end almost to the use of animal food', though he then added, gloomily, that this would only postpone the inevitable food crisis, and not for long either, since the lack of manure would reduce the fertility of the soil.[13]

Until well into the nineteenth century the regular consumption of meat was a sign of affluence, so most 'vegetarian' diets were imposed by poverty rather than by choice. However, this was not always the case, as Benjamin Franklin's brief spell of vegetarianism, noted elsewhere, seems to have proceeded from principle rather than necessity.[14] One observer of the beneficial effects of a diet including a variety of vegetables was Jonas Hanway (1712-86). An early career as a merchant trading with Russia was punctuated with disasters including that of having all his goods seized by a Moslem ruler in the Caspian Sea and further privations at the hands of pirates. Despite these setbacks he made a sufficient fortune from his business and from an account of his adventures to devote much of his life to philanthropy and to a series of sometimes eccentric campaigns. He was the first person to promote the use of the umbrella but was fiercely opposed to the increasingly popular practice of drinking tea and to the giving of tips – an activity which invoked the wrath of hackney carriage drivers. He devoted much of his abundant energy to campaigning on behalf of children, becoming a governor of the Foundling Hospital whose exemplary diet is discussed in chapter three and which he may have influenced. He took a generally dim view of the English diet, observing of overseas colonies that:

> When the French begin a settlement their first object is a fortification: but Englishmen provide a house where they may fortify themselves with liquor. Some foreigners remark that England appears to them as a country where half the people are employed to supply the other half with liquor.[15]

Hanway travelled throughout the kingdom compiling his observations on the condition of labouring families and published them in his *Letters on the Importance of the Rising Generation of the Labouring Part of our Fellow Subjects.* He noted that some families who could not afford much meat had found ways of making their portions go further, with beneficial results: 'With the addition of legumens, roots and vegetables, five pounds weight of meat will go as far as we generally make ten or fifteen and the consumer will be more free of the scurvy'.[16] These observations were made in 1767, some time before the relationship between scurvy and diet (discussed in chapter four) was widely accepted and appears to have been based upon the fact that vegetables were cheap and affordable rather than upon their nutritious qualities.

Shelley: 'A Thousand Screaming Victims'

In the following century vegetarianism gained some powerful advocates, the first being Joseph Ritson in his *Essay upon Abstinence from Animal Food as a Moral Duty* of 1802, but a more prominent figure was the Romantic poet Percy Bysshe Shelley, though his short and controversial life did not make him a model for many of his countrymen.

> **Percy Bysshe Shelley (1792–1822),** son of an MP, was educated at Eton and Oxford where he reputedly only ever attended one lecture, though read extensively. If true, this may be explained by his lifelong difficulty in forming lasting relationships with fellow human beings. Having been sent down from Oxford for a pamphlet advocating atheism, he married Harriet, a girl aged sixteen, but when his young wife rejected his ideas for an open marriage (i.e. sharing her with one of his friends) he abandoned her and their child in favour of Mary Godwin, also sixteen, daughter of William Godwin and of the early feminist Mary Wollstonecraft, author of *The Vindication of the Rights of Woman* who had died following the birth of her daughter. When Harriet drowned herself in the Serpentine in Hyde Park, Shelley married Mary Godwin, later author of *Frankenstein.* The couple travelled in Italy, some of their time in the company of Byron, while Shelley entered upon his poetical career, writing *Prometheus Unbound* while continuing to advocate politically awkward causes such as that of Irish nationalism. They settled in Pisa and in July 1822, aged twenty-nine, Shelley was drowned while sailing off the coast near Livorno. His body was cremated on the beach near Viareggio and his ashes interred in the Protestant cemetery in Rome. His death was celebrated in some conservative circles.

Shelley had become acquainted with a vegetarian called John Frank Newton (*c.*1770–1827) who had apparently overcome asthma by conforming to a vegetarian diet and established a vegetarian commune in Bracknell, Berkshire, in 1806 which advocated a vegetable diet and 'nakedism' (a respectable version of the 'Shakers' of John Robins). Newton, in 1811, wrote *The Return to Nature* which argued, against Malthus, that, if vegetable cultivation replaced pasture, ten times more nutrients would be produced from the same acreage.[17] Shelley joined the group and renounced meat in 1812, later writing two tracts on vegetarianism, *A Vindication of Natural Diet* and *An Essay upon the Vegetable System of Diet*. As already quoted at the start of the chapter, his claims for the vegetarian regime were characteristically immoderate:

> Hospitals are filled with a thousand screaming victims; the palaces of luxury and the hovels of indigence resound alike with the bitter wailings of disease; idiotism and madness grin and rave among us and all these complicated calamities result from the unnatural habits of life to which the human race has addicted itself during innumerable ages of mistake and misery.[18]

Shelley compared the vicious and disease-plagued existence of carnivorous mankind with the gentle and supposedly healthier orang-utan and believed that the adoption of a vegetarian diet would, given time, expel from humanity the diseases which had accumulated in the human physiology through centuries of inappropriate diet:

> Disease is hereditary and the mass which is now existing in the world has been produced by a mistake of unfathomable antiquity. With what rapidity the adoption of vegetable food might diminish this accumulation it is impossible to predict.[19]

He advised his readers, in capital letters, 'NEVER TAKE ANYTHING INTO THE STOMACH THAT ONCE HAD LIFE', and assured them that 'the author and his wife have lived on vegetables for eight months. The improvements of health and temper here stated is [sic] the result of his own experience'. He also gave examples of supposed vegetarians who had lived to great ages including 'Old Parr' (152), 'A shepherd in Hungary' (126) and 'James the Hermit' (104).[20] Given Shelley's notoriously unstable temper, this was not the strongest of recommendations.

Nevertheless, in the century that followed, vegetarianism gained a more significant following in Britain and elsewhere, beginning in 1847 with the formation of the Vegetarian Society at Ramsgate in Kent, thereby adding the word *vegetarian* to the language.[21] It was the brainchild of Joseph Brotherton, MP (1783–1857), who embraced a number of philanthropic causes including free elementary education, public libraries, the abolition of slavery and the ending of capital punishment. His wife was also a vegetarian and her contribution to the cause was to write vegetarian cookbooks which substituted loaves and melons for the loaves and fishes of the Biblical miracle. In Britain the most prominent and outspoken vegetarian was the playwright George Bernard Shaw (1856–1950) whose vegetarianism was mitigated by his consumption of vitamin B12 extracted from liver, to prevent pernicious anaemia, and by Mrs William Morris who surreptitiously fed him a pudding containing suet.

In the United States a similar organisation was formed in 1850 under the leadership of Sylvester Graham (1794–1851), one of its most prominent members being Dr William Alcott, kinsman of the writer Louisa May Alcott. Graham, who styled himself a doctor, observed that there was no beef in Eden and he advocated following the diet of Adam and Eve (except, presumably, for the apple). Graham developed a nutritious, wholemeal bread free from the alum and other chemical additives commonly used by bakers to make their bread whiter and he appears to have been motivated by a desire to suppress lust which, he believed, was promoted by a carnivorous diet. Besides a vegetarian diet he advocated hard beds, cold baths and chastity on the grounds that ejaculation was debilitating. His *Lectures on the Science of Human Life* asserted that 'the enormous wickedness and atrocious violence and outrages of mankind immediately preceding the flood strongly indicate, if they do not prove, an excessive indulgence in animal food'. On the other hand, 'a single pound of rice absolutely contains more nutritious matter than two pounds and a half of the best butcher's meat; and three pounds of good wheat bread contain more than six pounds of flesh; and three pounds of potatoes more than two pounds of flesh'.[22] This advice, which was made more believable to his credulous followers by the primitive methods of nutritional analysis then available, was not appreciated by all and it is hardly surprising that his appearance at speaking engagements was often disrupted by butchers who regarded him as a threat to their livelihoods.[23] In Russia the most prominent vegetarian was Leo Tolstoy (1828–1910) who corresponded with his fellow-vegetarian Mahatma Gandhi and gave his support to a pacifist, vegetarian sect called the Doukhobors who, persecuted for their beliefs in Tsarist Russia, emigrated to Canada where they still practise their beliefs. In the twentieth century vegetarianism was strengthened by the growing realisation that vegetables contained certain elements essential to life and health that were lacking in meat – vitamins. There are at present about four million vegetarians, of different degrees of commitment, in the United Kingdom and no supermarket is complete without a range of vegetarian foods.

'The Great Masticator'

Late in the nineteenth century vegetarianism was joined, and in some respects rivalled, as a dietary system by 'Fletcherism', the brainchild of Horace Fletcher (1849–1919), an American who argued that the key to healthy eating was mastication. The British Prime Minister W.E. Gladstone (1809–98) had been a great advocate of chewing thirty-two times (one chew for each tooth), but he excluded liquids from the regime whereas Fletcher included them (though by what method they should be chewed he failed to specify). Chewing thirty-two times at the rate of 100 times per minute before swallowing would, he believed, increase the energy output of the foods while reducing the quantity required. It was thus a form of dieting as well as a way in which to increase the nutritional value of the food consumed. Moreover, food should only be eaten when one was hungry and happy. Fletcher's credibility was enhanced by his demonstration, while in his fifties, of several feats of physical strength and endurance in competition with young athletes from Yale, and his followers were not deterred by his insistence that they examine their excrement carefully to ensure that it gave off no evil smell. In support of this aspect of his theory Fletcher adopted the habit of sending small samples of his own excrement by post to his followers as evidence of its odourless character.[24] The results of such activities are nowhere recorded, but his ideas attracted a substantial and reputable following. Fletcher claimed that his diet was a cure for, amongst other conditions, haemorrhoids, adenoids and moral turpitude.[25] Horace Fletcher certainly prospered in his theories and was able to retire to a stylish palazzo on Venice's Grand Canal. The writers Henry James and Mark Twain and the millionaire John D. Rockefeller were among his admirers and mastication was a subject of great interest to *The Lancet* in the early years of the twentieth century. In 1903 it published ten items on the subject with titles like *Observations on Mastication*; *The Vigorous Use to which jaws and teeth are put among existing primitive peoples*; *Too much food is eaten*; and *Inefficient mastication conduces to excessive eating*. Dr Harry Campbell of Wimpole Street, who initiated the material with a series of articles, caused some offence to the dental profession when he suggested that brushing and mouthwashes could damage the teeth because bacteria 'play a useful part as scavengers'.[26]

Fletcher's experiments on tramps whom he provided with free meals were, in his opinion, such a success that, if his formula were widely adopted, 'there would be such a reduction in the numbers of the impoverished that the problem of the poor might be regarded as solved'.[27] Some of Fletcher's more eccentric followers, like Bishop Fallows of Chicago, believed that inappropriate diets promoted vicious behaviour, warning his flock that 'vice can be fed into children via their stomachs',[28] a claim which prompted *Punch* to advise its readers that the consumption of Welsh rarebit and pickles could have injurious consequences and that the only really safe food for children was boiled rice.[29] Seeing his chance, a murderer called Edgar Burnz in Sing Sing prison claimed that his crimes were due to his juvenile diet and claimed that he had been reformed by adopting Fletcherism.[30] The potentially evil consequences of Welsh rarebit were happily avoided and Fletcherism passed into history leaving mankind with the problem of surplus energy and inadequate exercise.

During the First World War, Fletcherism enjoyed a fresh, if brief, moment of glory when it was embraced by Kennedy Jones, co-founder of the *Daily Mail*, who for six months was director of food economy at the Ministry of Food. Jones published a pamphlet which argued that Fletcherite mastication would increase the nutritional value of food and consequently reduce the quantity of produce that would need to be imported through the dangerous Atlantic shipping lanes. His arguments were ridiculed by the Royal Society and the pamphlet, along with Kennedy Jones, disappeared from history, though the Royal Society's record itself was not without blemish. It argued against the importation of fruit on the grounds that 'its nutritive value is far below that of wheat', this at a time when the role of vitamins in a healthy diet, as expounded by one of its most eminent Fellows, Frederick Gowland Hopkins, was not yet fully understood.[31]

The Holy Palate Tavern

Horace Fletcher was joined in his attempts to create a more healthy diet for the twentieth century by the Italian 'futurist' Filippo Marinetti (1876–1944). Marinetti, who enjoyed the benefits of a private income and could consequently afford to take a lofty view of the traditional Italian diet, declared that pasta was 'Italy's absurd gastronomic religion', too ponderous for the pace of the twentieth century.[32] Consumers of pasta were 'slow and pacific, while meat eaters [were] quick and aggressive'.[33] He advocated the installation in kitchens of ultra-violet lamps and 'ozonisers' to impart 'active properties' to foods and to remind them that the days of 'physical work' were being replaced by technology (a correct and relevant insight, though not in the kitchen). One of his admirers, a journalist of *Gazzetta del Popolo*, wrote to congratulate Marinetti on his work and recommended that the Italian diet should be:

Three quarters composed of the marvellous vegetable products for which we are envied throughout the world and a scant quarter of animal products. These [i.e. the animal products] must be used very frugally, especially by intellectual workers, while soldiers, manual workers and in general those who engage in a great deal of physical activity can eat more of it (the opposite of what normally happens).[34]

His comments on the relative needs of 'intellectual' and physical workers were, of course, prescient, but such subtleties are hard to discern in the *Taverno di Santo Palato* (Holy Palate Restaurant) in Turin, which opened in 1931 to give Marinetti's ideas edible form. It served such delicacies as 'intuitive antipasto' and 'aerovictuals', the latter consisting of olives, fennel and candied bitter orange, to be consumed while stroking sandpaper and listening to Wagner.[35] It was not a success, despite Marinetti's assurances that 'meals will be less frequent but perfect in their daily provision of equivalent nutrients'. He approved of the violence and misogyny of Mussolini's Fascists but was a somewhat equivocal supporter of the movement and died before it collapsed. His dietary ideas died with him and when last observed, the site which the *taverno* occupied was being converted from a travel agency to a pizza restaurant.[36]

The No Breakfast Association

A twentieth-century figure of more lasting fame than Horace Fletcher adopted an approach to diet which, according to him, originated in Manchester. Mahatma Gandhi, who was famously ascetic by inclination and slight in build, nevertheless harboured his own anxieties about diet and health. He became convinced that his recurrent headaches and constipation were due to over-eating and recorded in his *Autobiography* that 'About this time I read of the formation of a *No Breakfast Association* in Manchester. The argument of the promoters was that Englishmen ate too much, that their doctors' bills were heavy because they ate until midnight and that they should at least give up breakfast if they wanted to improve this state of affairs'.[37] The headaches and constipation persisted and so, on the advice of a German vegetarian, he decided, in addition to foregoing breakfast, that he would live off fruit and nuts, 'the natural diet of man'. It is not clear that this worked either.

Exotica

During the nineteenth and early twentieth centuries some wild ideas concerning human nutrition really gathered pace. Lydia Pinkham (1819–83), born in Massachusetts, appears to have developed her 'vegetable compound' in response to her husband's declining fortunes and its precise formulation remains a mystery, but this did not inhibit the claims made for it by its inventor. It allegedly disposed of 'all ovarian troubles' while curing constipation, biliousness and liver troubles. By the 1920s its sales reached almost $4 million and in the 1960s *Pinkham's Medicinal Compound* was the subject of a popular song. In the early 1900s a Swiss doctor, Maximilian Bircher-Benner, suggested that cooking deprived foods of their nutritional value (as indeed boiling can) and informed his followers that, since food received all the cooking it needed by exposure to the sun, it should be eaten raw – especially a mixture of fruit, nuts and grains which he called by the Swiss word, *muesli*, later adopted for a range of breakfast cereals. In 1928 Johanna Brandt, a South African immigrant to the United States, published *The Grape Cure* in which she claimed to have fought off cancer by fasting for twelve hours a day and eating nothing but grapes for the other twelve hours. It was publicised by a strange character called Bernarr [sic] Macfadden who, between running for Governor and President of the United States, made a fortune from a chain of health farms and magazines. The medical profession was alarmed and in 1950 Macfadden offered $10,000 to anyone who could prove that grapes did not cure cancer – of course, an impossible task. Macfadden himself survived to the age of eighty-seven, having made a parachute descent three years earlier to mark his eighty-fourth birthday.[38] Perhaps the most bizarre, because the most surprising, advocate of an unconventional diet was Linus Pauling (1901–94). Having won two Nobel Prizes, one for chemistry and one for peace, Pauling became convinced that vitamin C played a crucial part not only in mankind's early diets but also in fending off illnesses in modern humans, ranging from colds to cancer. When his wife was found to be suffering from cancer Pauling declined all medical intervention in favour of large doses of vitamin C. She died and, although his ortho-molecular medicine still has a following, especially in the United States, it has not persuaded the broader medical profession of its merits.[39]

Raw Recruits

In the twentieth century, as the science of chemistry was applied to that of nutrition by more conventional practitioners, concerns about the human diet took on a more responsible tone, though no less alarming for that. In his seminal work *The Englishmen's Food*, first published in 1939, Sir Jack Drummond declared that 'The opening of the twentieth century saw malnutrition more rife in England than it had been since the great dearths of mediaeval and Tudor Times',[40] much of this being due to ignorance rather than simple poverty, as the role of essential dietary elements such as vitamins was only slowly coming to be understood. During the Boer War, and again during the First World War, the British and American governments became concerned about the number of young male volunteers for military service who had to be rejected because they were too short, too skinny or suffered from such conditions as rickets. The problem was averted, rather than solved, by the creation of 'bantam battalions' in the British Army for recruits who were undersized. In the United States many volunteers from the Mid-West were found to be suffering from goitre, an unsightly swelling of the thyroid glands in the neck. It is normally caused by a shortage of iodine in the diet and is associated with areas where there are low concentrations of iodine in the soil, and hence in cereal and vegetable crops grown there. This was the case both in the American Mid-West and in the English Midlands where the condition was known as 'Derbyshire Neck'. From the 1920s goitre was largely eliminated by the addition of iodine to table salt, an early example of a medical condition treated by the fortification of a common product. By the time that the United States entered the Second World War the role of vitamins and minerals in diet was coming to be understood, and in the year that America entered the war, 1941, the breakfast cereals industry began to restore nutrients which were lost in processing, thereby remedying some of the worst deficiencies of the diets of American recruits. In 1955 the first fortified cereal (Kellogg's Special K) was launched, containing vitamins and minerals in excess of those naturally occurring in the raw materials from which it was made, and in 1961 General Mills countered by launching Total, a cereal which contained in a standard serving 100 per cent of the daily requirement of the principal vitamins and iron. By 1973 at least 85 per cent of breakfast cereals were fortified at least with vitamins, but an attempt by the Swift meat packing company to arouse the interest of consumers in the nutritional content of its products was met with indifference, which was a harbinger of future events. In response to an offer of nutritional information on 15 million packs, Swift received 251 requests.

The British Diet

Concerns about the quality of the British diet between the two world wars was expressed in the work of the National Birthday Trust Fund, which was founded in 1928 and flourished in the late 1930s during the Depression of that decade. It was the brainchild of three well-connected ladies: Lucy Baldwin, wife of the prime minister; Lady Cholmondeley; and the immensely wealthy Marchioness of Londonderry whose Park Lane mansion was a bizarre meeting place for an organisation, designed to support malnourished pregnant women in the distressed regions. Midwives had drawn attention to the rising figures of mortality amongst their clients in these areas, due to the fact that, when food was short, the mother normally ensured that her husband and children received such meager rations as were available, at the expense of her own well-being. As a result, maternal deaths in areas like the Rhondda Valley in Wales had risen from seven to eleven for every 1,000 births, whereas at the turn of the century a figure of two per 1,000 births had been regarded as excessive.[41] The declared aim of the National Birthday Trust Fund was to collect one shilling (5p) from all citizens on their birthdays, giving a total of 42 million shillings or a little over £2 million which would be used to supply nourishing foods to these women. This noble idea overlooked the fact that hardly any of the army of unemployed, amounting to 2½ million,[42] not to mention their spouses and children, could afford a shilling for anything.

Nevertheless, the organisation raised enough money from wealthy patrons and the moderately affluent to begin their work which was later supported by the government in the form of the Commission for the Special Areas. They began by distributing jars of Marmite (rich in B-group vitamins, notably folic acid, essential for pregnant women) and dried milk in South Wales and later extended this to other areas of Wales and to the north east whose coalfields were also badly afflicted by unemployment. They later added beef drinks, Ovaltine and milk-based foods, and the result was a drop in mortality to fewer than five deaths per 1,000 – still a figure which would have been regarded as high thirty years earlier, but an improvement nevertheless.[43] Unfortunately this charitable exercise in nutritional science was marred by the event which was held to mark its success. This occurred on 28 March 1939, when a lavish celebratory dinner was held at the Guildhall, London, attended by Queen Elizabeth who was provided with a guard of honour of debutantes. Two hundred women who had benefited from the scheme were brought to London from the distressed areas, virtually as exhibits, each being provided with a ninepenny picnic luncheon box from J. Lyons for the occasion, while the celebratory feast proceeded in an adjacent room. Presumably the organisers felt that the rich food they were themselves enjoying would have been too much for these poor women. Perhaps they were right.[44]

The advent of the Second World War six months after the dinner solved the problem of unemployment, and the high standard of the British diet during the shortages and privations of the war has already been noted.[45] In the years that followed the war the widespread take-up of school meals and the improved dental and health care which followed the foundation of the National Health Service helped to maintain standards. In 1980, however, the first Thatcher government removed the requirement for local authorities to maintain minimum nutritional standards in school meals and this measure, combined with the earlier decision of Margaret Thatcher as Education Secretary to reduce the availability of free school milk, led to a deterioration in children's diets which was noted with alarm by *The Lancet*. In August 1986 the journal featured an article headed *Britain needs a Food and Health Policy: the Government must face its Duty*, which drew attention to the effects of the decline in the quality of school meals and commented that the British diet was 'one of the least likely among comparable countries to promote health and longevity'.[46] Forty per cent of energy in the British diet was being derived from fat against a recommended level of 30 per cent, and a survey carried out jointly by the Ministry of Agriculture and the Consumers' Association had revealed that, when a representative sample of consumers was questioned on the subject, 'over ninety per cent wanted nutritional labelling', though this left unanswered the difficult question of what they meant by 'nutritional labelling', a matter that was to perplex nutritionists and politicians for decades. The situation was to be further complicated by the lobbying of powerful interest groups who were interested in the marketing of products such as sugar and fats which were rich in kilocalories but deficient in much else, such as protein, vitamins and minerals.

Politicians

In the meantime, in the United States nutritional standards had become a serious political issue as a result of the activities of the Kennedy Clan.

In March 1962, President John F. Kennedy declared that information about the quality of food was a basic consumer right and three years later his brother, Robert Kennedy, shortly to be a presidential candidate, led a 'hunger march' in the southern states of the USA to draw attention to the existence of malnutrition (especially in the black community) in the world's richest economy. A television documentary by CBS entitled 'Hunger in America' further dramatised the issue.[47] At about the same time, two United States government agencies were conducting their own research into the nutritional health of its citizens.

The first of these, the result of a ten-year study, was published by the Department of Agriculture in 1968 entitled *Dietary Levels of Households in the US* and showed that in the years 1955–65, a period of rapidly increasing prosperity, there had actually been an increase in the number of households with diets lacking in one or more important nutrients.[48] A particularly surprising revelation was that poor diets were often associated with families of above-average income. The second study was carried out by the Department of Health, Education and Welfare in 1968–70. It was concerned with 30,000 low-income families in ten states and presented evidence of iron-deficiency anaemia in many of the families studied, as well as a shortage of protein in pregnant women and shortage of vitamins A and D in ethnic minority groups.[49] The fact that there were malnourished groups in the world's most prosperous society was variously attributed to: the increasing consumption of snack and 'fun' foods by teenagers; the gradual reduction in family meal occasions and the habit of 'grazing' on convenience foods, especially by younger people; and the staggering of school hours in some areas which meant that some children ate (or failed to eat) breakfast unsupervised.

These reports, and the attention they received in the media, led to a flurry of political activity. President Nixon, in an address to the US Congress in 1969, congratulated the powerful US food industry on the advances it had made in processing and packaging, but drew attention to the resulting burdens on those who were less well off and less sophisticated in the ways of the modern marketplace. He was tactfully expressing a view that has been shared by many others and which argues that ingeniously devised processed foods, with formidable polysyllabic chemicals in their lists of ingredients, sometimes leave consumers with only the vaguest idea of what they are buying. A Harvard professor was appointed by President Nixon as his special adviser, a White House Conference was called, panels and task forces were created, the great and the good were enlisted and a bulky tome was duly produced whose conclusions included a recommendation that some kind of labelling

should be devised which would convey to consumers the nutritional content of the product within. In the words of the conference report:

> Every manufacturer should be encouraged to provide truthful nutritional
> information to consumers about his products to enable them to follow rec-
> ommended dietary regimes ... The use of Madison Avenue [i.e. advertising]
> methods to get this information to the general public is essential.[50]

These recommendations were uncontroversial but hinted at two problems which were to bedevil attempts to encourage consumers to eat more
healthy diets. The first was contained in the phrase 'truthful nutritional
information' and the second concerned the use of advertising to arouse and
sustain the interest of busy consumers in the information thus conveyed.

What is Nutrition and Who Cares?

Nutrition is a complex science. Intelligent people spend years at universities studying the subject and a lifetime refining and applying what they
have learned. Expressing 'truthful nutritional information' on a small food
label may be compared with describing 'health' or 'virtue' in a similar space.
Over forty dietary elements are known to be necessary for health, ranging from the protein, carbohydrate and fat which give us our energy, or
kilocalories, to minerals and vitamins which are essential to our well-being
– some in amounts so small that it is very difficult to measure them. It is
not made easier by the fact that some substances are more or less benign
according to their source. Thus Omega 3 fatty acids, which are widely promoted as a remedy against heart disease, are regarded in responsible quarters
as being more beneficial when obtained from fish than from vegetables.
The consumer can be excused for being confused! The US introduced
Recommended Daily Allowances (RDAs) for seventeen such elements in
1943, a move prompted by alarm at the number of young men rejected for
military service in the Second World War owing to poor nutrition. Some
idea of the complexity of the subject may be gained by reflecting on the
fact that the present list of RDAs includes allowances for the following:

Energy (expressed as kilocalories)
Protein (a component of the energy requirement)
11 vitamins
8 minerals

Moreover, these twenty-one elements are separately calculated for ten gender/age groups, giving a total of 210 separate values. Some idea of the differences may be inferred from a comparison of the recommended allowances for twenty-four-year-old males and females. Males need about 2,500 kilocalories a day and females about 2,000. However, whereas males need only 10mg of iron a day, females need as much as 18mg, the latter figure influenced by the fact that women who are pregnant or breastfeeding need unusually high levels of iron in their systems. In the circumstances a great deal of thought had to be devoted to defining the White House Conference Report's 'truthful nutritional information' before the results could be handed over to Madison Avenue for transmission to the public.

Unusual Diets

A study of differing diets throughout the world indicates that, while human beings can tolerate such differences, they are often associated with widely varying medical conditions. There is some evidence that the 'Mediterranean' diet associated with southern Europe, which is rich in fruit, vegetables, cereals, olive oil, wine and fish, is good for the heart because it is low in saturated fats and tends to lower blood sugar levels and blood pressure. Similar claims have been made for the Japanese diet which is rich in rice, fish and vegetables and low in red meat, dairy foods and the fats associated with them. One of the most extraordinary diets is that of the Inuit who inhabit the Arctic regions of Canada, Alaska and Greenland. In 1976 the British nutritionist Hugh Macdonald Sinclair (1910–90) visited Greenland to test the Inuit diet. Sinclair already had a substantial reputation in the field, having lectured at Oxford and at University College, London, and conducted the *Oxford Nutrition Survey* for the Ministry of Health during the Second World War.[51] This had involved taking mobile teams to industrial towns and carrying out assessments of the nutritional status of the local populations, taking samples of urine and blood and testing their ability to see in poor light (a test of the adequacy of the quantity of vitamin A available). Towards the end of the war he was sent to Holland. In September 1944, in an attempt to end the war quickly, British and American paratroopers had seized key towns and bridges in the vicinity of Eindhoven and Arnhem in southern Holland. The enterprise failed but attracted much support from the local Dutch population so, when the Allies withdrew, the German occupiers imposed a blockade on the south of the country, leading to very serious food shortages. Sinclair and his team assessed the situation in two weeks and recommended the right feeding regimes to bring relief to the starving population, an effort he repeated shortly afterwards in the British zone of occupation in Germany.

He had long been intrigued by the Inuit diet, and he had lectured on it in Trondheim, Norway, in 1966. In 1976 he returned to the subject, visiting Greenland and subjecting himself to the Inuit diet for 100 days. The diet consists mostly of fish and sealmeat, though it also includes some berries, including blueberries, which grow within the Arctic Circle and are a good source of vitamin C. Conventional theories held that a diet so dependent upon flesh would lead to a build-up of fatty deposits in the arteries caused by cholesterol and consequently a high incidence of heart attacks and thromboses, but in fact the Inuit suffered very little from these afflictions. Sinclair's study suggested that it was not fat which caused a build-up of cholesterol and heart attacks but the *wrong type* of fat. Fish oil contains Omega 3 polyunsaturated fatty acids which actually lower the level of cholesterol and explain the healthy condition of the Inuit. This probably also explained the Inuit's tendency to nosebleeds (which are caused by a thinning of the blood), a phenomenon which Sinclair noted in himself as he conducted the experiment.

Explaining Nutrition

In the months that followed President Nixon's speech to Congress in 1969, the Food and Drug Administration (FDA) carried out extensive consultations with nutritionists, consumer representatives, dieticians and the food industry about the best way to proceed, and a shortlist was drawn up of elements to be included in food labelling. The Food and Nutrition Board of the National Academy of Sciences (an impeccably respectable organisation which may be compared with the Royal Society) led the exercise, and the research amongst consumers which followed was conducted by Cornell University, resulting in the following list of eleven elements being identified as critical to an understanding of nutritional needs:

Kilocalories
Protein
Carbohydrate
Fat

Vitamin A

Vitamin B group: Niacin

                     Thiamin

                     Riboflavin

Vitamin C

Calcium

Iron

Cornell also carried out an extensive study of different methods of conveying the information, involving home interviews of 2,195 consumers and tests of three different types of label in four supermarket groups. The research arrived at two significant conclusions. First, it showed that interviewees were most comfortable with labels which expressed the nutritional content of a serving of the product as a percentage of Recommended Daily Allowances. The second conclusion was more disappointing, since only just over 9 per cent of the sample claimed to use the information. Moreover, those most likely to make this claim were well-educated, affluent consumers who were least likely to be victims of malnutrition while minority ethnic groups, whose dietary problems had originally prompted the actions of Robert Kennedy, were least likely to use them. It is well known that in such studies consumers tend to overstate their usage, further suggesting that the labels really were not reaching the people who most needed to understand them. It is hard to escape the conclusion that the Cornell study, while identifying the best available method of labelling, had also demonstrated that it wouldn't do much good. The 'traffic light' system described in the opening sentences of this chapter is a further attempt to overcome this problem, and its effectiveness will be judged by time unless it is frustrated by the opposition of retailers and manufacturers, as may yet happen.

'Read the Label; Set a Better Table'

In 1973 the nutrition labelling regulations were published, following the model proposed by Cornell. The eleven elements were shown, with the contribution of each to the Recommended Daily Allowance. In each case the RDA chosen as a measure was that of the group with the greatest need, so that for kilocalories, for example, the reference group was young males, while for iron it was pregnant or breastfeeding women. In the words of the handbook on RDAs, they were 'estimated to exceed the requirements of most individuals and thereby ensure that the needs of nearly all are met'.[52] In addition, manufacturers could, if they wished, include information on twelve others, including other vitamins, iodine and zinc. The labelling was voluntary unless a supplier made any kind of nutritional claim in advertising or packaging, in which case it was compulsory. It was also compulsory for baby foods in which case the RDAs were, of course, based on the needs of infants. The regulations were more burdensome for products normally eaten with other foods, such as breakfast cereals. In these cases the suppliers had to declare the nutritional values without the milk added and could, if they wished, declare it with the milk added. This they invariably did, giving two sets of values and making the labels very complicated – a problem only partly mitigated by the fact that cereal packets, being large, can accommodate this plethora of data. In certain circumstances the consumption of grossly excessive quantities of vitamins (such as carotene, vitamin A) can be harmful to health and so, in order to prevent what the Food and Drug Administration (FDA) called 'a nutrition horsepower race', it specified that, where the addition of nutrients to products was grossly disproportionate, the label should bear the following warning:

> The addition of [x] at the level contained in this product has been determined by the United States government to be unnecessary and inappropriate and does not increase the dietary value of the food.

The introduction of nutrition labelling was accompanied by an ambitious publicity campaign financed by the US government and devised by the well-known Madison Avenue advertising agency, J. Walter Thompson. It produced a series of television and radio advertisements featuring well-known personalities like Dick Van Dyke and urging consumers to 'Read the label; set a better table'. A film, slide show and pamphlets were made available to schools and community groups and a booklet entitled *Food is more than just something to eat* was distributed by the FDA. The extensive publicity campaign no doubt helped to ensure that virtually all suppliers adopted nutrition labelling for their products, despite its voluntary nature, with the exception of products like tea and coffee whose nutritional (as distinct from restorative) values were negligible. Suppliers tended to err on the side of under-declaring nutritional values in order to avoid falling foul of the inspectors whose task it was to check that the regulations were being observed.

There were, however, many who had reservations about the system. Prominent amongst these were the manufacturers of health foods whose highly fortified products often contained nutrients vastly in excess of the RDAs and who thereby risked not only incurring the dreaded warning label quoted above but, in some cases, found themselves being regulated under the much tougher drugs regulations. A campaign of letter writing prompted by a health food magazine suggested that RDAs had been set deliberately low in order to show health foods and supplements in a poor light. There was no evidence to support this contention since, as indicated above, RDAs tended to err on the high side, but this did not prevent the lobby from securing the support of Senator William Proxmire, one of the more colourful members of Congress. Proxmire accused the highly respected Food and Nutrition Board of the US National Academy of Sciences of being in the pay of the food industry and setting RDAs low so as to penalise the health food industry. Neither Proxmire, nor the letter writing, nor the lawsuits that were launched against the FDA by members of the industry prevailed in the face of the nutrition labelling campaign, but they are an indication of the passions that are aroused by the unassuming science of human nutrition.

Senator William Proxmire (1915–2005) was elected as Senator for Wisconsin in 1957 in place of the recently deceased, and unlamented, Senator Joseph McCarthy. He remained a senator for the state until 1989, being elected by large majorities despite his refusal to raise campaign funds, preferring simply to greet citizens at public events with a handshake. An exceptionally conscientious legislator, he voted in 10,252 consecutive Senate votes between 1966 and 1988, more than three times the previous record for a senator. He was an early and vociferous critic of the Vietnam War and he gave his support to a number of causes more deserving than the health foods industry, and with more effect. For example, faced with the reluctance of the Senate to ratify the Convention on the Prevention and Punishment of the Crime of Genocide he gave the same short speech on the subject over 3,000 times, over a period of twenty years, until the Senate finally ratified the measure in 1986. He is probably best remembered for his *Golden Fleece* awards to organisations which had, in his view, made wasteful use of Federal taxes in pursuit of such studies as 'Why people fall in love', the activities in a Peruvian brothel, the dimensions of airline stewardesses' buttocks and an investigation into why prisoners wanted to leave gaol. He was an early advocate of physical exercise and retired from the Senate in 1989, dying in 2005, aged ninety, after a struggle with Alzheimer's.

A more reasoned reservation came from the Gerber Baby Foods company who knew from their own research that iron-deficiency anaemia was still quite common amongst infants under three years old and feared that the new regulations made it difficult to draw attention to this problem without losing it amongst an abundance of other information about other nutrients which were not at risk. Some manufacturers took a positive attitude towards the new labelling and attempted to build on it by educating consumers about the meaning of chemical terms. One of the more enterprising was a series of advertisements run by General Foods with headings like *Di-Hydrogen Oxide: what's it doing in your food?* It went on to explain that di-hydrogen oxide was otherwise known as water and that long chemical names did not always indicate sinister substances. The campaign was short-lived.

E-Numbers

In the years that followed, American consumers continued to show their customary apathy towards healthy diets and to consume ever larger quantities of sugary drinks, hamburgers, chips and other products whose nutrition labelling would not have recommended them to anyone who bothered to read them and take note of what they said. European consumers stumbled along in their wake, fitfully aided by the system of E-numbers which the European Union introduced as a standardised means of indicating that flavourings, colourings, sweeteners and other additives were approved as safe. For the really well-informed and conscientious it is even possible to discover both the purposes of these substances and the feats of chemistry by which they have been devised. At present they number more than 600 and there is no evidence that they do much more than alarm some consumers who see them listed on food packets and vaguely feel that they are not good for them. The list is revisited at regular intervals by the EU organisation which oversees it, the European Food Safety Authority based in Parma, Italy, the purpose of these reviews being to examine evidence that the approved substances are still suitable for inclusion in human foods – or not, as the case may be.

Particular anxieties have recently come to surround the question of hydrogenation, a process by which hydrogen is added to vegetable oils whereby they become solid, saturated fats, a cheap substitute for animal fats that are used in margarine and known as *transfats*. They have excellent preservative qualities, for example for cakes and products of the baker's art, and are commonly used in deep-fried fast foods and snack foods, but they are also associated with a greater risk of coronary heart disease. In 2003 Denmark regulated their use in food products and in December 2006 New York City Council banned some of them from use in the city's restaurants. This followed an article in the respected *New England Journal of Medicine* which calculated that between 12 and 20 per cent of cardiovascular episodes could be eliminated if transfats were removed from the diet.[53] Further concerns have been expressed by some nutritionists about high fructose syrups, derived from corn (maize) and often used as a sweetener in the United States as a substitute for sugars, which are subject to heavy import tariffs. There is some evidence that these products are even more 'addictive' than ordinary sugars and that they stimulate the production of insulin, with which they work to produce body fat.

Since the 1970s governments in Europe and America have gradually become more insistent about the need to show the nutritional values of processed foods on packaging, though a good deal of latitude still exists concerning the way in which this is done. The current controversy in Britain over the relative merits of 'traffic light' indicators and Guideline Daily Amounts is a case in point, and it is hardly surprising that confectionery companies and others whose products are richer in kilocalories than in nutrients should choose labelling methods that do not draw attention to these facts. Nor should we be too surprised at the regular emergence of 'miracle diets' that promise health and beauty in the traditions of Fletcher, Marinetti and others. Nutrition is a complex subject which is not easily reduced to a few lines and figures on the back of a wrapper. Some of the consequences of these uncomfortable facts are discussed in chapter seven.

'Deadly Adulterations and Slow Poisoning'

There shall be standard measures of wine, ale, and corn (the London quarter), throughout the kingdom.

Magna Carta, clause 35

There is Death in the Pot
From the title page of Fredrick Accum's book on food, *Adulteration*, 1820

The whole of the twenty-four samples of bread examined were adulterated with alum ... genuine mustard, whatever the price paid for it, is scarcely ever to be obtained

Arthur Hill Hassall, reporting on his analysis of common foods, 1855

'Judgements of the Pillory for Putrid Meat'

The temptation to adulterate products in order to increase profits is as old as human history itself and the greatest temptation naturally applies to the most expensive products, like wine, and the most commonly consumed, like bread. Some of the most alarming adulteration, however, arose through ignorance. In his *Six Weeks Tour Through the Southern Counties of England and Wales*, published in 1771, Arthur Young described approvingly the way in which vegetables were taken from rural areas to the London markets on waterways and then added that, on the return journey, the barges carried 'nightsoil' – human excrement.[1] Sanitary regulations governing the quality of food are to be found in the teachings of Moses, while ancient Greece and Rome had wine inspectors to safeguard the quality of the products, though Pliny the Elder (23–79 AD) drew attention to the process by which wine could be made from honey and water: 'Keep the mixture exposed to the rays of a hot sun for forty days after the rising of the dog star ... this beverage is known as hydromeli and with age acquires the flavour of wine'.[2] Pliny also complained that bakers added chalk to bread, an accusation that was to be repeated for millennia. The Mead which was a popular drink in Anglo-Saxon England appears to have been similar to Pliny's 'hydromeli' though permitted additives included spinach, strawberry leaves, pepper and roses but not hops, which were regarded as an adulterant, though they acted as a preservative.[3] In 1421, 'information was laid against one for putting an unwholesome kind of weed called Hopp into his brewing' and Henry VIII also forbade their use by his brewer. The addition of hops to ale to produce beer was finally authorised by Edward VI.[4] During the reign of Edward the Confessor a brewer who had adulterated his product was drawn about London in a cart which had previously been used for collecting refuse.[5] Reference has already been made to the *Assize of Bead and Ale* of 1266 which established the procedures for checking the quality of the products and setting their prices, but half a century earlier the *Magna Carta* itself had laid down standard measures for certain products in Clause 35:

> There shall be standard measures of wine, ale, and corn (the London quarter), throughout the kingdom. There shall also be a standard width of dyed cloth, russett, and haberject, namely two ells within the selvedges. Weights are to be standardised similarly.

Punishments for infringing standards could be savage and depended on ridicule as well as on other penalties. Thus the selling of putrid meat led to the 'Judgements of the Pillory' in which offending traders would be exposed to severe danger as well as scorn since their fellow citizens were able, and often encouraged, to pelt those confined to the pillory with anything that came to hand (dead cats being popular missiles) with occasionally fatal results. The *Liber Albus*, compiled in 1419 at the request of the mayor of London, Richard Whittington, describes processes by which the quality of ale was checked by elected officials called ale-conners. When a brewer 'shall have made a brew, send for the Ale-conners of the Ward wherein they dwell, to taste the ale, so that he or she sell no ale before that the said ale-conners have assayed the same, under pain of forfeiture of the said ale'.[6] If the ale was suspected of containing too much sugar then the test was to pour a pint on a wooden bench and sit on the damp patch in leather breeches until it was dry. If the breeches stuck to the bench the ale was over-sugared.[7] *Liber Albus* also records penalties for bakers whose loaves were found to be defective, for example if they contained sand:

> If any default shall be found in the bread of a baker of the City, let him be drawn upon a hurdle from the Guildhall to his own house, through the great streets where there may be most people assembled, and through the great streets that are most dirty, with the faulty loaf hanging from his neck. If a second time he shall be found committing the same offence, let him be drawn from the Guildhall though the great street of Chepe, in manner aforesaid, to the pillory and remain there at least one hour.

If these humiliations were insufficient to deter a third offence, then the baker would be forbidden to practise his trade.[8] For brewers, penalties were comparatively mild, possibly because, at this time, the trade was almost entirely in the hands of women, though professional brewing was 'reckoned among the callings of low repute'.[9] Home brewing, which was a branch of domestic cookery, was respectable, one of the more prominent brewers being Joan, wife of Oliver Cromwell (according to *Mrs Cromwell's Cookery Book*, published in 1664 by one of her former servants).[10]

Contemporary records make many references to 'stinking rabbits' and 'stinking or putrid poultry' and, in a specific warning, 'on the baskets of fishmongers', the merchants were told that only one type of fish may be held per basket and those who infringed, or hid rotten fish beneath a covering of fresh, were threatened with gaol. Similar prohibitions were applied to the practice of soaking ginger or saffron in water to increase its weight, though in the twentieth century the practice of injecting chickens with water both to make them look more appetising and to increase their weight is well established.[11] Chaucer's *Pardoner's Tale* mentions the practice of adulterating wine and a contemporary record reminds us of the fate of John Penroe, a London merchant, who was convicted of that offence in November 1350. He was sentenced to drink copious quantities of his defective vintage, had the rest poured over him and was banned from trading in wine for five years.[12] The following century a German wine merchant convicted of a similar offence was obliged to drink *six quarts* of the offending produce and, unsurprisingly, died.[13] This is all the more surprising because, at this time, a body in Frankfurt drew up a register of the products that could legitimately be added to wine and they included milk, clay, loam, copper sulphate and alum.[14] It was followed by the celebrated *Rheinheitsgebot* regulations (sometimes described as 'German beer laws') dating from the early sixteenth century, which were supposedly designed to protect the purity of German beer but which were used well into the twentieth century to protect German producers of cereals from foreign, including European, competition and which survived until the creation of the Single European Market in 1992.

The Grocers

In some cases trade associations were themselves entrusted with monitoring and maintaining standards. Thus the Grocers were granted the office of 'garblers', the word referring to sifting. A fourteenth-century statute decreed that 'no merchandise that ought to be garbled should in future be weighed or sold before it has been cleansed and garbled by a man appointed for the purpose by the said grocers'.[15] The authority of the Grocers, one of the City's oldest livery companies, was extended to products such as sugar, confectionery ingredients and later tobacco. In the Middle Ages pepper was a valuable commodity that was sometimes used in paying taxes, Alaric the Goth having demanded payment in pepper when he besieged Rome in AD 408. Consequently the temptation to 'bulk up' pepper by adding foreign substances was exceptionally great and in the reign of Elizabeth I merchants were encouraged to export consignments of pepper which were considered too foul for the English market.[16] Despite the savage punishments inflicted on those who were convicted of adulterating their goods, the primitive state of science, especially chemistry, and the absence of effective microscopes to examine suspicious consignments, meant that the enforcement of such regulations as existed was unreliable and intermittent.

By the following century scientists like Robert Boyle (1627–91) were beginning to apply some crude but systematic analysis of the more commonly adulterated foods and Boyle himself declared that 'most of the cinnamon and cloves that is [sic] brought to these Western regions is defrauded in the Indies of much of the finest and subtlest aromatic parts before it is sent into Europe'.[17] In 1688 one of the first statutes of the reign of William and Mary had created a penalty of £300 for adulterating wine, but since the definition of 'adulteration' was far from clear and since the science of chemical analysis was in its infancy, there was no effective means of enforcing the statute. Boyle made an early record of the sophistication that was brought to bear on the production of expensive products like wines, writing:

I had many years ago a wine which, being coloured with cochineal, or some such tinging ingredient, was taken for good raspberry wine not only by ordinary persons but among others by a couple of eminent Physicians, one of whom pretended to an extraordinary criticalness of palate on such occasions.[18]

British Wines, 'English Claret'

Shakespeare himself celebrates the art of wine adulteration when in *King Henry IV, Part I* he has Falstaff complain: 'there's lime in this sack [sherry]'. There were helpful guides for those who wished to practice the art of unconventional winemaking. Thus *The Innkeeper's and Butlers' Guide for Making and Managing British Wines with Directions for the Managing, Colouring and Flavouring of Foreign Wines and Spirits* offered a recipe for 'English claret' which included 6 gallons of water and 2 gallons of cider into which 8lb of raisins should be stirred. After a fortnight the 'winemaker' should add the juice of barberries, raspberries and black cherries and, finally, a pinch of mustard seed. This would give the required flavour, texture and colour without the expense of importing the genuine article from Bordeaux. Further recipes were English Port, Sack (sherry) and Champagne, the last consisting of water, sugar, currants and yeast, and all the recipes untainted by grapes which, since they had to be imported, were presumably considered an extravagance.[19] The fact that such guides were openly available for sale suggests that the practices were scarcely disreputable, let alone illegal. Some guides appear to have had innocent, if naïve, aims. Thus a guide of 1596 entitled *A Book of Secrets* suggests that the addition of plaster of Paris to cheap sherry will both preserve the sherry and enhance its taste, a recipe for whose effectiveness there is no evidence.[20] In some respects the practice of chemistry by the adulterers was at the cutting edge of the science of its time. Thus France, the home of claret, was well advanced in the adulteration of one of its most iconic products. In 1750 the Farmers-General (tax collectors) became alarmed at the huge quantities of *vin gaté* (soured wine) that were being brought to Paris, ostensibly to make vinegar. Investigations revealed that the vinegar was being converted into wine by the addition of lead oxide, which reacts with and neutralises acids and lead acetate to give additional 'body' to the by now toxic liquid.[21] The use of lead for this purpose (and the contamination of wine by lead drinking and storage vessels) may also account for two other historical phenomena. Lead poisoning can lead to sterility among males and it has been suggested that the failure of Roman emperors to produce heirs may be connected with the contamination of their wine by lead; and the ingestion of lead salts may account for the high incidence of gout amongst the aristocracy of the eighteenth and nineteenth centuries.[22] If winemakers and others were not sure how to acquire the necessary toxins they could turn to *Watson's Chemical Essays*, published in 1787 by The Rev. Richard Watson, Fellow of the Royal Society and Regius Professor of Divinity at Cambridge, which gave clear instructions on the processes required to produce them in their own kitchens.[23]

Moreover, a contemporary manual gave advice to brewers on unconventional methods of producing alcoholic drinks. One, published in 1703, was called *A Guide to Gentlemen and Farmers for Brewing the Finest Malt Liquors*. It advised that stagnant water gave a stronger drink with less malt and, more alarmingly, that:

> Thames water, taken up above Greenwich, which has in it all the fat and sullage of the City of London, makes a very strong drink: it will of itself alone, being carried to sea, ferment wonderfully, and it will be so strong that sea commanders have told me it would burn, and has often fuddled mariners.[24]

Another century would pass before London's sewage was officially, rather than just surreptitiously, discharged to the river, but one is left wondering which agency caused the river water to 'ferment' in the manner applauded by the would-be brewer. In 1738 further advice was proffered to brewers by *The London and County Brewer and Cellar Man*,[25] who provided a recipe free of malt, barley, hops or any other ingredients normally associated with ale, but recommended suspending a young cockerel in the brew and adding the gravy from lean beef. Later in the century, in 1795, another writer published *Valuable Secrets of the Arts and Trades*, which gave detailed instructions for enterprising traders on the use of quicklime, mutton fat and sulphuric acid to adulterate products.[26] Coffee and chocolate, also expensive and increasingly fashionable drinks were, like pepper, vulnerable to adulteration by unscrupulous traders. Coffee and chocolate houses had begun to appear in the City of London in the 1660s, Pepys recording a visit to one in his diary on 24 November 1664, and it is from this time that evidence of adulteration of the products begins to appear in the form of Acts of Parliament mentioning specific additives which attracted penalties. These included roasted peas and beans, butter, dandelion, parsnip and, astonishingly, lard. Some allowances were made for the temperaments of the drinkers since, according to one contemporary writer, 'the other ingredients for making up chocolate may be varied according to the constitutions of those that are to drink it'. For drinkers with 'cold constitutions', nutmegs, cloves and lemon peel could be added; for 'hot consumptive tempers', almonds and rhubarb were recommended, while rhubarb alone should be added for 'young green ladies'.[27]

Poison Detected, or Frightful Truths …

Other eighteenth-century writers were less complacent. The early years of the Seven Years' War (1756–63) were times of food shortages when the temptation to adulterate food would have been greater, so it is probably no coincidence that in 1757 there appeared a work whose title, in a pattern that was to become common, told the reader all he needed to know about the volume's contents. It was called *Poison Detected, or Frightful Truths and Alarming to the British Metropolis in a Treatise on Bread and the Abuses Practised in Making that Food*, the anonymous author describing himself as 'My Friend, a Physician', probably a Dr Peter Markham. In addition to the usual charges that bread contained alum, lime and chalk, it added that of including ground up bones to the recipe, asserting that 'the charnel houses of the dead are raked to add filthiness to the food of the living' and that 'Chickens are said to die of eating London bread'.[28] The author hinted that white lead was used to colour the bread and claimed, wrongly, that the population of London had fallen from 2 million to 1 million because of the poisons administered by the bakers. It was further asserted that a test of adulteration was to see whether a loaf floated. If not, it was adulterated – a process reminiscent of mediaeval witchcraft trials and probably as reliable. Other writers came to the defence of bakers. Thus *A Modest Apology in Defence of the Bakers*, also published in 1758, argued against 'some of the Most Frightful Untruths that ever alarmed the British Metropolis', adding that a fall in population would lead to fewer accidents, less vice and more employment: besides, bodily suffering was good for the soul.[29] This riposte may have been produced tongue in cheek but in the same year a chemist called Jackson in *An Essay on Bread* wrote a balanced assessment of the case against the bakers and argued that, while alum was undoubtedly widely used, the claims for chalk and bone were much more doubtful, not least because they would have the effect of reducing the weight of the bread when all the efforts of the crooked baker would be directed to increasing it. A later writer found some of the recipes for adulterated bread impossible to prepare. Despite these refutations the charges stuck. Smollett's *The Expedition of Humphry Clinker*, published in 1771, records the principal character, Matthew Bramble, complaining: 'the bread I eat in London is a deleterious paste mixed up with chalk, alum and bone ashes'. He went on to give a further account of the horrors of food as prepared and consumed by Londoners:

> Wine is a vile, unpalatable and pernicious sophistication, balderdashed with cider, corn-spirit and the juice of sloes ... you can hardly believe they can be so mad as to boil their greens with brass halfpence in order to improve their colour ... It was but yesterday I saw a dirty barrow-hunter in the street, cleaning her dusty fruit with her own spittle ... milk, the produce of faded cabbage leaves, frothed with bruised snails, carried through the streets in open pails, exposed to spittle, snot and tobacco-quids from foot passengers ... table-beer, guiltless of hops and malt, vapid and nauseous.[30]

Friedrich Christian Accum: 'Death in the Pot'

The first sustained attempt to draw attention to the extent to which food and drink were being adulterated was made by the son of a Jewish-turned-Christian soapmaker and a Huguenot Mother. Friedrich (later anglicised to Fredrick) Accum (1769–1838) was born in Westphalia, Germany, and trained as a pharmacist before coming to England in 1793. He attended William Hunter's anatomy school in Windmill Street, off the Tottenham Court Road, before becoming an assistant to Sir Humphry Davy at the recently founded Royal Institution. Accum became chemist to a gas, light and coal company and later founded a company which manufactured apparatus for chemical laboratories, the newly emerging American universities of Harvard and Yale being amongst his first customers. His training as a chemist enabled him to detect foreign substances in food and drink which would have eluded earlier analysts.

In 1820 he published a book which set out the results of his examinations of many common foods and whose first page bore a quotation from the Second Book of Kings: *There is Death in the Pot.*[31] If that wasn't enough to frighten his readers then the title of the book was: *A Treatise on Adulteration of Food and Culinary Poisons, Exhibiting the Fraudulent Sophistications of Bread, Beer, Wine, Spirituous Liquor, Tea, Coffee, Cream, Confectionery, Vinegar, Mustard, Pepper, Cheese, Olive Oil, Pickles and Other Articles Employed in Domestic Economy and Methods of Detecting Them.* The tone of the book was set in its opening pages where he declared: 'The eager and insatiable thirst for gain is proof against prohibitions and penalties; and the possible sacrifice of a fellow-creature's life is a secondary consideration among unprincipled dealers'. He added that 'the man who robs a fellow subject of a few shillings on the highway is sentenced to death … he who distributes a slow poison to the whole community escapes unpunished.'[32] He distinguished in his analysis between ingredients of 'inferior quality' (such as unrefined flour, which later centuries showed to be beneficial to human health) and substances which were 'highly deleterious' and frequently poisonous and he sometimes confined himself simply to giving sensible advice which condemned no particular party. For example, he argued that water should not be kept in lead reservoirs.[33] In a few cases he examined products which were not foods but medicines. One of these was Peruvian bark which had been used in Europe as a remedy for malaria since the seventeenth century, but Accum revealed that the 'Peruvian bark' available in some pharmacies was, in fact, sawdust from good English oak, which cost the chemist one-quarter of the genuine article and was useless for malaria.

In an echo of the work of Adam Smith half a century earlier, Accum drew attention to the extent to which the growing sophistication and specialisation of manufacturing had contributed to the ease with which products could be corrupted. In *Wealth of Nations* Smith had drawn attention to the productivity gains which arose from the division of labour, also writing that:

> Consumption is the sole end and purpose of all production; and the interest of the producer ought not to be attended to, only so far as it may be necessary for promoting that of the consumer. But in the mercantile system the interest of the consumer is almost constantly sacrificed to that of the producer.[34]

Accum may have been familiar with Smith's great work and drew attention to the fact that 'the division of labour which has been so instrumental in bringing the manufactures of this country to their present flourishing state should have also tended to facilitate and conceal the fraudulent practices in question'. By this he meant that it was easier to escape blame and detection when a production process involved many people, each responsible for one or two of the activities involved in the whole.

The book contained sixteen chapters, each of which examined a separate product, ranging from common commodities like bread and vinegar to more expensive ones like coffee, wine and anchovy sauce. Each chapter, besides giving the results of Accum's analysis, gave the means by which adulteration could be detected and examples of the results of such practices. Thus the chapter on wine explained how spoilt cider was turned into 'port'; gave recipes for 'British Champagne' and 'Southampton Port'; explained how potash could be used to impart colour to red wine; and advised how to clarify cheap white wine: 'Put a pound of melted lead, in fair water, into your cask pretty warm and stop it close'. One of the casualties of such practices was poor Mr Bland of Newark who died, poisoned, after drinking 'Port Wine'.[35] The chapter on beer quoted, disarmingly, a book called *A Practical Treatise on Brewing* which explained that 'Malt, to produce intoxication, must be used in such large quantities as would very much diminish, if not totally exclude, the brewer's profit'. This no doubt explained why the samples that Accum examined contained molasses, honey, vitriol and opium. He also listed twenty-nine grocers and chemists who had recently been fined for providing brewers with forbidden substances.[36] He also named fifty-three brewers who had corrupted their products.

Some of the practices he revealed suggested a degree of enterprise and ingenuity on the part of the traders. Until well into the nineteenth century tea was an expensive, luxurious product. In 1666 the East India Company presented King Charles II with 22lb of tea at a cost of 50s (£2.50) per pound – an enormous sum at the time. The following century, Acts of Parliament imposed heavy fines for adulterating tea with liquorice (sometimes used to dye used tea leaves), elder and ash leaves, molasses and clay.[37] In 1818 Hatton Garden magistrates fined a tea merchant for including in his products finely ground leaves of elder and ash. This was a comparatively innocuous process compared with some of the practices revealed by Accum in the trade of coffee and tea. The preferred method was to purchase used tea leaves and coffee grounds from London hotels and coffee shops, boil them with ferrous sulphate and sheep's dung, and then restore their colour with chemicals like verdigris or carbon black before reselling them. This trade was a significant industry until well into the nineteenth century, one case being brought before magistrates involving an enterprise which was entirely devoted to this recycling process.[38] Green pickles commanded a higher price than brown and the preferred colour could be imparted by boiling them in copper vessels together with a copper halfpenny while olive oil went further if the oil of crushed poppy seeds was added, giving a more profitable, if toxic, mixture. The most resourceful merchants were those who converted black pepper into the more expensive white pepper. This was done by steeping the black pepper in a mixture of sea water and urine (whether human or animal was not entirely clear) and leaving it to dry in the sun.

Accum's work attracted a great deal of attention, not only in England. It was quickly published in Philadelphia and, in translation, in Leipzig and the *Literary Gazette* wrote: 'we are almost angry with Mr Accum for the great service he has done the community by opening our eyes, at the risk of shutting our mouths for ever'.[39] As one would expect, Accum made many enemies as the result of his work, some of them being members of the Royal Institution where he had conducted much of his analysis and of which he was at one time librarian. He was accused of stealing books from the library and a search of his house revealed some pages which might have come from the library or might have been his own property. The charges were dismissed by a magistrate but Accum was then charged with mutilating books and a trial date was set. Accum fled to his native Germany and never returned to England, no doubt to the relief of many interests in the food, drink and pharmaceutical businesses. Another thirty years was to elapse before others took up the cause.

Deadly Adulterations and Slow Poisoning ...

In 1831, *The Lancet* joined the struggle against adulterated food though a further twenty years passed before its campaign became relentless. The journal had been founded by Thomas Wakley in 1823 to campaign against abuses in the medical profession, and in particular the purveyors of quack medicines, but Wakley's attention was soon drawn to the problems associated with the strange and sometimes poisonous substances which were being added to common foods by ignorant or greedy merchants.

Thomas Wakley (1795–1862) was the son of a Devon squire whose main interest lay in breeding racehorses. Thomas, the youngest of eleven children, was apprenticed to an apothecary in Taunton and later qualified as a surgeon at Guy's Hospital, London. While practising as a doctor in London, Wakley became friendly with the radical journalist and later MP William Cobbett (1763–1835), who persuaded Wakley to publish *The Lancet* with a view to reforming the medical profession. Publication began in October 1823, and the journal was relentless in its campaigns against the autocratic and self-serving colleges of surgeons, physicians and apothecaries. He also campaigned against the Corn Laws, which inflated the price of bread for the poor; against slavery; against the stamp duty on newspapers; and for Parliamentary reform – all of which causes eventually triumphed. In 1835 he was elected to Parliament and spoke so effectively against the conviction of the Tolpuddle Martyrs that, when they were eventually reprieved, Wakley held the place of honour in the celebration of their pardons in 1838. He was also instrumental in securing the passage of the Medical Act of 1858, which set up the General Medical Council.

In January 1831 *The Lancet* reviewed a book whose title tells its readers all they need to know about its contents. The book was called *Deadly Adulterations and Slow Poisoning, or Disease and Death in the Pot and Bottle; in which the Blood-empoisoning and Life-Destroying Adulterations of Spirits, Beer, Bread, Flour, Tea, Sugar, Spices, Cheesemongery, Pastry, Confectionary [sic], Medicines etc. are laid open to the Public, with Tests and Methods for ascertaining and detecting the Fraudulent and Deleterious Adulterations and the good and bad Qualities of those Articles: with an Expose of Medical Empiricism and Imposture, Quacks and Quackery, Regular and Irregular, Legitimate and Illegitimate; and the Frauds and Malpractices of Pawnbrokers and Alehouse Keepers. By an Enemy of Fraud and Villainy, 1830.*

Both the author and the reviewer were anonymous, though the reviewer was probably Wakley himself who described the volume as a 'strange but interesting book' by an author who 'writes in a tone of half-mad honesty … nothing that we eat or drink, according to the author, has escaped the infernal traffickers'. Amongst the highlights of the book's contents were the revelations that turpentine, sugar and lime were found to have been added to gin while green Stilton cheese was converted from white by the addition of verdigris. The only popular myth rebutted by the author was the one that claimed that calves were fed on chalk in milk to whiten their flesh. Otherwise it was black marks all round.[40]

The effectiveness of this onslaught was, of course, diminished by the fact that the author was anonymous and no offending traders were specifically named, presumably for fear of the laws of libel. Over the years that followed the journal made intermittent sallies upon the world of food marketing while concentrating its fire upon the obvious charlatans such as James Morison, whose wealth and status were such that he rode in a carriage decorated with a coronet and attended by footmen. *The Lancet* headline 'Murder by Morison's Pills' in 1836 summed up Wakley's views on Morison's Vegetable Universal Pills, which were recommended for consumption at up to thirty a day and claimed to cure virtually all known illnesses, including cholera. The promotion of such remedies was, of course, assisted by the development in the eighteenth century of newspapers and magazines which, from an early stage, were happy to welcome advertisements for patent medicines in their pages. In the circumstances the addition of turpentine to gin may have seemed a relatively harmless activity, though the journal's campaigns were also no doubt influenced by the fact that the techniques of chemistry and microscopy were still relatively young, so the analysis of the constituents of food was far from the exact science that it needed to be if potentially libellous charges were to be made.

Chemistry

By the early nineteenth century chemistry had emerged from the shades of alchemy and was progressing towards the status of a scientific discipline, as its sister physics had done a century earlier in the hands of Isaac Newton (1642–1727). Much of this progress, as it affected food, was due to the work of two Frenchmen, Antoine-Laurent Lavoisier (1743–94) and Joseph Gay-Lussac (1778–1850), as well as the Englishman Sir Humphrey Davy (1778–1829). Lavoisier developed a hydrometer which was accurate enough to measure the specific gravity of liquids and used it to analyse the content of spa water. He also demonstrated that water, one of Aristotle's four 'elements', was in fact made of *two* elements, hydrogen and oxygen, and Lavoisier thereby introduced the distinction between elements and compounds. His younger contemporary Gay-Lussac developed methods to determine the composition of soluble salts like copper sulphate which was used as a colourant in some foodstuffs, and whose presence in foods could henceforward be detected with some confidence. Gay-Lussac, like Lavoisier, was an early victim of the French Revolution when his father was arrested, but this did not prevent Joseph from being educated at the prestigious Ecole Polytechnique and there was no question of his sharing Lavoisier's fate under the blade of the guillotine.[41] At the same time Humphrey Davy was using electricity to break down water molecules into their constituent elements, oxygen and hydrogen, as Lavoisier had done by other means.

Two centuries earlier, Anthony van Leeuwenhoek (1632–1723) had made some significant advances in the development of powerful microscopes. He was born in Delft, the son of a basket maker and worked variously as a draper, surveyor and civil servant. He helped to wind up the estate of his contemporary, the painter Jan Vermeer, who died bankrupt and was probably a childhood friend of Anthony. He appears to have been influenced by the book *Micrographia,* published in 1665 by the scientist Robert Hooke (1635–1703) whose magnified illustrations of plant and animal life forms inspired Anthony to grind lenses, make microscopes and use them to make observations. His highly developed skills enabled him to make microscopes that magnified over 200 times, far greater than any previous instrument, and in the 1670s he began a correspondence with London's Royal Society that lasted half a century in which he described and illustrated the objects he had seen through his microscopes. Many of his letters were translated from Dutch and printed in the *Philosophical Transactions of the Royal Society.* These led to his election as a Fellow of the Royal Society in 1680, thus joining a company which included Robert Hooke himself as well as Christopher Wren, Robert Boyle and Isaac Newton. In September 1683 he reported the results of his examination of the plaque from his own teeth where he observed 'many very little living animalcules, very prettily a-moving. The biggest sort had a very strong and swift motion and shot though the spittle as a pike does through the water'. These later became known as bacteria. Over the years that followed Leeuwenhoek's discoveries, microscopy languished as a branch of medicine but in 1840, ten years after *The Lancet* began its campaign against adulterated food, the Microscopical Society of London was formed. So by about 1840 the techniques of chemistry and microscopy had advanced to a point where the analysis of substances, including foods, could be undertaken with some confidence.

The Lancet and the Analytical Sanitary Commission

Thomas Wakley's interest in the subject seems to have been re-awakened by an experience he had in his capacity as a coroner for Middlesex in 1850. A number of pauper children died of a gastric condition and Wakley concluded that the cause lay in the oatmeal they had eaten which had been 'expanded' by the addition of cheap ground barley, a powerful laxative.[42] Fortified by the evidence he had gathered, Wakley wrote to Dr Arthur Hill Hassall (1817–94), a London physician who was building a reputation as a highly accomplished analyst, using his skills to detect impurities in food and drink both by use of the microscope and by chemical tests. In the same year the pauper children died, Hassall had published a critical report on London water, his microscopic analysis revealing impurities which were invisible to the naked eye. *Punch* subsequently published a cartoon which purported to show the alarming creatures which such an analysis of London's water would reveal. Wakley wrote to Hassall inviting him to collaborate in publicising impurities in the food supply and to this Hassall enthusiastically agreed. In the months that followed Hassall proceeded to collect and examine samples of a wide variety of food and drink, using both his microscope and the rapidly developing techniques of chemical analysis not only to identify impurities, but also to publicise the practices themselves and the traders who used them, under his own name and with the authority of *The Lancet* itself. In his first article he made the menacing declaration that a 'highly important feature will be the *publication of the names and addresses* [his italics] of the parties from whom the

different articles were purchased; the advantages of such a course of pro-
ceeding require no explanation'.[43] Hassall also identified traders who sold
products of high quality. Wakley, who had such confidence in Hassall's
competence that he in effect indemnified him against any costs arising
from legal proceedings, published the findings under the rather pompous
title, *The Analytical Sanitary Commission*, implying an official status which
it did not have.

That did not matter. Over a period of four years, 1851–54, Hassall
purchased about 2,500 samples for analysis, describing his method of collection thus: 'These nocturnal excursions brought us into many curious
parts of London and gave us a wonderful insight into the habits and ways
of life of people in the poor districts'.[44] The extent of his activities may
be judged by the fact that there were thirteen separate reports in the first
six months of 1851, covering foods and drinks in common use. Potatoes
were found adding weight to a wide variety of foodstuffs including bread,
coffee, cocoa and sugar. Milk, to no one's surprise, had been diluted with
water which was itself often foul, as Hassall's earlier study would have led
readers to expect. More alarmingly, some dairies offset the effects of the
water by adding snails to the mixture, their mucus acting as a thicken-
ing agent while producing a pleasant and reassuring froth on the surface
of the liquid. Red lead and arsenite of copper were used to give colour,
while sulphuric acid and powdered glass imparted smell and texture to
foods and snuff.[45] Sugar contained large quantities of wood, lime, iron
and, more worryingly, living insects and lead. Since lead was expensive as
well as poisonous, it must be assumed that this, along with other foreign
substances, had probably entered the food chain by accident rather than by
design. Each article was followed by a warning of the identity of the next
substance to be examined, but this does not seem to have deterred the
adulterers since, although bread was advertised as being next on the list and
duly examined, 'the whole of the twenty-four samples of bread examined
were adulterated with alum', including three samples from 'The League
Bread Company', whose advertisements proudly boasted that its bread
contained no alum.[46] Only in 1876 was it forbidden to add alum, a toxic
substance, to bread. Malt vinegar was found to comprise mostly dilute
sulphuric acid and marmalade contained turnips, while Cayenne Pepper
consisted mostly of brick dust and sawdust with a dash of red lead to
impart the correct colour. An analysis of tea revealed a rich mixture of
china clay, rice and a chemical dye called Prussian Blue while even well-
known brands were not exempt from guilt. Fortnum and Mason, which
had been founded by a royal footman and earned the highest reputation

for quality when supplying officers with delicacies during the Peninsular War (1808–14), was found to be colouring its 'greengage' jam with copper! Various derivatives of lead were especially popular in colourings used for cakes and sweets consumed by children, while 'genuine mustard, whatever the price paid for it, is scarcely ever to be obtained'.[47] Hassall's revelations attracted some alarming support from other chemists. Thus in 1853 Mr Albert Bernays, from Derby, wrote to *The Lancet* with an account of his own experience with gooseberries:

> I had bought a bottle of preserved gooseberries from one of the most respect-able grocers in this town and had its contents transferred into a pie. It struck me that the gooseberries looked fearfully green when cooked and on eating one with a steel fork its intense bitterness sent me in search of the sugar. After having sweetened and mashed the gooseberries with the same steel fork, I was about to convey some to my mouth when I observed the prongs to be com-pletely coated with a thin film of bright metallic copper.[48]

The main exceptions to the general rule that products had been adul-terated came in the brewing trade, provided that the beer was bought directly from the brewery. Thus the bitter and India Pale Ale from Bass and from Allsopp's breweries was 'malt and hops and the constituents of pure spring water', and Guinness was similarly praised. Whitbread and Truman beer contained 'rather much salt', but as a rule 'the admirers of the bitter beer manufactured by the celebrated brewers we have mentioned may enjoy with advantage this, their favourite beverage'. However, there was a very different tale when the same products were purchased from public houses. In many such cases the alcohol content was 25 per cent less than the brewers' product which indicated the degree to which the beer had been watered.[49] Others were even less reassuring. Thus in 1848 John Mitchell, in his *Treatise on the Falsification of Foods and the Chemical Means to Detect them*, analysed 200 beers and he later informed a Parliamentary Select Committee that all were contaminated (which normally meant watered down) except for some samples taken directly from breweries. Of the samples taken from publicans, not a single one was within 20 per cent of the strength at which it had left the brewery.[50]

Hassall devoted particular care to the examination of coffee, an expen-sive but increasingly popular drink of the time. He had expected to find that it contained chicory and in this he was not disappointed, but he also discovered quantities of wheat. When taxed with this the government, in the person of the Chancellor of the Exchequer, Sir Charles Wood,

complained that 'an army of excisemen' would be required to monitor
the quality of the nation's victuals and that 'there were no possible tests by
which chicory could be detected when mixed with coffee'.[51] The following month Hassall refuted this claim by a method which he frequently
used in his analyses to persuade the doubting: he included a drawing of
a sample of coffee and another of coffee mixed with chicory and wheat
as revealed by the microscope. The drawings, which were magnified by a
factor of 350, made clear the distinction.[52] The articles which appeared in
The Lancet were closely followed both by *The Times* and *Punch*, thus drawing them to the attention of a much wider readership. *Punch* lampooned
Sir Charles Wood for his stance over coffee and chicory, reminding its
readers that 'we have been drinking a concoction and decoction of
chicory, corn and potatoes' disguised as coffee, and addressed a series of
Punch's Sermons to Tradesmen, including bakers, confectioners (who were
accused of lacing their products with arsenic) and grocers, for putting
potato in chocolate and milk, chocolate also being fortified with brick
dust.[53] At about the same time, 1850, an even wider audience learned
of the criticisms levelled against those providing them with sustenance
when Charles Dickens placed some barbed comments in the mouth of
Mr Spenlow in *David Copperfield*. Spenlow paid 'Honour to the soil that
grew the grape, to the grape that made the wine, to the sun that ripened
it and to the merchant who adulterated it.'[54]

Food and its Adulterations

In 1855 Hassall published a compendium of his findings in a volume entitled
Food and its adulterations,[55] which he dedicated to Sir Benjamin Hall ('Big
Ben', 1802–67), chairman of the General Board of Health, and in the same
year, in response to the publicity generated by the campaign in *The Lancet*,
a Parliamentary Select Committee was established to examine the issues it
had raised. Hassall had written a separate book called *Adulterations Detected,
or Plain Instructions for the Discovery of Frauds in Food and Medicine,*[56] explaining to his readers how they could identify foreign substances in their food,
but a contemporary encyclopaedia, drawing attention to the complexity
of the subject, commented that 'there is room for someone to write a key
to the book entitled *How to Understand the Instructions*'. It observed that if
householders followed Hassall's guide and armed themselves with such
aids to detection as the bottles of sulphuric acid he recommended, then
disasters could be expected.[57]

Hassall had demonstrated that adulteration was so common as to be the rule rather than the exception in many markets, but it was by no means clear that these practices were illegal. One is led to conclude that our Victorian ancestors had robust constitutions since most of them survived such a diet. The Select Committee took evidence from, amongst other people, Thomas Blackwell,[58] whose Soho Factory had been found to be selling tins of 'anchovies' which were in fact miscellaneous fish coloured with china clay. Blackwell acknowledged that the use of copper salts to add colour to green vegetables, and of iron compounds to impart a red colour to potted meats and sauces, was common practice and professed ignorance of any danger to health that might be thus caused. The result of the committee's deliberations was the first Adulteration of Food and Drink Act, passed in 1860 in the face of considerable opposition from the food industry and, more surprisingly, from the reforming MP John Bright. Bright protested that the adulteration of food was the sign of a vigorous and competitive economy following the well-established principles of *laissez-faire* and proposed an amendment to the Bill which would have weakened it. He attracted vigorous support from Mr Hardy, MP for Leominster, who complained that the Bill amounted to 'a very objectionable system of informing and spying in respect of articles of food sold in this country', because town councils would be able to 'appoint one or more persons possessing competent medical, chemical and microscopical knowledge as analysts of all articles of food'.[59] In the face of such opposition, Mr Wise, MP for Stafford reminded the House of Commons of some of the evidence which had been brought before the Select Committee whose work had led to the introduction of the Bill:

> Large quantities of tea were mixed with silkworms' dung; it was sold as 'gunpowder tea'. Of course the Committee did not venture to taste it but it found a large market in the poorer parts of the metropolis as the silkworms' dung gave it the appearance of great strength.[60]

In the face of such evidence the Adulteration of Food and Drink Act was passed in 1860 and the fear it engendered in suppliers may be judged by the fact that, the following year, they came together to launch the magazine *The Grocer* to defend their practices against the reformers. *The Grocer* continues to thrive in the twenty-first century, but the Food and Drink Act itself was ineffective because of the reluctance of local authorities to appoint public analysts to enforce it. The exception lay in Dublin where Dr Cameron examined 2,600 samples, found 1,500 of them adulterated and secured 342 convictions. In the whole of England there were fewer than 300 examinations.[61] The Act was swiftly supplanted by subsequent legislation which raised fines from a derisory £5 to £50 plus six months in gaol, and which required all local authorities which had police forces to appoint public analysts, one of the first being Henry Letheby (1816-76) who, in 1855, became medical officer to the City of London and campaigned strongly and effectively against the adulteration of its food. His reputation was damaged towards the end of his life when, in 1867, he cleared the water companies of responsibility for the cholera outbreak of the previous year.[62] The Society of Public Analysts, of which Letheby was a prominent member, developed procedures and methods for the inspection of food but many years passed before their work was effective. For example, one of the tricks of 'jam' manufacturers was to fashion tiny wood chips to resemble raspberry chips and the practice went unnoticed until the suffragette Sylvia Pankhurst denounced the exploitation of the women engaged in the trade. Mrs Pankhurst then opened a factory to produce jam from fruit but the venture failed, as did other similar enterprises whose proprietors discovered that many people preferred cheap, adulterated products to more expensive, healthy ones.[63] Nevertheless, the Victorian legislation was significant not only in creating some basic standards and the beginnings of an inspectorate, but in placing the onus on suppliers to ensure that no adulteration had taken place and that, in the words of the 1875 Sale of Food and Drugs Act, the food supplied 'shall be of the nature, substance and quality demanded'. This philosophy continues to underpin later legislation, notably the Food Safety Act of 1990.

Twentieth-Century Alarms

The passage of legislation designed to ensure that food was 'of the nature, substance and quality demanded' did not end the problems of earlier centuries. Twenty-one years after the passage of the Food and Drugs Act in 1896, an investigation into the sale of whisky in thirty public houses in Glasgow revealed that only two were selling genuine Scotch.[64] In 1914 in *The Flying Inn*, G.K. Chesterton wrote *The Song against Grocers* which includes the lines:

> He sells us sands of Araby
> As sugar for cash down;
> He sweeps his shop and sells the dust
> The purest salt in town ...

As the century progressed the most crude and egregious examples of adulteration, such as the watering of beer and the addition of potatoes to anything that needed bulking up, gave way to more sophisticated methods and more exotic forms of contamination, some of them not just criminal but murderous, and not only to the consumers. In 1906 the American writer Upton Sinclair (1878–1968), who enjoyed the rare distinction of being an American socialist, published *The Jungle*, a lurid account of practices in the Chicago meat-packing industry, which left the reader in little doubt that immigrant workers who disappeared on the notoriously unsafe production lines were likely to emerge in a can. The *New York Times* followed up Sinclair's book with its own enquiries which left nothing to its readers' imaginations in describing how meat was shovelled from dirty floors and filthy railway wagons into processing plants. Sinclair's intention had been to highlight the plight of the workers, but its main effect was to alarm consumers, leading to America's own food legislation, the Pure Food, Drink and Drugs Act of 1906, with Harvey Wiley in charge of its implementation. Sinclair later observed that his book had been aimed at the heart (or conscience) of the American consumer but had, instead, hit the stomach.

However, the new century saw one significant change from previous ones. In earlier periods all classes had been affected by contamination and, in the case of some commonly adulterated products like wine, the wealthier classes had been struck more than most by conditions like gout. In the twentieth century contaminated food tended to have its most devastating effects on the poorer classes. Thus in Spain in 1981–82, some 20,000 people were affected by toxic oil syndrome when contaminated industrial rapeseed oil was sold by itinerant vendors as a cooking oil to poorer families. Fever, vomiting, breathing difficulties and thrombosis resulted, with deaths numbering over 350.[65]

As in previous centuries the popularity of wine amongst the more affluent and the profits that can be made from adulterating it have attracted the attention of some of the most ingenious manipulators. In June 2001, *USA Today* reported a scandal that had broken in Beaune, wine capital of Burgundy, when police arrested local traders accused of labelling mediocre wine as top flight vintages from Meursault, Nuits St Georges and Beaune. If so the French, facing fierce competitive pressures from the wines of Australia and New Zealand, were only following where other European producers had led. In the 1970s a previously reputable wine merchant was found to have used sediment from the holds of banana boats to add flavour and colour to his wines, but a more extraordinary case occurred in Austria during the following decade when a businessman included a claim for the costs of large quantities of antifreeze in his income tax return. He had been adding it to cheap Austrian wine to add sweetness and texture before exporting it, mostly to Germany.[66]

A Bad Decade

The 1980s were bad for food and drink safety, the events occurring through poor management and poor judgement rather than fraud. This was the decade in which Bovine Spongiform Encephalopathy (BSE) made its presence felt – a condition affecting cows which, when transmitted to humans, can prove fatal in the form of a new variant of the condition Creutzfeldt-Jacob Disease. Paradoxically BSE arose from an attempt to make safer for humans the business of rendering offal. This was to be achieved by removing dangerous flammable solvents from the rendering operation and lowering the temperatures at which the offal was processed. The effect of these changes was to leave in the resulting offal harmful prions which were able to survive the lower temperatures and remained active in animal-based feeds, which were fed to the normally herbivorous cows. Some of them developed BSE which was passed to humans via the meat they produced.

Later in the decade, on 6 July 1988, a tanker conveyed 20 tons of aluminium sulphate to a water treatment plant at Lower Moor near Camelford, Cornwall. The chemical is used in small quantities during the treatment of drinking water but the driver mistakenly deposited the entire load in the drinking water reservoir itself, raising the level of the chemical to 250 times the permitted level and causing gut complaints, sore throats and blisters to many of the 20,000 users of the water in and around Camelford.[67]

On 16 December 1988 the Health Minister Edwina Currie resigned from her post following some indiscreet references to the prevalence of salmonella in eggs, though in fact in the year ending October of that year 13,004 salmonella cases were indeed reported, 1,000 of them arising from eggs. Paradoxically, following the bankruptcy of a number of egg producers consequent upon Mrs Currie's remarks, eggs had to be imported from the Netherlands where salmonella was rife. Salmonella returned eighteen years later in Cadbury's Marlbrook plant in Herefordshire, when it was found that about 1 million chocolate bars were contaminated by waste leaking from a faulty pipe. The company was fined £1 million. In 1989, the year after Edwina Currie's comments, The Lancet commented that

'Consumers were just coming to terms with salmonella when its place at the forefront of media attention was taken by listeria', a fairly common condition in products like soft cheese which is harmless to most people but dangerous for pregnant women. This followed a series of conflicting statements from the government departments responsible for agriculture and health which 'served to perplex the public and infuriate French cheese producers' who felt that their soft cheeses had been unfairly tainted in the media-driven controversy.[68]

A problem peculiar to the twentieth century arose in the form of industrial sabotage: disaffected employees or criminals contaminating, or threatening to contaminate food products either in order to work out grievances against a company or to extort money. Thus in October 2006 glass and needles appeared in Kingsmill loaves, produced by Allied Bakeries while in July 2007, fourteen Tesco stores had to be closed following threats from an extortioner. An arrest followed.

Scares about the safety of food have generated counter-attacks, sometimes from unlikely quarters. Thus a publication of FOREST (which campaigns on behalf of smokers) traced the onset of what it called 'food fascism' to a barely credible source: the work of the Nobel Peace Prize winner John Boyd Orr. In a careful study carried out in 1935 Boyd Orr had demonstrated that there was a close relationship between income and health indicators like children's weight and stature. The authors of the FOREST publication, however, asserted that 'food fascism' was:

> not just a recent phenomenon. It can certainly be traced back to the pre-war era when Sir John Boyd Orr in his study *Family, Health and Income* [in reality it was entitled *Food, Health and Income*] argued that a high fat diet composed primarily of meat, milk and dairy products was healthy.

This is such a travesty of Boyd Orr's careful and balanced study that, combined with the fact that the FOREST authors got the title wrong, one wonders whether they actually read it. Other 'food fascist' targets of the authors included the former editor of *The Lancet* and Tim Lang, director of the London Food Commission and later professor of food policy at London City University, who was accused of working with the 'so-called Catholic' Institute of International relations who were accused of 'consistently supporting Marxist causes' – a rare case, had it been true, of Catholics and Marxists agreeing on anything at all. The authors detected in all this 'a shift from the traditional discredited forms of socialism. Instead they [presumably the food fascists] are constructing a new form of political control'.[69]

The work concludes with a warning that after eating would come drinking, boxing and gambling, the authors hinting that these pleasures would be next on the fascist hit list. It should be emphasised that the food industry itself has extended no great welcome to its unlikely champions. Others have shown concerns about the impact of food scares on companies and the industry as a whole, arguing that 'Young, talented people are more likely to rule out the food industry as one of their career options' and that share prices could be depressed by such events.[70] There is little, if any, evidence that these fears are well-founded.

In the twenty-first century it appears that the most egregious adulterants like lead, alum, sand and verdigris have been eliminated from human foods, at least in the developed world. However, even if one sets aside the wilder accusations of 'food fascism', some doubts remain about many substances that are added quite legitimately to our diets. Reference has already been made to the fact that more sugar is being added to processed foods,[71] and similar problems have been identified in other additives, some commonly known and some not. In 1996 a health pressure group was formed called Consensus Action on Salt and Health (CASH), its mission being to reduce salt consumption by 25 per cent, arguing that this would be followed by a significant reduction in heart attacks and strokes. Its activities were implicitly endorsed by the government's chief medical officer, Sir Liam Donaldson, who in his annual report for 2001 stated that 'A major initiative by the food industry to reduce the salt content of processed and catered foods could help save lives in the long term'.[72] The pressure group also published a list of common products which contained high levels of added salt together with a list of low-salt alternatives, and the high degree of interest in the subject was reflected in the coverage it received in the national press. The news was not all bad. Marks and Spencer, for example, had halved the amount of salt in its bread.[73] But has salt, along with the new E-numbers, with their artful colourings and flavour enhancers, taken over as one of the new poisons? It seems unlikely that the argument will ever end.

7

A Century of Excess

The global increase in the availability and accessibility of food and the reduced opportunities to use physical energy

The World Health Organisation's summary of the cause of the European obesity epidemic

There is compelling evidence that humans are predisposed to put on weight by their biology. This has previously been concealed in all but a few but exposure to modern lifestyles has revealed it in the majority ... Obesity is a consequence of abundance, convenience and underlying biology.

UK government's *Foresight* report, 2007

'Obesogenic Environment'

In November 1996 the expression 'obesogenic' entered the language, if not the dictionary, in the columns of *The Independent*. The author explained it as follows:

Our environment is obesogenic. The level of physical activity it encourages is extremely low. Parents are loath to allow their children to play outside because it's dangerous, riding a bike is suicidal and trying to find the stairs in a building is an exercise only in ingenuity. On the other side of the equation our food supply has gone from low energy, high roughage to being dominated by fat.[1]

The word is not an elegant addition to our vocabulary but the concepts that it expresses – a combination of a less physically active lifestyle with a diet high in surplus energy – is perhaps the greatest challenge to human health and longevity that mankind faces. It has been suggested that, unless the challenge is met, future generations could have shorter lifespans than their elders, for the first time in recorded history. What is the extent of the problem and what are the potential remedies?

The Wartime Diet

The twentieth century was not always thus. Reference has been made in chapter one to the fact that, at the beginning of the twentieth century, 40 per cent of volunteers for the Boer War were rejected because of their physical condition. Reference has also been made to the heroic experiments of Robert McCance, Elsie Widdowson and their young assistants to evaluate the effects of the British wartime diet, with beneficial results for the population.[2] Britain's agricultural policies from about 1870 onwards had been based upon the principles of free trade which meant that most agricultural produce was imported from low-cost producers like Australia, New Zealand and the Americas, while Britain concentrated on producing manufactured goods and services to pay for the imports. This had devastating effects upon British agriculture which fell into a depression. For example, only 20 per cent of bacon consumed in Britain was from home production, the remainder coming from Denmark, Ireland and further afield.[3] Consequently, when the First World War left the country dependent upon shipments across the vulnerable shipping lanes of the oceans, serious food shortages occurred, with prices of many commodities rising by 60 per cent in the first two years of the war. Poorer members of society went short, food riots ensued, soup kitchens appeared in many areas and, eventually, food rationing was introduced rather haphazardly in 1918.[4]

In anticipation of another such emergency the government of Neville Chamberlain set up a Food (Defence Plans) Department as early as 1936 which, upon the outbreak of war, became the Ministry of Food, soon to be headed by Lord Woolton. It did not get off to a promising start despite a number of encouraging precedents, One of these was the Glossop Sandwich which had been devised in 1934 by a school medical officer to be made available free of charge for under-nourished schoolchildren in the High Peak area of Derbyshire. It included milk, fruit, wholemeal bread, vitamin-enriched margarine, oily fish, cheese, watercress and yeast and had been effective and popular. By contrast the Basal diet which was first proposed for the British population by the Ministry of Food at the outbreak of war included fat but no meat or fish, and prompted Winston Churchill to write to Lord Woolton: 'The way to lose the war is to try to force the British public into a diet of milk, oatmeal, potatoes etc. washed down on gala occasions with a little lime juice'.[5] Magnus Pyke, who was employed by the Ministry at the time and later became a well-known television presenter on the subject of food, recalled that at one point it was proposed to encourage the British public to eat their pets – an idea wisely abandoned.

Woolton was a man of vision whose ambitions stretched beyond a simple programme of ensuring that the food available was shared equally between classes regardless of means. He later wrote: 'I determined to use the powers I possessed to stamp out the diseases that came from malnutrition, especially those among children such as rickets.'[6] To this end in July 1940 he launched the National Milk scheme which ensured that priority was given to allocating supplies of milk to schoolchildren, remaining supplies then being shared amongst adults. Otherwise, all adults registered themselves and their children with local food retailers who received produce in accordance with the number of registered customers they had. Special recipes were promoted making use of produce which was reasonably readily available. The best known is probably Woolton Pie, a vegetable pie whose recipe was devised in the kitchens of the Savoy Hotel and consisted of potatoes, swedes, parsnips, carrots, onions, cauliflower, turnips and oats topped with potato-based pastry and sprinkled with grated cheese. Woolton was also responsible for the fact that the production of cereals and vegetables had by 1942 increased by 50 per cent compared with pre-war levels, priority being given to the production of vegetable food rather than livestock, as this made more efficient use of the available land. At the same time every effort was made to ensure that no food was wasted, even potato skins:

Those who have the will to win,
Eat potatoes in their skin,
Knowing that the sight of peelings
Deeply hurts Lord Woolton's feelings.

Such rhymes were, of course, easily mocked, but the Ministry of Food, and Lord Woolton, were amongst the great successes of the war. Woolton showed some imagination in enlisting the assistance of skilled cooks and nutritionists whose post-war reputation owed much to their wartime activities. Prominent amongst these was Marguerite Patten, OBE, whose

Victory Cookbook was followed, during the period of rationing which
continued after 1945, by *Post-War Kitchen*. Recipes promoted by the
Ministry of Food included such dishes as Parsnip and Sage Soup, Leek
and Smoked Haddock Kedgeree and Venison Hot Pot while, since meat
like mutton and beef was in relatively short supply, such alternatives as
moorhen, coot, squirrel and sparrow were also recommended.[7] Not all
recipes were well received. Notoriously *snoek*, a fish from South Africa,
failed to tempt the British palate, but the wartime diet was undoubtedly
beneficial and made a significant contribution to victory. When munitions
factories were established early in the war in areas of high unemployment
and severe social deprivation like South Wales, it was observed that their
productivity was lower than elsewhere, a characteristic attributed to the
weakened state of the population who had been malnourished for much
of the 1930s. However, by 1942 marked improvements in the health of the
people of such areas was noted.[8]

The British wartime diet was thus, by default, much more vegetarian
than it had ever been, and despite the trust earlier shown in 'mighty roast
beef' and red meat as the most appropriate diet for Englishmen,[9] there was
a significant improvement in the nutritional health of the population as a
whole. At the end of the Second World War, most of the British population, after six years of war shortages, rationing and queues, was better fed
than it had ever been – and probably better fed than it is over sixty years
later in 2008. Curiously, at the same time, scientists in Hitler's Germany
were conducting research which identified the dangers of eating too much
meat and using too many additives and preservatives. Fibres, fruits and
vegetables were promoted as the basis of a healthy National Socialist diet,
but this research, years ahead of its time, was disregarded after 1945 because
of its association with the Nazi regime and was rediscovered in 1999 by an
historian at Pennsylvania State University, Robert Proctor.[10]

Return to Fletcher

In 2006 the World Health Organisation (WHO), a branch of the United
Nations Organisation, held a conference in Istanbul on the problem of
obesity in the European Region (a region which, for the purposes of
the conference, included a number of Central Asian republics, formerly
part of the Soviet Union). The resulting report on obesity in Europe, *The
Challenge of Obesity in the WHO European Region and Strategies for Response*,
published in 2007, summarised the causes of the problem as 'the global

increase in the availability and accessibility of food and the reduced opportunities to use physical energy'.[11] It went on to examine each of these issues in more detail, beginning with diet, and suggested that a move away from high-fibre to carbohydrate-rich diets could have encouraged obesity since 'the bulky nature of high-fibre food, with increased demands on chewing and gastric distension, may increase satiety and curtail energy intake'.[12] This almost sounds like a return to Fletcherism. Horace Fletcher, whose exploits and theories have been discussed in chapter five, believed that lengthy mastication not only improved the nutritional value of food but reduced the quantity required to satisfy the appetite. It is no coincidence that within a year, in October 2007, the UK government, working through its *Foresight* programme based in the Department for Innovation, Universities and Skills, published its own report entitled *Tackling Obesities: Future Choices*. The plural form of the noun, 'obesities', was significant and drew attention to the fact that many factors contribute to the problems it causes: it is not just a case of people eating too much and being lazy; 'obesity is a consequence of abundance, convenience and underlying biology'.[13] In the late twentieth century environmental factors began to drive the human body in new directions – directions with which it was not designed to cope.

Health and Height

The last 100 years have presented affluent western societies with challenges never before faced by the human body: less exercise and more (if not more nutritious) food than it has ever encountered before. At first the signs were promising. At the end of the nineteenth century the average adult Englishman was about 5ft 7in tall (1.7m) which itself reflected a steady increase since the advent of cheap imported food from about 1870, though the benefits were at that time unevenly distributed between social groups. By 1970 the average adult male had gained about 2.5in (6cm) in height. The marked regional and class differences which had characterised Victoria's reign had also waned. The cotton operatives of Lancashire whose growth had been stunted by child labour and poor diet had been replaced by prosperous office workers who were no longer 3in shorter than the offspring of middle-class families in the south.[14] Seebohm Rowntree's book *Poverty: a Study in Town Life*, published in 1901, had demonstrated that poverty was not a problem peculiar to the immigrant rookeries of London. He estimated that in a prosperous provincial capital like York, with its philanthropic

Quaker confectionery manufacturers, 30 per cent of the population lived in poverty and 10 per cent in dire need. Malnutrition was especially common amongst working-class wives. When food was in short supply, priority was given to the male breadwinner who was most likely, for example, to receive any meat that the family could afford. The resulting malnutrition of mothers and daughters, combined with the rigours of multiple childbirths, helps to explain why diseases associated with poor living conditions like tuberculosis were more common amongst women than men. We should be thankful that organisations like The National Birthday Trust Fund, whose activities in the 1930s were described in chapter five, are no longer so urgently necessary to combat malnutrition amongst married women.[15] However, this should not be allowed to conceal the fact that the twenty-first century faces nutritional challenges which are in many ways more insidious.

Agriculture, Mining and the Weekly Wash

The increases in stature which marked the twentieth century (in all age groups, regions and in both sexes) were a reflection of a more adequate diet, but another factor must not be overlooked. The decline of physical exertion as a characteristic of much work, movement and home life meant that, as the calorific (energy) intake increased with the availability of more food, so the need for energy-rich foods declined. The two lines crossed some time in the second half of the twentieth century, since when we have become steadily fatter. Some clue as to the change in the nature of work may be found by examining the decline in employment in two activities associated with rigorous physical exertion: agriculture and mining. Others, like 'heavy industry', are sometimes included in such comparisons, but the category does not lend itself to precise definition and the development of mechanised processes in such industries would no doubt also reflect a decline in the need for as much physical exertion as in the past. The figures are as follows and relate to the numbers employed in the male workforce in Great Britain:

	1901	1951	2006
Agriculture, horticulture, forestry and fishing	1,390,000	1,131,000	215,000
Mining and quarrying	931,000	675,000	56,000

In 1901 these two physically demanding activities had accounted for 14 per cent of the total British labour force, and fifty years later (when food rationing prevailed) they were still major sources of employment. By 2006 their share had fallen to 1 per cent of the workforce. In 2006 the largest single source of employment, accounting for almost 4.5 million jobs, lay in the retail and wholesale sector, while 74 per cent of all employment is in the services sector overall. These jobs no doubt have stresses of their own, though not, on the whole, of the kinds associated with vigorous physical work.[16] The services sector did not even receive a separate entry in 1901. Moreover, the physical burdens of agriculture and mining have themselves diminished as human beings have shied away from unnecessary burdens of physical labour as is, in the view of some, an inevitable evolutionary trend.[17] Combine harvesters and powerful cutters have largely replaced the scythes, pitchforks, picks and shovels of the nineteenth century, just as production lines, pallets, fork-lift trucks and containers have eased the burdens of manufacturing and distributive trades. Similar processes have been evident in the home. The days have passed when Mondays were allocated to doing the family laundry with hot tubs, scrubbing boards, Sunlight Soap and dolly pegs – the last being three-legged wooden devices topped by a t-bar with which the housewife agitated the weekly wash amidst much steam, sweat and energy. So have the days when carpets were hung on washing lines and beaten vigorously amongst clouds of dust to make them clean. Mr Hoover and his many followers have seen to that, reducing previously energetic household chores to gentler routines. The consequences of this combination of more food and a less physically active lifestyle were quick to make themselves felt and are summed up in the *Foresight* report:[18]

> We evolved in a world of relative food scarcity and hard physical work – obesity is one of the penalties of the modern world, where energy-dense food is abundant and labour-saving technologies abound.

Fitness and Fatness

The most common means of measuring health in relation to weight is the Body Mass Index (BMI). This is calculated by taking a person's weight in kilos and dividing it by the square of his or her height in metres. In the 2007 boat race one of the competitors weighed in at 15st 10lb (100kg) – a big fellow, but he was over 6ft 6in tall; just 2m. His body mass index was therefore 100 divided by 4, giving a BMI of 25. A BMI of 20–25 is regarded as healthy; less than 20 is underweight; 25–30 is overweight and over 30 is obese, with attendant health problems. It should be added that these rather neat limits, conveniently divisible by five, have an anecdotal element about them and their strictly medical basis is open to question. Certain prominent and very healthy sportsmen would, by these criteria, be recommended to diet. That said, they are a helpful guideline, particularly when a BMI of 30 is reached. The National Diet and Nutrition Survey into adults aged nineteen to sixty-four carried out in 2000–2001 revealed that the average BMI of those surveyed had risen to 27.2 for men and 26.4 for women, showing that the average citizen is now overweight and representing a 10 per cent increase in BMI over the last fifteen years.[19] In the period 1980 to 2005 adult obesity rates have quadrupled to a point where nearly 25 per cent of adults and 10 per cent of children are obese and, if the trends continue, then 'by 2050, Britain could be a mainly obese society'.[20] Obesity causes 30,000 deaths annually and costs society as a whole about £7.4 billion a year, this including the cost of 18 million days lost through obesity-related sickness according to estimates by the National Audit Office. A further half of the adult population is at present overweight.[21] Overweight people are particularly susceptible to type-2 diabetes, hypertension (high blood pressure), cardiovascular diseases and certain types of cancer. At present obesity accounts for about 1.4 per cent of the NHS budget, a figure that could increase to 9.3 per cent by 2050.[22]

A Wider Problem

This is not a problem which is peculiar to Great Britain. In 2007 the World Health Organisation (WHO) report, based on the proceedings of the Istanbul conference, drew attention to the trend throughout the developed world towards 'the passive consumption of energy-dense diets', a phrase which underlined the fact that, as our diets have become more generous in kilocalories, our work, leisure pursuits and means of transport have become less physically demanding. WHO estimated that, by 2010, 150 million people would be overweight or obese in the European region with consequent increases in type-2 diabetes, cardiovascular complaints, some cancers and osteoarthritis, with mortality rates approaching those associated with cigarette smoking. The report went on to examine levels of physical activity conducive to good health within Europe. It was estimated that the Dutch were the most physically active, with about 44 per cent undertaking an appropriate level of exercise compared with less than 29 per cent in the United Kingdom. This may be due to the fact that many Dutch city dwellers (normally the most sedentary element of the population) cycle to work, though it does not explain why the Germans also score highly with a figure of 40 per cent. The Dutch also eat well, accounting for 700g per day of fruit and vegetables compared with 619g for the British, though the Italians are well ahead with 847g. Reported obesity levels in Italy and the Netherlands are less than half those of Britain, suggesting that cycling to work and following a 'Mediterranean' diet offer more than anecdotal routes to health. On the other hand the United Kingdom enjoys the doubtful distinction of being the leader in the consumption of soft drinks, accounting for, on average, some 200ml per household per day, whereas the Italians fail to reach 50ml.[23] In the space of a century, it seems, much of the European population has moved from famine to feast and beyond. The problem in the United States is even worse, one authoritative judgement being that almost half of all Americans can now be defined as obese or suffering from an eating disorder. It is also sobering to reflect that in Japan, obesity levels remain at 2 per cent, unchanged in thirty years.[24]

The United States was the first nation to feel the effects of affluence as it affected diet and in the twenty-first century is its most acute victim.[25] In 1888 the United States Department of Agriculture appointed Wilbur Atwater (1844–1907), a professor of chemistry, as its director of research. Atwater's interest lay in human nutrition and he devoted his time to identifying the diets that would best serve the needs of his fellow citizens. He recommended that Americans consume 3,500 kilocalories per day, significantly more than the levels recommended in the twenty-first century (2,000–2,500) and more than his contemporary European physiologists considered necessary, Atwater's reasoning being that Americans worked harder than Europeans.[26] He did some early work in the analysis of the fat, protein and carbohydrate content of food and recommended that a substantial proportion of the kilocalories be from protein and fat, thus paving the way for an American diet based first upon the belief that Americans should eat more, and secondly upon the view that Americans should consume large quantities of meat. This habit was to dominate the twentieth century and posed problems of its own. Atwater's revelation that certain beans provided as much protein as meat was overlooked by immigrant communities who associated vegetable diets with the poverty of their European homelands and regarded the consumption of large quantities of meat as an essential element of their 'Americanisation'.[27] In 1900 the principal causes of premature death in the United States were tuberculosis and pneumonia, accounting for 21.5 per cent of the total, these conditions frequently associated with poor living conditions and inadequate diet. After a century of ever-increasing consumption of kilocalories, heart diseases accounted for the largest share of deaths in 2000, accounting for 31.4 per cent of the total. Deaths from strokes added another 6.9 per cent and, like heart disease, these are frequently associated with diets rich in fats.[28] In the meantime, powerful lobbyists had arisen to protect the interests of the cattlemen whose prosperity depended upon the Americans' love of meat.

When Marion Nestlé, chair of the Department of Nutrition and Food Studies at New York University, moved to Washington to work for the Public Health Service, she was informed that, regardless of what her research told her, the report she was preparing 'could not recommend "eat less meat" as a way to reduce intake of saturated fat, nor ... suggest restrictions on intake of any other category of food'. If she were unwise enough to do so then 'producers of foods that might be affected by such advice would complain to their beneficiaries in Congress, and the report would never be published.'[29] A more public demonstration of the power of interest groups followed the publication, in 1977, of a Senate Committee's *Dietary Goals for the United States*, which moved away from the Atwater 'eat more calories, especially meat' approach towards an 'eat fewer calories, especially less meat' recommendation. The then Senator Robert Dole (later presidential candidate) discussed with the president of the National Cattlemen's Association, Wray Finney, the controversial recommendation, 'decrease consumption of meat', and suggested instead the use of the words 'increase consumption of lean meat'. Finney agreed: 'Decrease is a bad word, Senator'.[30]

World Food Production

The world is not short of food, though its distribution amongst the world's population is grossly inequitable. Adult men are estimated to require about 2,500 kilocalories per day and adult women about 2,000, with some variation caused by stature and differences arising from varying levels of physical activity required by occupations and living conditions. WHO estimates that from 1961 to 1998 global food availability increased from 2,300 kilocalories per day to 2,800, so, allowing for the fact that children need fewer kilocalories than adults, the world's production of food should be sufficient to meet the energy requirements of its population. Some 800 million people are under-nourished because so much food is consumed by those, mostly in the West, who would be better off without it and because much is wasted. The increase in food availability has been particularly pronounced in Western Europe where, since about 1960, following the end of post-war rationing, there has been an increase of about 400 kilocalories per day, representing an increase of about 15 per cent of daily intake. No wonder we are putting on weight.[31] Moreover, as income levels rise and appetites are satisfied, there is a tendency for humans to move from cheap low-energy and nutrient-rich vegetable products of the kind associated with the British wartime diet to the more expensive meat, fat and sugar-based diets. These tendencies are further exacerbated as people move from the countryside to towns and cities where occupations are more sedentary and incomes higher, with a consequent increase in demand for meat and for processed foods. These trends are now making themselves felt in China, having already penetrated western countries, including the former Eastern bloc states which have joined the European Union. The speed with which sugar penetrated European markets in earlier centuries has already been noted,[32] and this has now been matched by the switch from diets based on inexpensive cereals to those based on more expensive (and fatty) meats. WHO estimates that in high-income countries, where household expenditure on food has fallen from 25 per cent of household income to 13 per cent over a generation, share of expenditure on cereals is less than half that of low-income countries while the share devoted to meat rises with income.[33] Moreover, the cereals eaten in towns are different from those in rural areas where small farmers may eat their own rice, maize or bread. When the farm workers move to towns to work in factories for higher incomes they are more likely to be able to afford, and to choose, convenience foods, a tendency encouraged by suppliers of food who wish to protect their businesses and their profits.

World Food Prices

It has been estimated that the real price of rice, wheat, maize, fat and sugar fell by about 60 per cent between 1960 and 2000, probably to its lowest in history. This was only partly due to the improvements in agricultural methods which occurred in the twentieth century, and particularly its second half, which led to huge increases in the production of grain, much of which was devoted to animal feed in Europe, the Americas and Australasia. The increase in the availability of meat, which was welcomed by the populations who were recovering from the healthy but limited diets of the Second World War, led to a higher intake of saturated fats than was previously possible or, indeed, desirable from the point of view of human health.

However, much of the decline in prices may be attributed to policy decisions taken by framers of protectionist farm policies. These include those of
the much-criticised Common Agricultural Policy of the European Union;
the subsidies offered to farmers in the United States; and the actions of the
Japanese government to preserve their rice-growing industry despite its
competitive disadvantages in comparison with those of its Asian neighbours. Thus the European Union is the world's third largest sugar producer
(after India and Brazil) but the second largest exporter despite having the
highest costs, the discrepancy being due to the subsidies paid to European
farmers. This practice distorts the world sugar market, penalises producers
in developing countries and dumps large stocks of cheap produce on the
world market, encouraging food processors to find uses for it by producing foods which are richer in kilocalories than nutrients. The resulting
conflict between the needs of consumers and the interests of producers
has been termed 'food wars',[34] from which flow two consequences. First,
the fall in prices of cereals and other crops has brought the commodities themselves within the purchasing range of increasing numbers of the
world's population and has also made more affordable the meat (and fat)
which has resulted from the growing use of surplus stocks as animal feeds.
Consequently the kilocalories consumed have increased, as shown in the
following table over three decades:[35]

Kilocalories consumed per person in:	1964/6	1997/9
World average	2,358	2,803
Developing nations	2,054	2,681
Industrialised nations	2,947	3,380

The second, less beneficial consequence of the dumped surpluses is that
food processors, in an understandable effort to protect their sales and
profit margins in the face of falling commodity prices, have 'added value'
by turning these products into increasingly sophisticated prepared meals
which are denser in the energy they contain than in the nutrients that
we need. This is seen at its most obvious in the market for breakfast cereals, supposedly low-energy, nutrient-rich products to which the addition
of sugars and fats is commonplace. Early in the twentieth century per
capita consumption of sugar in Europe was about 5 kilos per year; at the
beginning of the twenty-first century it is about 50 kilos a year, most of it
consumed in processed foods. These practices are particularly damaging to
the diets of poorer people.

Poor Diets for Poor People

It is a great paradox that obesity and poor nutrition are frequently linked, but it is easily explained by distinguishing between 'energy-dense' foods that are rich in kilocalories and 'nutrient-dense' foods that are low in kilocalories but rich in nutrients such as vitamins and minerals. The problem is at its most acute amongst people of low income and poor education, for whom convenience foods, heavy with fats, sugars, colourants and flavourings, are often cheap and attractive. The situation in the United States may be taken as representative of that of other Western societies with protectionist farm policies which ensure that the nation produces almost twice as much food as its citizens need, particularly in the fields of grain and fats. This, in turn, encourages food processors to protect their shareholders' interests in two ways: first by promoting over-consumption of foods; and secondly by 'adding value' to the surplus raw materials like fat and sugar through the use of sophisticated processing and marketing techniques. Thus it has been estimated that the 'farm value' of products like canned tomatoes and cornflakes – the share of the price that is taken by the farmer – struggles to reach 10 per cent of the sum paid by the shopper.[36] In the words of two of America's most prominent researchers into the subject:

> Highest rates of obesity and diabetes in the United States are found among the lower income groups ... Refined grains, added sugars and added fats are among the lowest-cost sources of dietary energy. They are inexpensive, good-tasting and convenient. In contrast the more nutrient-dense lean meats, fish, fresh vegetables and fruit generally cost more.[37]

The problems of poor diets amongst poor people is exacerbated by the fact that nutrition labelling, which should help consumers to distinguish energy-dense for nutritious foods is a complex subject, as explained in chapter five. The labels are consequently much more likely to be heeded by those with higher incomes and better education who are least likely to suffer from obesity or poor nutrition.

In the west, poorer education and lower socio-economic status has been associated with a lower intake of fresh fruit and vegetables and higher consumption of snack foods, sugar and fat.[38] This has not been helped by the fact that, over the period 1985–2000, the prices of soft drinks, fats, sugars and starches fell in relation to those of fresh fruit and vegetables. While the consumption of 'raw' sugar (for example, in tea and coffee) fell during this period, the fall was more than offset by a rise in consumption in soft drinks,

confectionery and snacks. The consumers' taste buds were outwitted by the
processors of these branded products.[39] Children in lower socio-economic
groups are also less likely to participate in family meal occasions where
parents can exercise some control over their choice of food and more
likely to eat in fast food outlets where they will be encouraged to consume
energy-dense foods rich in sugars and fat.[40] Nor are adults exempt from
such influences. As early as 1990, a British government survey of adults
revealed that:

> Twenty-seven per cent of food energy was consumed out of the home. Foods
> eaten out of the home contained a lower proportion of protein than the diet
> as a whole and they contained more sugars and less fibre, iron and vitamins per
> unit of energy.[41]

Given that sugar and fat are readily available at historically low prices, it
is hardly surprising that catering outlets make generous use of them to
flavour and preserve their products and to bolster their profit margins.
There is more than anecdotal evidence to suggest that eating in fast-food
restaurants increases body mass index. Studies in America confirmed that
frequency of eating out was associated with an increase in body fat amongst
healthy adults, with women particularly vulnerable to an increased BMI
if they made frequent use of fast-food restaurants. There is also evidence
to suggest that serving sizes in fast-food outlets and in supermarkets have
tended to increase, especially with the growth of larger portion sizes in
'value meals' and the more extensive use of 'all-you-can-eat' buffets.[42] In
the 1950s in the United States a soft drink would normally contain 8oz of
soda whereas in 2002, a 'child-size' cola drink at a fast-food outlet would
be 12oz and a large cola could be as much as 32oz. By that time also a
portion of 'Super Size French Fries' could be three times the size which
applied twenty years earlier. In Western countries, where many food and
confectionery markets are mature, growth has been concentrated on
eating out, most particularly in fast-food restaurants. In the United States
the proportion of meals consumed away from home grew from 6 per cent
in the late 1970s to 20 per cent in the late 1990s,[43] while in Britain a survey
of adults in 1990 showed as many as 29 per cent of meals being eaten away
from home.[44] The problems thus posed are further exacerbated by the
fact that restaurant meals give no indication of their calorific content. A
single dish in a pizza, pasta or hamburger restaurant often exceeds the total
calorific content recommended for an adult for a whole day, but very few
people realise this. In New York fast-food chains are obliged to show the

calorie content of dishes, but this is not a requirement in Britain and there are no proposals to make it so.[45]

Bad Habits Spread Fast

Evidence from Eastern European countries which emerged from the Soviet Union tends to support the anecdotal tales of earlier centuries in the West when the fat, jolly squire of novels like *Tom Jones* was seen in contrast with the under-nourished rural labourer. Eastern Europeans had to wait for later centuries before they could experience the obesity that can come with affluence, though in the case of Eastern Europe the transition appears to have occurred very quickly. The experience of the Ukraine, the Baltic Republics and Poland suggests that, following their emergence from the experience of Soviet economic penury, obesity was first seen as an affliction of the more prosperous classes – but this problem quickly passed to the lower-income groups as cheap, energy-dense foods began to emerge from factories and retailers inspired by Western models and often financed by Western investment,[46] leading to the enthusiastic adoption of sugary, salty, fatty foods by these groups. In the 1990s most inward investment by western corporations in the area's food and agriculture went not into the production of grain, fruit and vegetables, but into two markets; those of confectionery and soft drinks, neither of them conducive to good eating habits.[47] In Poland, in the period 1999–2004, sales of chocolate rose by 26 per cent, sugar confectionery by 22 per cent and soft drinks by more than 50 per cent.[48]

Children

Particular concerns have been expressed about the marketing of energy-dense products to children who are especially vulnerable and who may develop poor dietary practices that may last lifetimes. In 2004 the United States Congress expressed concern about the fact the childhood obesity rates had grown from 5 per cent in the 1960s to 16 per cent by the turn of the millennium.[49] A report was commissioned from the Institute of Medicine which revealed the 'Orwellian' methods by which the food industry 'intentionally targets children who are too young to distinguish advertising from truth and induces them to eat high-calorie, low nutrition "junk" foods … at least thirty per cent of the kilocalories in the average child's diet derive from sweets, soft drinks, salty snacks and fast food'. Reference was also made to the sophisticated research which provided a 'basis for exploiting the suggestibility of young children', leading to product placements and the use of text messages as well as the more conventional television advertising messages.[50] The reviewer of the report in the *New England Journal of Medicine*, Marion Nestlé, who has considerable experience of the field, argued that the US should follow Australia, the Netherlands and Sweden in banning advertisements for foods and confectionery to children, and should also ban the use of cartoons and celebrity endorsements in all such advertisements. In the same issue of the *Journal,* an article headed *Obesity: the New Frontier of Public Health Law* considered the legal implications of the childhood obesity problem.[51] It estimated that children are exposed to 40,000 advertisements each year of which 72 per cent are for candy, cereal and fast food, and it reviewed the legal hurdles involved in their regulation. As early as 1978 the Federal Trade Commission's attempts to impose restraints on non-nutritious foods aimed at children were frustrated by arguments deployed by skilled and powerful lobbyists who invoked constitutional rights to 'free speech', buttressed by supposed difficulties in defining 'nutritious' and identifying programmes aimed at children. These arguments have been compared with those advanced in defence of tobacco advertising in earlier decades. Attempts in some individual states to deter purchases of unhealthy soft drinks and confectionery have run into difficulties of distinguishing the good from the bad. Some on/off attempts have been made to invoke civil law in prosecuting companies who are supposedly central to the problem of poor nutrition, notably a case brought on behalf of obese children, claiming that a fast-food corporation failed to warn them of the risks associated with consuming their products.[52] However, the authors concluded, with a sigh, that self-regulation might have a better chance of succeeding, given the legal obstacles in the USA.

Where America leads, Britain follows. In 2002 it was estimated that children and adolescents spent, on average, about 860 hours a year in school classrooms and significantly more than that, about 1,200 hours a year, watching television or playing computer games.[53] Within Europe the United Kingdom had the largest number of advertisements per hour within programmes aimed at children and the largest category of such advertisements were for fast-food restaurants, confectionery and sweetened breakfast cereals. At this rate, therefore, a child would be exposed to over 7,000 advertisements for food each year on television alone. Moreover, a study published in 1996 demonstrated that the great majority of such advertisements would be for fatty and sugary foods such as confectionery, sugar-fortified breakfast cereals, ready-prepared foods, savoury snacks and fast-food restaurant meals: 'Food advertising represents a grossly unbalanced nutritional message. Fatty and sugary foods account for a disproportionately large percentage of all food advertising.'[54] The strength of the messages has been further fortified by the imaginative use of sporting and other heroes in such advertise-ments, the use of the football star and commentator Gary Lineker to market Walker's Crisps being instrumental in promoting the growth of this snack food sector overall, as well as the brand which employed him in its advertise-ments. And lobbyists can also be as effective in Britain as in America. In 1984 Saatchi and Saatchi, then at the height of its influence in government circles as the advertising agency to Margaret Thatcher's Conservative Party, won an industry award for their *Look After Yourself* series of four advertisements drawing attention to the harmful nutritional effects of fat, starch, salt and sugar. Except that the sugar advertisement never appeared: it included such statements as 'a sweet tooth can become no tooth at all' and was withdrawn, evidently at the behest of the Department of Health which was paying for the advertisements. It had to wait for the awards ceremony to be seen by a small group of industry executives![55]

Other techniques besides advertising have been used to influence chil-dren, one of the most invidious being the invocation of 'pester power' by the practice of placing products such as confectionery within the reach of small hands at checkouts. A survey of major supermarket chains showed that Asda and Morrisons had such displays at all their checkouts, though in the case of Morrisons a very small proportion were at child height. Marks and Spencer had such temptations at over 80 per cent of their checkouts while Tesco (at 10 per cent) and Waitrose (virtually none) brought up the rear. When it came to price promotions only Marks and Spencer devoted as many promotions to fruit and vegetables as to fatty and sugary foods (27 per cent each), while for Somerfield the figures were 7 per cent for fruit and vegetables against 31 per cent for fatty and sugary products.[56]

The campaign to promote poor diet has also been carried into schools. Exclusive contracts to install vending machines in school premises in return for payment by manufacturers of soft drinks and snack foods have proved to be tempting to those authorities who are struggling to balance school budgets. Coupons on such products have been offered with the inducement that they can be exchanged by the schools for computers, sports equipment and other necessary or desirable accessories. In other cases logos have appeared, in return for payment, in programmes for school sporting events, on furniture and on workbooks. These practices are most advanced in the United States, but have made themselves felt elsewhere.[57]

Remedies

The *Foresight* report identified a number of factors which influence our ability to maintain a balance between the food we eat and the energy we expend. Four were shown as critical to the maintenance of a healthy life-style. The first was the mechanism of appetite control in the brain which in many people amounts to 'an underlying biological tendency to put on weight and retain it'.[58] The second factor was the 'force of dietary habits': at its simplest a sweet tooth, like smoking, is an easy habit to acquire, but a hard one to discard. The third was the level of physical activity undertaken which, for strong social reasons in an age of cars, mechanisation and service industries, is usually inadequate. The fourth was 'psychological imbalance in making lifestyle choices', expressed not only in activities like excessive social consumption of alcohol but also in choice of convenience foods by busy people despite lurking suspicions that they may contain more kilocalories than nutrients. To sum up the effects of these challenges, 'the pace of technological change has outstripped human evolution'.[59] From the *Foresight* report emerges a warning that unless radical steps are taken, then by the middle of the twenty-first century, 'it will become normal to be obese'.[60] It also advises of the 'futility of isolated initiatives': advertising campaigns telling people of the virtues of exercise will achieve little if the roads are too dangerous for children to walk or cycle to school; and exhortations to eat fewer unhealthy snacks will do no good if such snacks are cheaper than healthy ones and if school meals are beyond the purses of poorer parents.

This message has been understood, if not acted upon, in the United States, whose Surgeon-General suggested in 2001 that the avoidance of ill health arising from obesity was more than a personal responsibility, declaring:[61]

> Many people believe that dealing with overweight and obesity is a personal responsibility. To some degree they are right, but it is also a community responsibility. Where there are no safe, accessible places for children to play or adults to walk, jog or ride a bike, that is a community responsibility. When school lunch-rooms or office cafeterias do not provide healthy and appealing food choices, that is a community responsibility.

He could have added that when politicians subsidise the price of sugar and allow companies to promote the sales of confectionery, snack foods and sugary drinks in schools, that is a community responsibility.

An Anti-Obesity Menu

Perhaps the approach to the obesity epidemic can be compared to a menu offering many courses. Few people will consume all the courses but most people will be expected to try several. Five approaches to the obesity problem suggest themselves. The first approach to obesity could be described as a search for the *medical* solution: a wonder drug which, when taken, will either cause the patient to undergo a healthy drop in appetite or to shed pounds in weight. So far the efforts of the pharmaceutical industry have met with little success. Pills certainly exist to help people lose weight, but drugs are rarely without side-effects and evidence to date suggests that, while weight is lost while the medication is being taken, it soon returns when the medication ceases. A report in the *British Medical Journal* in November 2007 revealed that Orlistat, a product of GlaxoSmithKline (GSK), could achieve a 10 per cent weight loss in about a quarter of those taking it, though the side-effects, including faecal incontinence, together with unrealistic expectations of weight loss, meant that it was rarely fully effective. The author of the article commented that as much would be achieved by 'leaving a few French fries on the plate, eating an apple instead of an ice cream or having 10–20 minutes of sex'![62] The same week a report in *The Lancet* suggested that another weight-loss drug, Rimonabant, was likely in many people to induce 'an increased risk of developing depressive mood disorders', while other weight-loss treatments had driven users to suicide.[63] In December 2007, Glaxo applied for a licence to market in the UK a drug called Alli, a low-strength version of the prescription drug Xenical which, it was claimed, would enable dieting users to increase weight loss by up to 50 per cent above that which would be achieved by dieting alone. The product is reported to be already on sale in the United States. Such remedies will no doubt have a place in the lives of those people who have serious genetic predispositions to being overweight, but for the rest of us they are probably best avoided. In 2007 scientists at Cambridge University announced their discovery that a variant of a gene (the FTO gene) could predispose humans to obesity and that almost half the UK population carried the variant.[64] This, together with other similar discoveries, will no doubt have stimulated Big Pharma to bring its determination and resourcefulness to bear on a huge and profitable market in the developed world, but there is no Prozac on the horizon and Prozac has its critics. A more modest initiative in the medical field may be built upon the discovery that breast-fed babies are less likely to become overweight than bottle-fed babies, and this revelation has been strengthened by further research by the Institute of Psychiatry, Kings College, London, which shows that breast-fed babies also enjoy higher IQs.[65]

Education

The second approach to obesity is education, but such attempts as have been made to educate consumers to eat healthily suggest that much effort brings about small improvements. An experiment conducted in Leeds and reported in the *British Medical Journal*[66] in 2001 involved 634 children aged seven to eleven in ten primary schools, a high level of information and support being made available for healthier meals, snacks and packed lunches and for an exercise programme. All this effort, over an academic year, led to a small increase in the consumption of fresh vegetables. Slightly more encouraging results were reported from three primary schools in England and Wales where the children, over a period of sixteen days, were shown videos featuring cartoon 'food dudes' who liked fruits and vegetables. They were also rewarded with stickers, pens and similar prizes. Over the period the children, at home and at school, consumed between 131 and 153 grams of fruit and vegetables more than they had in their diets before the experiment.[67] This is in the context of a situation in which 6 per cent of pre-school children are believed to be obese while 17 per cent have reached this condition by the age of fifteen. Furthermore, a much-publicised attempt by the television chef Jamie Oliver to improve the quality of school meals, substituting salads, fruit and pasta for chips, chocolate and crisps, while welcomed (and paid for) by the government, had some disappointing outcomes. Not only did the uptake of the new, healthy school meals decline; in some areas parents were filmed thrusting burgers and crisps through a school fence to rescue their children from healthy eating in scenes reminiscent of America in the era of prohibition.

In the United States itself an experiment was undertaken which was designed to persuade consumers in West Virginia, one of the poorest states in the Union, to switch from the consumption of high-fat milk to skimmed or fat-free milk. The small town of Wheeling, with a population of 35,000, was chosen for a campaign involving television, radio and newspaper advertisements, backed up by public relations events and costing $26,000 on the theme *1% or less*, referring to the fat content of the milk. The campaign resulted in the share of fat-free and skimmed milk sales rising from 29 per cent to 46 per cent of total consumption.[68] From these experiments we may conclude that changing dietary habits through educational measures of this kind can achieve some modest success, but it is undoubtedly very hard work.

Healthy school meals which were also free for all pupils would no doubt have the desired effects, but there is no sign that any government is prepared to entertain this idea.

Marketing Good Health: Some Encouraging Trends

The third approach to obesity calls upon the sophisticated marketing skills of the food industry, which have shown that it is possible, over time, to change people's habits for the better, notably in the consumption of bread, where more money can be made from wholemeal and flavoured breads (e.g. tomato bread) than from the standard white loaf. The *Family Food Survey* for 2005–6 shows trends in the consumption of certain foodstuffs which would gladden the heart of Jack Drummond, John Boyd Orr and others who fought to wean the British population away from white bread and on to more nutritious foods. The figures are given in grams per person per week over the period 1974–2005/6:[69]

	1974	2005/6
Fruit, including pure fruit juice	731	1292
Vegetables, excluding potatoes	1141	1156
White bread	860	336
Brown bread	65	41
Wholemeal bread	17	145
Cakes and pastries	158	130
Biscuits	214	165

Similar changes have been observed in other markets. Consumption of butter fell in the 1990s to a third of the level of the 1960s, while that of margarine has grown, a particularly marked increase being seen in the sales of low-fat spreads, with emphasis on their healthy characteristics rather than price. Likewise the sales of red meats (beef, veal, mutton and lamb) fell by half while that of poultry doubled.[70] In the year ending October 2005 the most rapidly growing market was drinking yoghurt, which recorded a sales increase of 51 per cent while frozen meals and pizzas fell by 9 per cent.[71] Perhaps the most remarkable marketing statistic of all is that weight-loss programmes like Weight Watchers now have an annual market value of £2 billion.[72]

Much of the credit for the increase in consumption of fruit, low-fat spreads, weight-loss programmes and drinking yoghurt, as well as wholemeal bread, may be awarded to the ways in which these have been marketed, in which there is perhaps a lesson for the future. The World Health Organisation, in its examination of the problem of obesity in Europe, observed the sophistication with which corporations had marketed foods which are not always the healthiest options, but it also appreciated that the information and expertise in the hands of such corporations might be enrolled in the interests of healthier diets.[73] If consumers can be persuaded to overcome their reluctance to eat wholemeal bread and to cover it with low-fat spreads instead of butter, why should they not be persuaded to abandon fatty, sugary foods? And if the European Union's infamous Common Agricultural Policy can manipulate the prices of milk, butter and sugar in the interests of producers, why should they not do the same for healthy foods in the interests of consumers?

Exercise: 'On Your Bike'

The fourth element in the struggle against obesity concerns exercise. The role of exercise in promoting good health, rather than just warding off illness, was recognised between the world wars by two visionary doctors. These were George Scott Williamson (1884–1953), who won the Military Cross in the First World War for his work in charge of field ambulances on the western front; and Innes Pearse (1889–1978), who met Scott Williamson while working at the Royal Free Hospital and later married him. After a false start in 1926 they created the Pioneer Health Centre in Peckham in 1935, which offered a mix of medical care, exercise and diet to promote health and well-being. Exercise took the forms of boxing, dancing, gymnastics and swimming in the centre's own pool. Food was provided from an organic farm in nearby Bromley, together with tuberculin-tested unpasteurised milk. Families, before the advent of the National Health Service (NHS) paid a small subscription to join the centre, which was in effect subsidised by charitable donations. The centre was successful and widely praised for the benefits it conferred on the local population. It attracted the attention of Aneurin Bevan as he established the NHS, but it did not survive the scrutiny of the statistician he sent to examine its activities, and it did not long survive the advent of the NHS itself, closing in 1950.[74]

As previously indicated in this chapter, insufficient people of either sex take adequate exercise, but the problem is particularly acute amongst women. On the day that the discouraging news about the effectiveness of anti-obesity drugs appeared in the *British Medical Journal*,[75] the Women's Sport and Fitness Foundation published the results of its own study of women's attitudes to sport and exercise. The findings were overwhelmingly negative. Eighty per cent of women took too little exercise and 25 per cent agreed with the statement: 'I hate the way I look when I exercise or play sport'. Participation in sport by women was half that of men.[76] These negative feelings had been acquired at school, owing to the rather unimaginative types of exercise schoolgirls are often encouraged to undertake. Such attitudes have their foundations in the nineteenth century, when there was anxious debate in women's magazines like the *Woman's Gazette* about whether outdoor games were suitable for schoolgirls with the attendant risks of catching cold – this at a time when the code of muscular, games-playing Christianity had taken a firm hold in boys' private schools. With some reservations about the effects on 'delicate girls', some games were introduced to schools, but not all young women wished to play hockey, lacrosse or netball in sunshine or in rain, and even in the twentieth century, young, talented women are sometimes put off sports by unimaginative schooling. Thus Catherine Bishop arrived at Pembroke College, Cambridge, in 1989, having learned at school that she had 'no aptitude for sport'. She was, with difficulty, persuaded to join the college boat club, where she thrived to the extent of winning a silver medal for Great Britain at the Athens Olympics in 2004.[77] Not every schoolgirl who fails to take to netball can take up rowing and win an Olympic medal, but a more imaginative approach to school sport might overcome the discouragement and aversion that many feel. Likewise children who lack the necessary physical accomplishments to excel at football, rugby, cricket and other sports are in some enlightened schools encouraged to become referees, umpires or scorers, skills which are in huge demand in the world of amateur and professional sport. Such professions encourage healthy outdoor activity often accompanied by strenuous exercise, and can actually earn money for the holders of these qualifications. Brentwood School in Essex pioneered a scheme of this kind in the 1980s.

Between 1975 and 2003 the average distance walked each year for purposes of 'transport', such as going to work or school, fell from 255 miles per person to 192, while the miles cycled for the same purpose fell from 51 to 34.[78] Sales of bicycles for adult use in Great Britain peaked in the 1960s and began to fall as car ownership increased. The decline was reflected in the decisions taken by major retail chains. Halfords, the chain which established itself as Britain's leading cycle retailer, joined the opposition by diversifying into motor car spares and accessories, while its smaller rival, Curries, abandoned bicycles altogether in favour of labour-saving 'white goods' like washing machines. The European Commission estimates that, in the twenty-first century, for every kilometre walked, its average citizen cycles about half a kilometre and travels about 27.5km by car. Leaving aside the effects of these habits on congestion and pollution, they also have clear implications for the amount of exercise we take.[79] More than 50 per cent of car journeys are shorter than 5km, a distance that could easily be covered by bicycle and, in crowded cities, could often be travelled more quickly. Only in Denmark and the Netherlands does cycling account for more than a negligible proportion of routine travel.[80] The World Health Organisation, in its review of the benefits of cycling to health, identified dangers from traffic, poor weather and exposure to crime as amongst the principal disincentives to cyclists.[81]

The widespread belief that cycling is too dangerous in streets dominated by motor cars is contradicted by independent studies, which have shown that the very small risk of sustaining injury while cycling is far outweighed by the health benefits of doing so. In 1989 the British Medical Association, concerned at the number of cycle injuries sustained in accidents, commissioned a study of the impact of cycling on health. They concluded that, 'even in the current hostile traffic environment', the benefits of cycling to health, particularly concerning weight, lungs and cardiovascular functioning, outweighed the small danger of serious injury, but recommended more cycle lanes, cycle parks and other cyclist-friendly measures to encourage British citizens to cycle to work like citizens of Denmark and Holland.[82] A later study in Denmark of over 30,000 people aged twenty to ninety-three years old demonstrated that 'those who did not cycle to work experience a thirty-nine per cent higher mortality than those who did'.[83]

Cycling is fighting back in Britain. From the late 1950s a series of initiatives encouraged people to take up cycling not as a means of transport, as in the past, but as a form of healthy exercise. An early example of such an initiative was the sponsorship of the annual tour of Britain by the Milk Marketing Board as 'The Milk Race' from 1958 to 1993, when the demise of the Board meant that sponsorship passed to other hands. In 1980 the Irish Health Education Bureau sponsored 'The Health Race', a nine-day 900-mile cycle race around Ireland with each town visited mounting a 'health week' to raise awareness of the role of diet and exercise in a healthy lifestyle.[84] It was repeated in Scotland the following year. More recent initiatives have included the *Sustrans* movement to create a national cycle network, often using canal footpaths and similar off-road facilities which are safe for cyclists to use. In London and other cities, steps have been taken to encourage cycling by the provision of cycle lanes as a means of reducing traffic congestion and pollution, and these are already bearing fruit in the capital in the form of more widespread bicycle use. Perhaps this will eventually produce healthier citizens. The *Foresight* report suggests that planning procedures for town and city developments need to take into account the needs of walkers and cyclists, if necessary at the expense of car owners, in order to promote these forms of exercise while conferring the additional benefits of cleaner, as well as safer, environments. The cycling capital of Britain is Cambridge, a city whose central area reluctantly tolerates rather than welcomes motor cars. Cambridge is particularly well supplied with cycle lanes and cycle parks, and a quarter of the population cycles to work, by no means all of them students.

Regulation

Finally, if public policies can create problems by subsidising the production of fats, sugars and starches, could they also be used to solve them? If the application of penal taxation to cigarettes can be justified on the grounds that they reduce deaths from cancer, could the use of taxes on sweet, fatty foods be justified on health grounds? Since such taxes would fall disproportionately on cheap foods popular with poorer citizens, they would be regressive, but perhaps that label is a price worth paying for better health. And if the proceeds of such taxes could be used to subsidise the prices of fresh fruit and vegetables rather than sugar, then the regressive element might soon vanish. But initiatives could go much further than this and in some cases they have, though not always with success. In Sweden, television advertisements to under-twelves have long been banned, but this prohibition is now evaded by satellite television which recognises no national borders. In Japan, food and drink advertisements are banned in schools and teaching materials are checked for promotional messages, while in Taiwan, soft-drink vending machines are banned in schools. In Latvia, a sales tax has been imposed on soft drinks.[85]

Reference has already been made to the difficulties experienced in the United States in using laws to govern the activities of corporations, but similar programmes in the past have sometimes borne fruit after long struggles. Few doubt that the drink-driving laws of the 1960s, backed by strong advertising campaigns, have reduced, though not eliminated, the scourge of drunken drivers. Likewise, smoking is now accepted as an unpleasant and dangerous habit to the extent that it is now banned in public enclosed spaces, but it took forty-five years for this to happen following the Royal College of Physicians' report *Smoking and Health*, first published in 1962.

Perhaps it will take just as long for public regulations and private tastes to re-align themselves over the question of diet and exercise as they did over drink-driving and smoking. Regulations on advertising of unhealthy foods will no doubt evoke cries of 'nanny state' from lobby groups, just as they did over smoking (and indeed over the compulsory wearing of car seat belts). If taxes are imposed on 'junk foods' richer in kilocalories than in nutrients, then there will be protesting cries from other interest groups, but food processors are, above all, ingenious, and if more money can be made from marketing healthy food than unhealthy food then they will adjust accordingly and their customers really will choose salads over hamburgers with French fries. Moreover, many of the measures proposed to combat obesity would have advantages for the other great contemporary menace: global warming. If more people cycled or walked to work or school then CO_2 emissions from cars would be significantly reduced. As if to emphasise this point, in November 2007 the Food Climate Research Network of Surrey University published a report which indicated the effects that diet can have on the amount of carbon discharged into the atmosphere. Evidently the rearing of livestock accounts for 8 per cent of the UK's greenhouse gas emissions and this, combined with the fact that much of the nation's food, especially meat, is imported from distant places like New Zealand and Argentina, enables a 'carbon value' to be placed on each plate of food. Thus Argentinian beef with a glass of Chilean red wine is carbon heavy; while organic vegan nut roast from local produce and a glass of locally brewed beer is carbon light.[86]

Criticisms have also been levelled at manufacturers of processed foods on the grounds that they use cartoon characters to advertise unhealthy snack foods, high in salt and sugar, to schoolchildren. The Consumer Association, which publishes *Which* magazine, provided evidence that Spiderman, The Simpsons, Shrek, the Pink Panther and even Winnie the Pooh, all popular with young children, were being used by companies like Kellogg's, Weetabix and Nestlé to promote products. A spokesman for the Food and Drink Federation described the *Which* report as 'bizarre', since a code of practice banned the use of licensed characters in advertising products which are high in salt, sugar or fat to young children. Kellogg's announced that it would cease the practice.

The Slow Food Movement

In October 2006 there assembled in Turin, Italy, the *Terra Madre* ('Mother Earth') conference of the Slow Food Movement.[87] This was begun in 1986 by a group of Italian gourmets who were offended by the opening of a McDonald's restaurant in Rome's historic *Piazza di Spagna*. The conference was attended by almost 5,000 delegates from 150 nations as diverse as Britain, Belgium, Armenia and Kirghizstan and serenaded by a choir of elderly women dressed in pinafores, red leggings and straw hats – the costume adopted by rice weeders who worked in the mosquito-infested swamps of Vercelli and Novara, between Turin and Milan, in the 1960s. Strangely the chorus was followed by one of Elgar's rousing marches. The gathering was addressed by the founding father of the movement, Carlo Petrini, born in 1949, a journalist, broadcaster, campaigner and founder of the Slow Food University whose aim is to promote the appreciation of good food and nutrition, an ironical echo of the McDonald's Hamburger University, founded in Illinois in 1960, with its rather different agenda. Petrini drew his audience's attention to the central paradoxes of world food consumption:[88]

> We produce enough food for 12 billion living souls, and there are only 6.3 billion of us on earth. 800 million people suffer from malnutrition or hunger; 1.7 billion suffer from obesity. Madness! It is madness to continue asking more from the earth, plundering resources and obeying the logic that says all consumption must be fast, abundant and wasteful.

Petrini's philosophy is summed up in the word *commensalita*, a word which translates into English as 'companionship at the table' and advocates gourmet values against the gluttony and excess which has characterised much of the twentieth century. He uses the expressions 'peasant' and 'peasant farmer' in a complimentary sense, whereas they have long been regarded as derogatory in many developed economies. The movement cherishes and promotes 'endangered' foods like Cornish pilchards, pecorino cheese, made in Sardinia from sheep's milk, and wild rice gathered by Native Americans, and it echoes the arguments of the Fair Trade Movement in its demands that the primary producers, the farmers, and those who harvest the products, should receive a fair proportion of the price paid by the consumer. These views are not confined to the Slow Movement whose foundation coincided with an effective boycott of Campbell's soups on behalf of migrant Hispanic harvest workers in Ohio.[89]

Some critics see the movement as elitist, as turning its back on cheaper methods of production and thereby denying access to cheap food for the poor. Petrini denies this and draws attention to the damaging impact of large-scale agriculture on the economy, by poisoning the soil with chemicals, filling the air with carbon dioxide as products are air-freighted around the world and driving local producers out of business by undercutting them. What chance does *Terra Madre* have in competition with McDonald's, KFC and the rest in the decades ahead? It is still a small movement, though represented in 150 countries and its activities are of sufficient interest to attract sponsorship from corporations like Lufthansa and Budget Rent-a-Car. In 1950, as the British re-asserted their preference for white bread against the healthier wholemeal bread which they had been obliged to eat during the war, no one would have guessed that, fifty years later, sales of white bread would be relentlessly declining while sales of healthier wholemeal bread, especially the previously despised rye bread, would be rising.[90] So perhaps we should not write off the chances of Petrini and his Slow Food Movement after all.

Moreover, there are some signs that there may be opportunities to grasp the problems of over-consumption in the developed world. In the latter half of 2007 the price of meat, grain, eggs and dairy products began to rise sharply. This was partly because of a growing taste for meat amongst the increasingly affluent consumers of India and China with a consequent increase in pressure on grain prices for animal feed. And it was partly due to the growing use of grains for the production of fuels like bio-diesel. There also appeared a steady flow of newspaper and magazine articles and television programmes drawing attention to the problems of obesity, the relative qualities of different foods and the need for governments to take an interest in the practices of fast-food restaurants which offer calorie-rich, nutrient-poor meals to their customers, especially children. In January 2008 the government announced that cookery lessons were to be re-introduced to those schools from which they had vanished, in an attempt to teach children about healthy eating. At the same time, the Health Secretary Alan Johnson issued his call to the food industry to adopt a system of nutritional labelling which would help, rather than confuse, citizens in their choice of healthy foodstuffs.[91] Is it too much to expect that the combination of rising food prices, government concerns and growing public awareness will make us change our eating habits for the better while worrying about the carbon footprints of the foods we eat?

Notes

Chapter 1: Fears, Fads and Fallacies

1. M.J. Daunton, *Health and Housing in Victorian London*, Medical History Supplement, 11, (1991), p. 130
2. W. Gratzer, *Terrors of the Table: the Curious History of Nutrition*, Oxford University Press, 2005, p. 3
3. J.C. Drummond and A. Wilbraham, *The Englishman's Food: Five Centuries of English Diet*, Pimlico edition, 1991, p. 403
4. Dr C. Singer, *A Short History of Medicine*, Clarendon Press, Oxford, 1928, p. 34 ff explains these theories and their consequences
5. G. Cannon, *The Politics of Food*, Century, 1988, p. 231
6. J. Thirsk, *Food in Early Modern England*, Hambledon Continuum, 2007, pp. 6–9 and 68
7. J.C. Drummond and A. Wilbraham, *The Englishman's Food: Five Centuries of English Diet*, Pimlico edition, 1991, p. 66
8. W. Gratzer, *Terrors of the Table: the Curious History of Nutrition*, Oxford University Press, 2005, p. 43
9. W. Gratzer, *Terrors of the Table: the Curious History of Nutrition*, Oxford University Press, 2005, p. 46
10. See chapter two for an account of the entry of potatoes and sugar to the European diet
11. J.C. Drummond and A. Wilbraham,, *The Englishman's Food: Five Centuries of English Diet*, Pimlico edition, 1991, p. 214
12. J.C. Drummond and A. Wilbraham,, *The Englishman's Food: Five Centuries of English Diet*, Pimlico edition, 1991, p. 235
13. M. Bragg, *On Giants' Shoulders*, Hodder and Stoughton, 198, p. 121
14. J.C. Smyth, (ed.), *The Works of the Late William Stark, M.D.*, London, 1788, pp. i ff describes Stark's early life
15. See chapter 4 for a discussion of the contemporary theories about remedies for scurvy
16. J.C. Smyth, (ed.), *The Works of the Late William Stark, M.D.*, London, 1788, p. 92

17. *The Lancet*, 24 August 1935, p. 460
18. J.C. Drummond and A. Wilbraham, *William Stark, M.D.: an Eighteenth Century Experiment in Nutrition*, published in *The Lancet*, 24 August 1935, pp. 459–62 describes the experiment in detail
19. J.C. Smyth, (ed.), *The Works of the Late William Stark, M.D.*, London, 1788 is the source of these quotations
20. See chapter three for an account of the early history of refrigeration
21. See chapter five for a fuller account of the work of Jonas Hanway
22. J. Hanway, *Letters on the Importance of the Rising Generation*, London, 1767, vol. 2, p. 193
23. Smith, W., *A Sure Guide in Sickness and Health in the Choice of Food and Use of Medicine*, London, 1776, pp. 57 and 59
24. *American Medical Recorder*, 1825, vol. 8, p. 230
25. W. Beaumont, *Experiments and Observations on the Gastric Juice and the Physiology of Digestion*, 1833, facsimile edition, Dover Publications, New York, 1996, p. 14
26. W. Beaumont, *Experiments and Observations on the Gastric Juice and the Physiology of Digestion*, 1833, facsimile edition, Dover Publications, New York, 1996, p. xvi
27. W. Beaumont, *Experiments and Observations on the Gastric Juice and the Physiology of Digestion*, 1833, facsimile edition, Dover Publications, New York, 1996, p. xxiii
28. W. Beaumont, *Experiments and Observations on the Gastric Juice and the Physiology of Digestion*, 1833, facsimile edition, Dover Publications, New York, 1996, p. xxvi
29. See p. 17 for an account of Spallanzani's work
30. *Oxford Dictionary of National Biography*, Oxford University Press, 2001, vol. 54, p. 403
31. W. Gratzer, *Terrors of the Table: the Curious History of Nutrition*, Oxford University Press, 2005, p. 62 ff gives a clear account of Rumford's theory
32. See pp. 14 and 19 above for these references
33. Rumford, *Of Food and Particularly of Feeding the Poor*, London, 1796
34. See p. 17 for a discussion of Antoine Lavoisier's contribution to the science of nutrition
35. J.C. Drummond and A. Wilbraham, *The Englishman's Food: Five Centuries of English Diet*, Pimlico edition, 1991, p. 285
36. W. Gratzer, *Terrors of the Table: the Curious History of Nutrition*, Oxford University Press, 2005, p. 90
37. *The Lancet*, 14 October 1865, p. 44 contains Liebig's claims
38. M. Ashwell, (ed.), *McCance and Widdowson, a Scientific Partnership of 60 years*, British Nutrition Foundation, 1993, contains a selection of writings on the work of this remarkable pair, many of the contributions coming from those who worked with them
39. *The Composition of Foods*, Royal Society of Chemistry, 6th edition, 2002, p. xi, introductory section by R. McCance
40. R.A. McCance, R.D. Lawrence, *The Carbohydrate Content of Foods*, Medical Research Council Special Report Series no. 135, H.M.S.O., 1929
41. R.A. McCance and H.L. Shipp, *The Chemistry of Flesh Foods and their Losses on Cooking*, Medical Research Council Special Report Series no. 187, H.M.S.O., 1929
42. For this insight into their relationship I am indebted to Sir Andrew Huxley, OM, FRS; interview at Sir Andrew's home, 10 December 2007
43. M. Ashwell, (ed.), *McCance and Widdowson, a Scientific Partnership of 60 years*, British Nutrition Foundation, 1993, pp. 20–21 describes the incident in McCance's own words

44. McCance's autobiographical fragment in *McCance and Widdowson, a Scientific Partnership of 60 years*, British Nutrition Foundation, 1993, p. 22
45. R.A. McCance and E.M. Widdowson, *The Chemical Composition of Foods*, Medical Research Council Special Report Series no. 235, H.M.S.O., 1940
46. *The Composition of Foods*, Royal Society of Chemistry, 6th edition, 2002
47. McCance's autobiographical fragment in *McCance and Widdowson, a Scientific Partnership of 60 years*, British Nutrition Foundation, 1993, p. 23
48. McCance's autobiographical fragment in *McCance and Widdowson, a Scientific Partnership of 60 years*, British Nutrition Foundation, 1993, pp 23–24
49. For these and other details of the Langdale regime I am indebted to Sir Andrew Huxley, OM, FRS; interview at Sir Andrew's home, 10 December 2007
50. *Oxford Dictionary of National Biography*, Oxford University Press, 2004, vol. 16, p. 960
51. J. Fergusson, *The Vitamin Murders: Who Killed Healthy Eating in Britain* Portobello, London, 2007, gives an account of Drummond's work and the speculation surrounding his death
52. Sir Andrew Huxley writing in *McCance and Widdowson, a Scientific Partnership of 60 years*, British Nutrition Foundation, 1993, p. 145
53. R.A. McCance and E.M. Widdowson, *Advice to a Young Scientist*, in *McCance and Widdowson, a Scientific Partnership of 60 years*, British Nutrition Foundation, 1993, p. 66
54. Bizarrely, Krebs's one-time collaborator, the half-Jewish Otto Warburg, was re-classified as one quarter Jewish on Hitler's orders because of Hitler's mistaken belief that Warburg had devised a treatment for cancer, a disease of which he had a particular dread
55. The processes of *Glycolysis* and *Oxidative phosphorylation*

Chapter 2: The Staffs of Life

1. J. Boyd Orr, *Food, Health and Income: Report on a Survey of Adequacy of Diet in Relation to Income*, Macmillan, 1936, p. 53 ff
2. J.R. McCulloch, *A Statistical Account of the British Empire*, London 1837, is the source of the earlier figures
3. G. Bourne, *Change in the Village*, Gerald Duckworth, London, 1966, p. 63
4. J. Boyd Orr, *Food, Health and Income: Report on a Survey of Adequacy of Diet in Relation to Income*, Macmillan, 1936, p. 39
5. J. Boyd Orr, *Food, Health and Income: Report on a Survey of Adequacy of Diet in Relation to Income*, Macmillan, 1936, pp. 21 and 61; these remain major constituents of the British diet in 2007; see *Annual Abstract of Statistics, 2007*, Office of National Statistics table 21.16
6. *Metropolitan Water Board 50 Years Review*, Staples Press, 1953, p. 223
7. Samuel Smiles, *Lives of the Engineers*, John Murray, 1874, vol. 1, p. 79
8. See below, p. 39
9. Ewbank Smith, *Victorian Farnham*, Phillimore, 1971, p. 11
10. *Parliamentary Papers*, 1828, vol. ix, p. 149
11. See panel on p. 50 for an account of Snow's life and work
12. *Illustrated London News*, 10, 17 and 24 September 1892
13. *Public Health*, vol. 9, 10 January 1897, p. 286, *Journal of the Incorporated Society of Medical Officers of Health*
14. J. Boyd Orr, *Food, Health and Income: Report on a Survey of Adequacy of Diet in Relation to Income*, Macmillan, 1936, p. 17 ff
15. R. Lacey, *Hard to Swallow*, Cambridge University Press, 1994, p. 16

16. Thomas Cogan, *The Haven of Health*, London, 1584, p. 112
17. W. Harrison, *The Description of England*, 1587, Cornell UP reprint, 1968, p. 116
18. P. Hentzner, *A Journey into England in the Year 1598*, Strawberry Hill, 1757, pp. 48–49
19. Francis Bacon, *Works of*, ed. Basil Montague, Philadelphia, 1848, vol. 2, pp. 82 and 116
20. The quotations which follow are taken from Newton's copy, held by the library of Trinity College, Cambridge
21. F. Slare, *A Vindication of Sugars against the Charge of Dr Willis*, London, 1715, pp. 5, 15, 21, 23, 43, 59 and 60
22. T. Tryon, *Letters Domestic and Foreign*, London, 1700, pp. 216–21
23. R.B. Sheridan, *Sugar and Slavery*, Caribbean University Press, 1974, p. 132
24. R.B. Sheridan, *Sugar and Slavery*, Caribbean University Press, 1974, p. 133
25. R.B. Sheridan, *Sugar and Slavery*, Caribbean University Press, 1974, p. 22
26. R.B. Sheridan, *Sugar and Slavery*, Caribbean University Press, 1974, p. 29
27. *Sunday Times*, 6 May 2007, p. 5, gives an analysis of the sugar content of common foods based on *McCance & Widdowson*, 1978 edition
28. *Annual Abstract of Statistics, 2007*, Office for National Statistics, table 21.16
29. Lord Horder et al, *Bread*, Constable, London, 1954, chapter 1 gives an account of the early technology of bread-making
30. Variations from one shilling to twenty-eight shillings per quarter (28*lb*) have been recorded
31. H.T. Riley, (ed.) *Liber Albus*, a compendium prepared in 1419 of the customs of the City at the behest of the Mayor, Richard Whittington
32. A.S.C. Ross, *Economic History Review*, vol. 9, no. 2, 1956, pp. 332–42
33. W. Harrison, *The Description of England*, 1587, Cornell UP reprint, 1968, p. 247
34. G.R. Elton, *The Tudor Constitution*, Cambridge University Press, 1960, p. 315; 21 November 1601
35. J. Thirsk, *Food in Early Modern England,*, Hambledon Continuum, 2007, pp. 108 ff
36. W. Harrison, *The Description of England*, 1587, Cornell UP reprint, 1968, p. 133
37. Thomas Cogan, *The Haven of Health*, London, 1584, pp. 24–25
38. J. Hanway, *Letters on the Importance of the Rising Generation of the labouring part of our Fellow-Subjects*, London, 1767, vol. 2, *Abuses in Bread*, pp. 261 and 280
39. A. Smith, *Inquiry into the Nature and Causes of the Wealth of Nations*, Dent, 1960, vol. 1, pp. 147
40. *The Lancet*, 8 August, 1829, p. 608
41. *The Lancet*, 22 August, 1829, p. 657
42. *The Lancet*, 4 July, 1857, vol. 2, pp. 4–5
43. J.R. McCulloch, *A Statistical Account of the British Empire*, London 1837, p. 586
44. See p. 12 for this reference
45. Sir Jack Drummond and Anne Wilbraham, *The Englishman's Food*, Pimlico, London, 1991, p. 454
46. See p. 90
47. G. Cannon, *The Politics of Food*, Century, 1988, p. 232
48. Sir Jack Drummond, *The Nutritive Value of Bread*, Sanderson-Wells lecture, 1947, p. 8
49. Sir Jack Drummond, *The Nutritive Value of Bread*, Sanderson-Wells lecture, 1947, pp. 7–8
50. *Annual Abstract of Statistics, 2007*, Office for National Statistics, table 21.16
51. See p. 76
52. R.D. Salaman, *The History and Social Influence of the Potato*, Cambridge University Press, 1970, p. 147

53. C. Clode, *Memorials of the Guild of Merchant Taylors*, London, 1875, p. 170

54. Royal Society Letters Book, vol. 1, p. 83

55. R. Bradley, *A General Treatise of Husbandry and Gardening*, London, 1724, p. 474 and *Botanical Dictionary*, London, 1728, p. 475

56. J.E. Austen-Leigh, *A Memoir of Jane Austen*, London, 1870, p. 5

57. A. Young, *Farmer's Tour Through the East of England*, London, 1771, p. 409

58. F.M. Eden, *The State of the Poor*, 1797, Routledge edition, 1921, pp. 102–3

59. A. Smith, *Inquiry into the Nature and Causes of the Wealth of Nations*, Dent, 1960, vol. 1, pp. 146 and 147

60. See p. 49

61. T. Malthus, *Essay on the Principle of Population*, Penguin, London, 1970, p. 117; see chapter one for an account of the work of Smith and Malthus

62. The peak was reached in 1945 with 1,398,000 acres; the figure for 2005 was 338,000 acres

63. W. Cobbett, *Rural Rides*, 24 June, 1822, Everyman Edition, 1973, p. 88

64. R.D. Salaman, *The History and Social Influence of the Potato*, Cambridge University Press, 1970, p. 530

65. R. Lovell, *The Complete Herbal*, Oxford, 1655, p. 347

66. R.D. Salaman, *The History and Social Influence of the Potato*, Cambridge University Press, 1970, p. 115

67. R.D. Salaman, *The History and Social Influence of the Potato*, Cambridge University Press, 1970, p. 578

68. *Annual Abstract of Statistics, 2007*, Office for National Statistics, table 21.3

69. *Annual Abstract of Statistics, 2007*, Office for National Statistics, table 21.16

70. Thomas Cogan, *The Haven of Health*, London, 1584, p. 153 ff

71. W. Gratzer, *Terrors of the Table*, Oxford University Press, 2005, p. 40

72. J. Hanway, *Letters on the Importance of the Rising Generation of the labouring part of our Fellow-Subjects*, London, 1767, vol. 1

73. W. Harrison, *The Description of England*, 1587, Cornell UP reprint, 1968, pp. 126 and 131

74. J. Thirsk, *Food in Early Modern England,*, Hambledon Continuum, 2007, p. 145

75. The edition used is that published by Routledge in 1928

76. J. Thirsk, *Food in Early Modern England*, Hambledon Continuum, 2007, p. 232

77. G.E. Fussell, *The English Dairy Farmer 1500–1900*, Cass, London, 1966, p. 301

78. F.M. Eden, *The State of the Poor*, 1797, Routledge edition, 1921, p. 106

79. J. Thirsk, *Food in Early Modern England,*, Hambledon Continuum, 2007, p. 192

80. G.E. Fussell, *The English Dairy Farmer 1500-1900*, Cass, London, 1966, p. 315

81. G. Sturt, *A Small Boy in the Sixties*, Harvester Press edition, 1977, p. 123

82. *The Lancet*, 16 December 1848, pp. 654–655

83. *The Lancet*, 18 May 1839, p. 314

84. R. Woods, and J. Woodward, (eds.), *Urban Disease and Mortality in Nineteenth Century England*, New York, 1974, Chapter 4, Cronjé, J., p. 81

85. W. Cheadle, *On the Principles and Exact Conditions to be Observed in the Artificial Feeding of Infants*, Smith Elder, London, 1889, p. 57

86. See p. 24

87. J.C. Morton, 'Town Milk' in *The Journal of the Royal Agricultural Society of England*, 1868, p. 95

88. *Annual Abstract of Statistics, 2006*, Office of National Statistics, 2007, p. 356

89. *Report on the Health of the City of Liverpool During 1915*, Liverpool, 1916, p. 42

90. *The Lancet*, 1928, vol. 1, pp. 202–3

91. *Family Spending*, 2006, Office for National Statistics, table A1

Chapter 3: 'Man's War against Nature'

1. J. Hanway, *Letters Upon the Importance of the Rising Generation*, London, 1767, vol. 1, p. 75 ff
2. J. Rendle-Short in *Medical History*, October 1960, pp. 288–309 gives an account of Cadogan's life; the quotation is from p. 293
3. W. Cadogan, *Essay upon the Nursing and Management of Children*, London, 1769, p. 1
4. W. Cadogan, *Essay upon the Nursing and Management of Children*, London, 1769, p. 41
5. R. Carson, *Silent Spring*, Penguin edition, 1965, p. 24
6. See p. 82 below for this curious development
7. *The Closet of Sir Kenelm Digby*, London, 1669, pp. 228 ff quoted in J. Thirsk, *Food in Early Modern England*, Hambledon Continuum, 2007, p. 134
8. *The Lancet*, 1 December 1984, p. 1255; incidence of reported childhood eczema had increased from 5.1 per cent of children in 1946 to 12.2 per cent by 1970, with a greater increase in breast-fed infants
9. *The Lancet*, 24 September 1983, pp. 715–6
10. J. Thirsk, *Food in Early Modern England*, Hambledon Continuum, 2007, p. 159
11. F.M. Eden, *State of the Poor*, 1797, Routledge edition, 1928, vol. 2, chapter 2, quoted in J. Thirsk, *Food in Early Modern England*, Hambledon Continuum, 2007, p. 227
12. J. Thirsk, *Food in Early Modern England*, Hambledon Continuum, 2007, p. 133
13. J.C. Drummond and A. Wilbraham, *The Englishman's Food: Five Centuries of English Diet*, Pimlico, 1991, p. 320
14. *The Lancet*, 1852, vol. 1, p. 52
15. *The Lancet*, 1852, vol. 1, p. 253, 6 March 1852
16. *The Lancet*, 18 February 1889, p. 383
17. S. Pepys, *Diary of Samuel Pepys*, 11 December 1663
18. J.C. Drummond and A. Wilbraham, *The Englishman's Food: Five Centuries of English Diet*, Cape, 1957, p. 323
19. Gamgee, A., *A Textbook of the Physiological Chemistry of the Animal Body*, London, 1880
20. D. Davies and A. Carr, *Fifty Years of Frozen Food in Britain*, Grantham, 1998, p. xi et seq.
21. T.N. Morris, *The Dehydration of Food*, Chapman and Hall, 1947, p. 3
22. T.N. Morris, *The Dehydration of Food*, Chapman and Hall, 1947, p. 1 et seq.
23. A.S. Wohl, *Endangered Lives: Public Health in Victorian Britain*, Methuen, 1983, p. 51
24. T.N. Morris, *The Dehydration of Food*, Chapman and Hall, 1947, p. 5
25. H.W. Von Loesecke, *Drying and Dehydration of Foods*, Chapman and Hall, 1955, p. 1
26. S. Cotson and D.B. Smith, (eds) *Freeze-Drying of Foodstuffs*, Columbine Press, 1963, p. 7 et seq.
27. *Oxford English Dictionary*, Oxford University Press, 1989, vol. 9, p. 364
28. W. Gratzer, *Terrors of the table, the Curious History of Nutrition Oxford*, 2005, p. 216
29. G. Cannon, *The Politics of Food*, Century, London, 1988, p. 175
30. Q. Seddon, *Spoiled for Choice*, Evergreen, Finchingfield, 1990, p. 87 describes the experiment
31. G. Cannon, *The Politics of Food*, Century, London, 1988, pp 163–164
32. G. Cannon, *The Politics of Food*, Century, London, 1988, p. 147
33. *The Lancet*, 11 August 1979, p. 294
34. R. Lacey, *Hard to Swallow*, Cambridge University Press, 1994, pp. 63–64

35. *The Lancet*, 20 November, 1982, pp. 1115–17
36. *The Lancet*, 27 July, 1985, pp. 177–80
37. *The Lancet*, 15 October, 1983, pp. 865–67
38. Dr J. Egger et al, *Journal of Paediatrics*, January 1989, pp. 51–58
39. *The Lancet*, 25 August 1984, p. 456
40. *The Independent on Sunday*, 27 May 2007, pp. 1–2 describes the study
41. W. Kim, the University of California, Los Angeles in *Nutrition Bytes*, vol. 9, no. 1, 2003, article 6
42. A. Cockburn, *Rumsfeld, an American Disaster*, Verso, 2007, pp. 62–72
43. *Food Chemical News*, 12 June 1995, p. 27
44. *European Journal of Oncology*, 2005, pp. 107–16
45. R. Carson, *Silent Spring*, Penguin edition, 1965, p. 24
46. R. Carson, *Silent Spring*, Penguin edition, 1965, p. 56 gives an example of this magnification
47. R. Carson, *Silent Spring*, Penguin edition, 1965, pp. 85, 110, 122, 140 et seq.
48. R. Carson, *Silent Spring*, Penguin edition, 1965, p. 223
49. R. Carson, *Silent Spring*, Penguin edition, 1965, p. v
50. *Meat Trades Journal*, 13 April 1975
51. E. Millstone, *Food Additives*, Penguin, 1986, p.10
52. J.S. Turner, *The Chemical Feast*, New York, 1970, p. vi, Introduction by Ralph Nader
53. J.S. Turner, *The Chemical Feast*, New York, 1970, pp. 5–25
54. Elizabeth M. Whelan, *Wall Street Journal*, 26 August 1999, p. A18 is the source of this and the comments which follow. Dr Whelan was the president of the American Council on Science and Health
55. J.S. Turner, *The Chemical Feast*, New York, 1970, p. 25
56. R. Lacey, *Hard to Swallow*, Cambridge University Press, 1994, p. 183
57. Elizabeth M. Whelan, *Wall Street Journal*, 26 August 1999, p. A18
58. *The Guardian*, 6 September 2007, p. 6
59. *The Guardian*, 6 September 2007, p. 7
60. M. Nestlé, *Safe Food: Bacteria, Biotechnology and Bioterrorism*, University of California Press, Berkeley, Ca., 2003, p. 265

Chapter 4: Diseases of Deficiency

1. S. Halliday, *The Great Filth: the War Against Disease in Victorian England*, Sutton, Stroud, p. 44
2. X. Baron, (ed.) *London, 1066–1914*, vol. 3, p. 409
3. The figures vary, of course, with stature and occupation; thus an athlete or manual worker needs more than an office worker
4. Published by Penguin Modern Classics
5. G. Sturt, *Change in the Village*, Duckworth, London, 1912
6. J. Drummond and A. Wilbraham, *The Englishman's Food*, Pimlico, London, 1991, p. 82
7. W. Gratzer, *Terrors of the Table: the Curious History of Nutrition*, Oxford University Press, 2005, chapter 9 describes Pekelharing's work
8. C. Funk, *Journal of Preventive Medicine*, vol. 20, p. 342
9. See p. 115 for an account of this discovery
10. F.G. Hopkins, *The Analyst and the Medical Man*, in *The Analyst*, November 1906, pp. 385–404; see panel on p. 31 for an account of Hopkins' career

11. F.G. Hopkins, *The Analyst and the Medical Man*, in *The Analyst*, November 1906, p. 395

12. K.J. Carpenter, *The History of Scurvy and Vitamin C*, Cambridge University Press, 1986, p. vii

13. J. Lind, *A Treatise of the Scurvy*, Navy Records Society, London, vol. 57, 1965, p. 9

14. K.J. Carpenter, *The History of Scurvy and Vitamin C*, Cambridge University Press, 1986, p. 1

15. K.J. Carpenter, *The History of Scurvy and Vitamin C*, Cambridge University Press, 1986, p. 1 et seq.

16. R. Hawkins, *Voyage into the South Sea in the Year 1593*, Hakluyt Society, London, 1847

17. See chapter 1 for a discussion of these

18. See p. 14, above

19. J. Drummond and A. Wilbraham, *The Englishman's Food*, Pimlico, London, 1991, p. 258

20. W. Cockburn, *An Account of the Nature, Causes, Symptoms and Cure of the Distempers that are incident to Seafaring People*, Newman, London, 1696, p. 17

21. W. Cockburn, *An Account of the nature, Causes, Symptoms and Cure of Loosenesses*, Strahan, London, 1706, pp. 229–30

22. Also spelt Bachstroem and Bachstrohm

23. Thanks to Ros Earis of Pembroke College, Cambridge, for providing the translation

24. J. Thirsk, *Food in Early Modern England*, Hambledon Continuum, 2007, p. 129

25. *The Voyages of Sir James Lancaster*, introduction and notes by Sir William Foster, Hakluyt Society, London 1940, 2nd edition, p. 79

26. J. Woodall, *The Surgions Mate*, Griffin, London, 1617, p. 185

27. C. Creighton, *A History of Epidemics in Britain*, 1891, p. 599

28. K.J. Carpenter, *The History of Scurvy and Vitamin C*, Cambridge University Press, 1986, p. 38

29. The word first appeared in English in 1565; *Oxford English Dictionary*, Clarendon press, Oxford, 1989, vol. 14, p. 768

30. K.J. Carpenter, *The History of Scurvy and Vitamin C*, Cambridge University Press, 1986, p. 45

31. Estimates of the numbers who perished from scurvy vary but half is, if anything, a conservative figure

32. *Oxford Dictionary of National Biography*, Oxford, 2004, vol. 33, pp. 810–13

33. W. Gratzer, *Terrors of the Table: the Curious History of Nutrition*, Oxford University Press, 2005, p. 20

34. *The Health of Seamen*, Navy Records Society, vol. 57, London, 1965, p. 21

35. J. Lind, *A Treatise of the Scurvy*, Millar, Edinburgh, 1753, pp. 13, 37 and 47–8

36. K.J. Carpenter, *The History of Scurvy and Vitamin C*, Cambridge University Press, 1986, p. 76

37. K.J. Carpenter, *The History of Scurvy and Vitamin C*, Cambridge University Press, 1986, p. 82

38. Copley Medal citation, from the website of the Royal Society

39. C. Lloyd, (ed.) *The Health of Seamen*, Navy Records Society, London, 1965, p. 133

40. J. Drummond and A. Wilbraham, *The Englishman's Food: Five Centuries of English Diet*, Pimlico, London, 1991, p. 270

41. The canning factory opened in 1812 having adopted the heat sterilisation methods developed by the Frenchman Nicolas Appert

42. See p. 133 for the disastrous consequences of Pauling's beliefs

43. Andrew B. Appleby, *Journal of Interdisciplinary History*, 1980, pp. 643–63 describes these famines and their consequences; see also A. Appleby, *Famine in Tudor and Stuart England,* Stanford, 1978
44. J. Strype, *Ecclesiastical Memorials*, vol. 2, London, 1822 p. 352, quoted in P. Williams, *The Later Tudors,* Oxford University Press, 1995, p. 48
45. See p. 59 above
46. J. Hanway, *Letters on the Importance of the Rising Generation of the Labouring Part of our Fellow Subjects,* London, 1767, vol. 2, p. 219
47. D. Whistler, *Disputatio medica inaugurales de morbo puerili Anglorum,* London, 1684, Cambridge University Library, microfilm
48. W. Fordyce, *New Inquiry into the Causes of Fevers,* Cadell, London, 1773, p. 207
49. J. Drummond and A. Wilbraham, *The Englishman's Food,* Pimlico, London, 1991, p. 273
50. See p. 74 for an account of Cullen's contribution to the science of refrigeration
51. See *The Works of William Cullen,* (ed. J. Thomson, 1827) for Cullen's views on rickets
52. J. Drummond and A. Wilbraham, *The Englishman's Food,* Pimlico, London, 1991, p. 275
53. See pp. 104–5 above for an account of Lind's work
54. E. Mellanby, *An Experimental Investigation on Rickets, The Lancet,,* vol. 196, 1919, pp. 407–12
55. *British Medical Journal*, vol. 291, 27 July 1985, pp. 239–42
56. *Dictionary of Scientific Biography*, ed. C.C. Gillespie, American Council of Learned Societies, New York, 1972, vol. 5, pp. 451–3
57. This experiment was witnessed by the author in 1974
58. *The Lancet*, 16 February 1980, p. 339 ff
59. Food Standards Agency website
60. *British Medical Journal*, vol. 292, 12 April 1986, leading article, pp. 969 et seq.
61. A. Gooch, et al, *British Journal of Psychiatry*, vol. 181, July 2002, pp. 22–28
62. BBC2's *The Truth abut Food*, 15 February 2007 considered some of these issues
63. ITV's *Tonight* programme, 13 July, 2007; see also website: www.foodforthebrain.org
64. *Sunday Times*, 27 January 2008, p. 13
65. BBC2's *The Truth about Food*, 17 July 2007

Chapter 5: Nutrition or Just Calories?

1. S. Mowbray, 'The Green Light for GDA Labels?' in *The Grocer*, 2006, 229 (7741), pp. 4–5
2. See p. 16
3. J. Thirsk, *Food in Early Modern England*, Hambledon Continuum, 2007, p. 2
4. J. Thirsk, *Food in Early Modern England*, Hambledon Continuum, 2007, p. 36
5. A. Maclaren, *Training in Theory and Practice*, Macmillan, 1866, pp. 63, 107 and 189 et seq.
6. See p. 128 for an account of its origin
7. Aristotle, *A Treatise on Government*, Book 1, chapter 8
8. Genesis chapter 9, verse 3
9. T. Stuart, *The Bloodless Revolution: Radical Vegetarians and the Discovery of India*, Harper Collins, London, 2006 examines the origins of the practice
10. T. Stuart, *The Bloodless Revolution: Radical Vegetarians and the Discovery of India*, Harper Collins, London, 2006, p. 15 ff

11. See p. 73

12. T. Stuart, *The Bloodless Revolution: Radical Vegetarians and the Discovery of India*, Harper Collins, London, 2006, p. 196

13. T. Malthus, *An Essay on the Principle of Population*, Penguin, London, 1970, p. 137

14. See p. 18

15. J. Hanway, *Letters on the Importance of the Rising Generation*, London, 1767, vol. 2, p. 186

16. J. Hanway, *Letters on the Importance of the Rising Generation*, London, 1767, vol. 2, p. 193

17. J.F. Newton, *The Return to Nature*, London, 1811, p. 38

18. P.B. Shelley, *An Essay Upon the Vegetable System of Diet*, Linden Press, London, 1940, p. 6

19. P.B. Shelley, *An Essay Upon the Vegetable System of Diet*, Linden Press, London, 1940, p. 10

20. P.B. Shelley, *A Vindication of Natural Diet*, in *The Prose Works of P.B. Shelley*, E. Murray (ed.), Clarendon Press, 1993, pp. 89, 90, 91

21. *Oxford English Dictionary*, Clarendon Press, Oxford, 1989, vol. 19, p. 476, 'due to the formation of the Vegetarian Society in Ramsgate, 1847'

22. J.C. Drummond and A. Wilbraham, *The Englishman's Food: Five Centuries of English Diet*, Pimlico edition, 1991, pp. 397–98

23. See *Lectures on the Science of Human Life* and *Lectures to Young Men on Chastity*, Boston, 1839 for Graham's views

24. D. Roth, *A Century of Change in America's Eating Patterns*, in *Food Review*, vol. 23, issue 1, US Department of Agriculture, 2000, p. 35

25. D. Smith, (ed.), *Nutrition in Britain*, Routledge, London, 1997, p. 17

26. *The Lancet*, 1903, vol. 2, pp. 216, 632, 788

27. D. Smith (ed.), *Nutrition in Britain, Science, Scientists and Politics in the Twentieth Century*, Routledge, London, 1997, p. 17

28. D. Smith (ed.), *Nutrition in Britain, Science, Scientists and Politics in the Twentieth Century*, Routledge, London, 1997, p. 17

29. *Punch*, 28 November 1906, 'Bishop Fallows on Diet'

30. D. Smith (ed.), *Nutrition in Britain, Science, Scientists and Politics in the Twentieth Century*, Routledge, London, 1997, p. 19

31. D. Smith, (ed.), *Nutrition in Britain*, Routledge, London, 1997, pp. 21 and 144 ff

32. J. Dickie, *Delizia, the Epic History of the Italians and their Food*, Sceptre, London, 2007, p. 273

33. F.T. Marinetti, *The Futurist Cookbook*, trans. S. Brill, Trefoil, London 1989, p. 41

34. F.T. Marinetti, *The Futurist Cookbook*, trans. S. Brill, Trefoil, London 1989, p. 46

35. J. Dickie, *Delizia, the Epic History of the Italians and their Food*, Sceptre, London, 2007, p. 271

36. J. Dickie, *Delizia, the Epic History of the Italians and their Food*, Sceptre, London, 2007, p. 270; the address is 2, Via Vanchiglia, Turin

37. M. Gandhi, trans. M. Desai, *An Autobiography or the Story of my Experiments with Truth*, Navajivan publishers, Ahmedabad, 1927, p. 198

38. These and other exotic fads, too numerous to mention here, are described well and with humour in W. Gratzer, *Terrors of the Table: the Curious History of Nutrition*, Oxford University Press, 2005

39. W. Gratzer, *Terrors of the Table: the Curious History of Nutrition*, Oxford University Press, 2005, p. 210

40. J.C. Drummond and A. Wilbraham, *The Englishman's Food: Five Centuries of English Diet*, Pimlico edition, 1991, p. 403

41. S. Halliday, *The Great Filth, the war against disease in Victorian England*, Sutton, Stroud, 2007, chapter 6 discusses the advances in maternity care in the late nineteenth century

42. P. Clarke, *Hope and Glory, Britain, 1900–2000*, Penguin, London, 1997, p. 153

43. A.S. Williams, *The Nutrition Work of the National Birthday Trust Fund*, in D. Smith (ed.) *Nutrition in Britain*, Routledge, London, 1997, chapter 5

44. A.S. Williams, *The Nutrition Work of the National Birthday Trust Fund*, in D. Smith (ed.) *Nutrition in Britain*, Routledge, London, 1997, p. 104 ff

45. See p. 29

46. *The Lancet*, 23 August 1986, pp. 434–6

47. S. Halliday, *Nutrition Labelling*, 1975, a report prepared by the present author for the Winston Churchill memorial Trust, is the source of this and much of the information that follows; the report is held by the Trust

48. *Dietary Levels of Households in the US*, United States Department of Agriculture, 1968

49. *Ten State Nutrition Survey*, United States Department of Health, Education and Welfare, 1970

50. White House Conference on Food, Nutrition and Health, Final report, 1970, conclusions, panels 3 and 4

51. J. Ewin, *Fine Wines and Fish Oil: the Life of Hugh Macdonald Sinclair*, Oxford University Press, 2001, is an account of his life

52. *Recommended Dietary Allowances*, National Academy of Sciences, Washington, D.C., 1974

53. D. Mozaffarian et al, *New England Journal of Medicine*, 13 April 2006, vol. 34, no. 15, pp. 1601–11

Chapter 6: 'Deadly Adulterations and Slow Poisoning'

1. J. Drummond and A. Wilbraham, *The Englishman's Food*, Pimlico, 1991 p. 192

2. F.A. Filby, *A History of Food Adulteration and Analysis*, Allen & Unwin, 1934, p. 109

3. F.A. Filby, *A History of Food Adulteration and Analysis*, Allen & Unwin, 1934, p. 108

4. F.A. Filby, *A History of Food Adulteration and Analysis*, Allen & Unwin, 1934, pp. 113–14

5. V.A. Kleinfeld, *Food, Drug, Cosmetics Law Quarterly*, 1946, p. 532

6. H.T. Riley (ed.), *Liber Albus*, Griffin, London, 1861, p. 312

7. J. Drummond and A. Wilbraham, *The Englishman's Food*, Pimlico, 1991 p. 45

8. H.T. Riley (ed.), *Liber Albus*, Griffin, London, 1861, p. 232

9. H.T .Riley (ed.), *Liber Albus*, Griffin, London, 1861, p. 307

10. J. Thirsk, *Food in Early Modern England*, Hambledon Continuum, 2006, p. 108

11. F.A. Filby, *A History of Food Adulteration and Analysis*, Allen & Unwin, 1934, p. 26

12. J. Drummond and A. Wilbraham, *The Englishman's Food*, Pimlico, 1991, p. 46

13. V.A. Kleinfeld, *Food, Drug, Cosmetics Law Quarterly*, 1946, p. 532

14. W. Gratzer, *Terrors of the Table*, Oxford University Press, 2005, p. 121

15. F.A. Filby, *A History of Food Adulteration and Analysis*, Allen & Unwin, 1934, p. 27

16. F.A. Filby, *A History of Food Adulteration and Analysis*, Allen & Unwin, 1934, p. 30

17. R. Boyle, *Works*, (ed. Birch), 1772, vol. 1, p. 320

18. R. Boyle, *Works*, (ed. Birch), 1772, vol. 4, p. 265

19. J. Davies, *The Innkeeper's and Butler's Guide*, Leeds, 1811, pp. 1 ff

20. F.A. Filby, *A History of Food Adulteration and Analysis*, Allen & Unwin, 1934, pp. 137 and 132

21. R. Watson, *Chemical Essays,*, London, 1787, vol. 3, p. 369
22. W. Gratzer, *Terrors of the Table*, Oxford University Press, 2005, p. 121
23. R. Watson, *Chemical Essays*, London, 1787, 5 vols; vol. 3, p. 361, tells how to produce white lead, a common additive for bread and wine
24. F.A. Filby, *A History of Food Adulteration and Analysis,* Allen & Unwin, 1934, pp. 115–16
25. F.A. Filby, *A History of Food Adulteration and Analysis,* Allen & Unwin, 1934, pp. 116–17
26. F.A. Filby, *A History of Food Adulteration and Analysis,* Allen & Unwin, 1934, p. 44 and original
27. C. Williamson, *The Natural History of Coffee, Thee, Chocolate and Tobacco,* London, 1682, section 3, p. 15
28. J. Drummond and A. Wilbraham, *The Englishman's Food,* Pimlico, 1991, p. 188
29. J. Drummond and A. Wilbraham, *The Englishman's Food,* Pimlico, 1991, p. 188
30. X. Baron (ed.), *London, 1066–1914,* Helm, Robertsbridge, vol. 1, pp. 799–800
31. Kings II, chapter 4, verse 40
32. F. Accum, *A Treatise on Adulteration of Food,* London, 1820, p. iv
33. F. Accum, *A Treatise on Adulteration of Food,* London, 1820, p. 73
34. A. Smith, *Wealth of Nations,* London, 1784, book 4, chapter 8
35. F. Accum, *A Treatise on Adulteration of Food,* London, 1820, pp. 98–110
36. F. Accum, *A Treatise on Adulteration of Food,* London, 1820, pp. 154–65
37. F.A. Filby, *A History of Food Adulteration and Analysis,* Allen & Unwin, 1934, p. 56
38. F.A. Filby, *A History of Food Adulteration and Analysis,* Allen & Unwin, 1934, p. 203
39. J. Drummond and A. Wilbraham, *The Englishman's Diet,* Pimlico, London, 1991, p. 291
40. *The Lancet,* 8 January 1831, pp 485–86
41. See chapter one for an account of Lavoisier's fate
42. W. Gratzer, *Terrors of the Table*, Oxford University Press, 2005, p. 128
43. *The Lancet,* 4 January 1851, p. 20
44. S. Hempel, *The Medical Detective,* Granta, London, 2000, p. 199
45. A.H. Hassall, *Food and its Adulterations,* Longmans, London, 1855, p. xiv
46. A.H. Hassall, *Food and its Adulterations,* Longmans, London, 1855, p. xiv
47. A.H. Hassall, *Food and its Adulterations,* Longmans, London, 1855, p. xiii
48. *The Lancet,* 15 January 1853, p. 66
49. A.H. Hassall, *Food and its Adulterations,* Longmans, London, 1855, pp. 456 ff
50. W. Gratzer, *Terrors of the Table*, Oxford University Press, 2005, p. 127
51. *The Times,* 20 March 1851
52. *The Lancet,* 26 April 1851, p. 466
53. *Punch,* 1851, vol. 20, pp. 116, 253, 13, 27 and 44 respectively
54. C. Dickens, *David Copperfield,* chapter 33
55. Longmans, London, 1855, the full title being: *Food and its Adulterations, comprising the reports of the Analytical sanitary commission of 'The Lancet' for the years 1851 to 1854 inclusive, revised and extended: being records of the results of some thousands of original microscopical and chemical analyses of the solids and fluids consumed by all classes of the public by Arthur Hill Hassall ... Illustrated by one hundred and fifty-nine engravings*
56. Longmans, London, 1857
57. R. Kemp, *Enquire Within Upon Everything,* London, 1865, p. 347
58. Co-founder of the later Crosse and Blackwell
59. Parliamentary Debates, 3rd Series, vol. 154, 7 July 1859, columns 846–47
60. Parliamentary Debates, 3rd Series, vol. 156, 29 February 1860, column 2027
61. J. Drummond and A. Wilbraham, *The Englishman's Food,* Pimlico, 1991, p. 295
62. See chapter 2 for a reference to the cholera epidemics
63. W. Gratzer, *Terrors of the Table*, Oxford University Press, 2005, p. 131

64. *The Magistrate*, the Magistrates' Association, London, vol. 63, no. 10, Winter 2007, p. 298
65. *The Lancet*, 4 June 1983, p. 1257
66. W. Gratzer, *Terrors of the Table*, Oxford University Press, 2005, p. 122
67. *The Lancet*, 20 August 1988, p. 465
68. *The Lancet*, 25 February 1989, p. 417
69. C. Tame and D. Botsford, *Not Just Tobacco: Health Scares, Medical Paternalism and Individual Liberty*, FOREST, 1996, pp. 6–19
70. J.V. Wheelock, *The Food Safety Crisis*, Bradford, 1989, p. 4
71. See p. 45 above
72. CASH website, 30 January 2007: www.hyp.ac.uk/cash/home/reports.htm
73. E.g. *The Daily Telegraph*, 29 January 2007, p. 7

Chapter 7: A Century of Excess

1. *The Independent*, 17 November 1996, pp. 52–3
2. See pp. 12 and 29, above
3. M. Brown et al, *The Ration Book Diet*, Sutton publishing, Stroud, 2004, p. 8
4. A.J.P. Taylor, *English History, 1914–45*, Oxford University Press, 1965, pp. 77–8
5. M. Brown et al, *The Ration Book Diet*, Sutton publishing, Stroud, 2004, p. 11
6. M. Brown et al, *The Ration Book Diet*, Sutton publishing, Stroud, 2004, p. 20
7. M. Brown et al, *The Ration Book Diet*, Sutton publishing, Stroud, 2004, p. 90 ff
8. M. Brown et al, *The Ration Book Diet*, Sutton publishing, Stroud, 2004, p. 50
9. See chapters 1 and 5 respectively
10. D. Roth, *A century of Change in America's Eating Patterns*, in *Food Review*, vol. 23, issue 1, US Department of Agriculture, 2000, p. 33
11. *The Challenge of Obesity in the WHO European Region and Strategies for Response*, WHO, Denmark, 2007, foreword, p. xii; www.bbc.co.uk/science/hottopics/obesity
12. *The Challenge of Obesity in the WHO European Region and Strategies for Response*, WHO, Denmark, 2007, p. 48
13. *Foresight* report: *Tackling Obesities: Future Choices*, 2007, p.17, http://s3.amazonaws.com/foresight/17.pdf
14. P. Clarke, *Hope and Glory: Britain 1900–2000*, Penguin Books, London, 1997, p. 41
15. P. Clarke, *Hope and Glory: Britain 1900–2000*, Penguin Books, London, 1997, p. 91; see also chapter five for the work of the National Birthday Trust Fund for malnourished mothers
16. B.R. Mitchell, *British Historical Statistics*, Cambridge University Press, 1988, pp. 104 and 107 and *Annual Abstract of Statistics*, Palgrave, London, 2007, pp. 91–2; also *Trends in Europe and North America*, UN Economic Commission for Europe, Geneva, 2003, p. 151
17. G.K. Zipf, *Human Behavior and the Principle of Least Effort: an Introduction to Human Ecology*, Hafner, New York, 1965, expounds this view
18. *Foresight* report: *Tackling Obesities:Future Choices*, 2007, p. 2, Introduction by Sir David King, Chief Scientific Adviser to HM Government: http://s3.amazonaws.com/foresight/17.pdf
19. *National Diet and Nutrition Survey*, Ruston et al, 2004, HMSO, Norwich, p. 20
20. *Foresight* report: *Tackling Obesities:Future Choices*, 2007, p. 6, available on the web, http://s3.amazonaws.com/foresight/17.pdf
21. *The Challenge of Obesity in the WHO European Region and Strategies for Response*, WHO, Denmark, 2007, p. 84

22. *Foresight* report: *Tackling Obesities: Future Choices*, 2007, p. 45, available on the web: http://s3.amazonaws.com/foresight/17.pdf

23. *The Challenge of Obesity in the WHO European Region and Strategies for Response*, WHO, Denmark, 2007, pp. 8, 38, 67, 68

24. *Foresight* report: *Tackling Obesities:Future Choices*, 2007, p. 24, available on the web: http://s3.amazonaws.com/foresight/17.pdf

25. F. Furedi, *Culture of Fear: Risk-Taking and the Morality of Low Expectation*, Continuum, 2002, p. 10

26. M. Nestlé, *Food Politics: How the Food Industry Influences Nutrition and Health*, University of California Press, Berkeley, Ca., 2002, p. 33

27. D. Roth, *A century of Change in America's Eating Patterns*, in *Food Review*, vol. 23, issue 1,US Department of Agriculture, 2000, p. 34

28. M. Nestlé, *Food Politics: How the Food Industry Influences Nutrition and Health*, University of California Press, Berkeley, Ca., 2002, p. 32

29. M. Nestlé, *Food Politics: How the Food Industry Influences Nutrition and Health*, University of California Press, Berkeley, Ca., 2002, p. 3

30. US Senate Select Committee on Nutrition and Human Needs, 24 March 1977

31. *The Challenge of Obesity in the WHO European Region and Strategies for Response*, WHO, Denmark, 2007, pp. 93, 65

32. See pp. 42–4, above

33. *The Challenge of Obesity in the WHO European Region and Strategies for Response*, WHO, Denmark, 2007, p. 96

34. T. Land, M. Heasman, *Food Wars*, Earthscan, London, 2004

35. *World Agriculture:Towards 2015/2030*, Food & Agriculture Organisation of the United Nations, Rome, 2002, p. 30

36. M. Nestlé, *Food Politics: How the Food Industry Influences Nutrition and Health*, University of California Press, Berkeley, Ca., 2002, pp. 1 and 17

37. A. Drewnowski and N. Darmon, *The Economics of Obesity*, in *American Journal of Clinical Nutrition*, 2005, vol. 82 (Supplement 1), p. 265

38. W.P. James et al, *Socioeconomic determinants of Health* in *British Medical Journal*, 1997, vol. 314, pp. 1545–9

39. W.P. James et al, *Socioeconomic determinants of Health* in *British Medical Journal*, 1997, vol. 314, pp. 1545–9

40. *The Challenge of Obesity in the WHO European Region and Strategies for Response*, WHO, Denmark, 2007, p. 77

41. J. Gregory et al, *Dietary and Nutritional Survey of British Adults*, HMSO, Norwich, 1990, p. 220

42. M.A. McRory et al, *Overeating in America :association between restaurant food consumption and body fatness in healthy men and women ages 19 to 8* in *Obesity Research*, 2000, vol. 7, pp. 564–71

43. J. Guthrie et al, *Journal of Nutrition Education and Behaviour*, 2002, vol. 34, pp. 140–50

44. J. Gregory et al, *Dietary and Nutritional Survey of British Adults*, HMSO, 1990

45. See chapter 5 for the problems concerning portion sizes in breakfast cereals

46. J. Pomerleau et al, *Nutrition and Lifestyles in the Baltic Republics*, London School of Hygiene and Tropical Medicine, 2000, pp. 51–2

47. *Impediments to Efficiency in the Agro-Food Chain in Bulgaria, Romania and Slovenia*, OECD, Paris, 1998, Agricultural Policy Papers, 1998–2002

48. *Consumer Eastern Europe2005–6*, Euromonitor, London, 2005; *Soft Drinks in Poland to 2008*, Datamonitor, Brussels, 2005

49. M. Nestlé, *New England Journal of Medicine*, 15 June 2006, vol. 354, no. 24, p. 2527

50. M. Nestlé, *New England Journal of Medicine*, 15 June 2006, vol. 354, no. 24, p. 2528

51. M. Mello et al, *Obesity, the New Frontier of Public Health Law*, 15 June 2006, vol. 354, no. 24, pp. 2601 ff
52. Pelman ex. rel. vs. McDonald's in New York State
53. *Daily Telegraph*, 20 October 2002
54. S. Dibb, *A Spoonful of Sugar: TV Food Advertising Aimed at Children*, Consumers International Programme for Developed Economies, London, 1996, p. 24
55. G. Cannon, *The Politics of Food*, Century, London, 1988, p. 111
56. S. Dibb, *Healthy Competition, how supermarkets can affect your chance of a healthy diet*, National Consumer Council, London, 2005
57. Commercial Activities in Schools, Report to Congressional Requesters, US General Accounting Office, Washington DC, 2000
58. *Foresight* report: *Tackling Obesities: Future Choices*, 2007, Executive Summary, available on the web: http://s3.amazonaws.com/foresight/17.pdf
59. *Foresight* report: *Tackling Obesities: Future Choices*, 2007, p. 48, available on the web: http://s3.amazonaws.com/foresight/17.pdf
60. *Foresight* report: *Tackling Obesities: Future Choices*, 2007, p. 13, available on the web: http://s3.amazonaws.com/foresight/17.pdf
61. *The Surgeon-General's Call to Action Prevent and Decrease Overweight and Obesity*, US Department of Health, 2001
62. G. Williams, *Orlistat over the counter*, 15 November 2007: http://www.bmj.com. cgi/content/full/bmj
63. R. Christensen et al, *The Lancet*, 11 November 2007, pp. 1706–13
64. Cambridge University website, 13 December 2007: www.admin.cam.ac.uk/news
65. *Foresight* report: *Tackling Obesities:Future Choices*, 2007, pp 44 and 47, available on the web: http://s3.amazonaws.com/foresight/17.pdf
66. P. Sahota et al, *British Medical Journal*, 2001, vol. 323, pp. 1027–32
67. C.F. Lowe et al, *European Journal of Clinical Nutrition*, 2004, vol. 58 (3), pp 510–22
68. W. Reger et al, *Using Mass Media to Promote Healthy Eating*, in *Preventive Medicine*, 1999, vol. 29, pp. 414–21
69. *Family Food: a Report on the 2005–6 Expenditure & Food Survey*, HMSO, Norwich, 2007, pp. 20 and 22
70. *Social Trends, 1994*, HMSO, London, p. 99, table 7.15
71. *Foresight* report: *Tackling Obesities:Future Choices*, 2007, p. 57, (information from A.C. Nielsen), available on the web: http://s3.amazonaws.com/foresight/17.pdf
72. *Foresight* report: *Tackling Obesities:Future Choices*, 2007, p. 70, available on the web: http://s3.amazonaws.com/foresight/17.pdf
73. *The Challenge of Obesity in the WHO European Region and Strategies for Response*, WHO, Denmark, 2007, p. 38
74. *The Times*, 28 March 1935, described its opening and *The Evening News*, 6 March 1950 its closure. Papers covering the centre's activities are held at the library of the Wellcome Foundation, Euston Road, London
75. See reference above, p. 189
76. *The Guardian*, 15 November 2007, p. 17
77. *Pembroke in Our Time*, ed. C. Gilbraith and C. Walston, Third Millennium, London, 2007, p. 144
78. *Foresight* report: *Tackling Obesities:Future Choices*, 2007, p. 52, available on the web: http://s3.amazonaws.com/foresight/17.pdf
79. *Energy and Transport in Figures*, European Commission, Brussels, 2002
80. *EU Transport in Figures Statistical Pocketbook*, European Commission, Brussels, 2000; also *Walcyng: How to enhance Walking and Cycling*, European Commission, Brussels, 2000

81. *The Challenge of Obesity in the WHO European Region and Strategies for Response*, WHO, Denmark, 2007, p. 214
82. *Cycling Towards Health and Safety*, BMA, Oxford, 1992, p. 121
83. L. Anderson et al, *Archives of Internal Medicine*, 2000, vol. 160, p. 1628
84. S.C. Doherty, *Health Education & the Media*, Pergamon Press, Oxford, 1981. pp. 77–8
85. *Foresight* report: *Tackling Obesities:Future Choices*, 2007, p. 73, available on the web: http://s3.amazonaws.com/foresight/17.pdf
86. *The Observer*, 11 November 2007, pp. 20–1
87. J. Dickie, *Delizia, The Epic History of the Italians and their Food*, Sceptre, London, 2007, p. 340 ff describes this event
88. J. Dickie, *Delizia, The Epic History of the Italians and their Food*, Sceptre, London, 2007, p. 342
89. R. Harrison (ed.,) et al, *The Ethical Consumer*, Sage, London, 2005, p. 60
90. See p. 191 above
91. See p. 122 above

Bibliography

Books and pamphlets including works of reference

Accum, F., *A Treatise on Adulteration of Food*, London, 1820

Appleby, A., *Famine in Tudor and Stuart England,* Stanford, 1978

Aristotle, *A Treatise on Government*, Book 1, chapter 8, Routledge, London, 1888

Ashwell, M., (ed.), *McCance and Widdowson, a Scientific Partnership of 60 years*, British Nutrition Foundation, London, 1993

Austen-Leigh, J.E., *A Memoir of Jane Austen*, London, 1870

Bacon, Francis, *Works of*, ed. Basil Montague, Philadelphia, 1848, vol. 2

Baron, X., (ed.) *London, 1066–1914*, vol. 3, Helm Information, Mountfield, Sussex, 1997

Beaumont, W., *Experiments and Observations on the Gastric Juice and the Physiology of Digestion*, 1833, facsimile edition, Dover Publications, New York, 1996

Boyle, R., *Works*, (ed. Birch), Millar, London 1744

Bradley, R., *A General Treatise of Husbandry and Gardening,* London, 1724

Bradley, R., *Botanical Dictionary*, London, 1728,

Bragg, M., *On Giants' Shoulders*, Hodder and Stoughton, London, 1988

Brown, M. et al, *The Ration Book Diet*, Sutton publishing, Stroud, 2004

Cheadle, W., *On the Principles and Exact Conditions to be Observed in the Artificial Feeding of Infants*, Smith Elder, London, 1889

Cadogan, W., *Essay upon the Nursing and Management of Children*, London, 1769

Cannon, G., *The Politics of Food*, Century, London, 1988

Carpenter, K.J., *The History of Scurvy and Vitamin C*, Cambridge University Press, 1986

Carson, R., *Silent Spring*, Penguin edition, London, 1965

Clarke, P., *Hope and Glory, Britain, 1900–2000*, Penguin, London, 1997

Clode, C., *Memorials of the Guild of Merchant Taylors*, London, 1875

Cobbett, W., *Rural Rides*, Everyman Edition, London, 1973

Cockburn, A., *Rumsfeld, an American Disaster,* Verso, 2007

Cockburn, W., *An Account of the Nature, Causes, Symptoms and Cure of the Distempers that are incident to Seafaring People*, Newman, London, 1696

Cockburn, W., *An Account of the nature, Causes, Symptoms and Cure of Loosenesses*, Strahan, London, 1706

Cogan, T., *The Haven of Health*, London, 1584

Cotson S. and Smith, D.B., (ed.) *Freeze-Drying of Foodstuffs*, Columbine Press, Manchester, 1963

Creighton, C., *A History of Epidemics in Britain*, Oxford University Press, 1891

Davies, J., *The Innkeeper's and Butler's Guide*, Leeds, 1811

Dibb, S., *A Spoonful of Sugar: TV Food Advertising Aimed at Children*, Consumers International Programme for Developed Economies, London, 1996

Dibb, S., *Healthy Competition, how supermarkets can affect your chance of a healthy diet*, National Consumer Council, London, 2005

Dickens, C., *David Copperfield*, Purnell, London, 1988

Dickie, J., *Delizia, the Epic History of the Italians and their Food*, Sceptre, London, 2007

Dictionary of Scientific Biography, ed. C.C. Gillespie, American Council of Learned Societies, New York, 1972

Doherty, S.C., *Health Education & the Media*, Pergamon Press, Oxford, 1981

Drummond, J.C. and Wilbraham, A., *The Englishman's Food: Five Centuries of English Diet*, Pimlico edition, London, 1991

Eden, F.M., *The State of the Poor*, 1797, Routledge edition, London, 1928

Elton, G.R., *The Tudor Constitution*, Cambridge University Press, 1960

Ewin, J., *Fine Wines and Fish Oil: the Life of Hugh Macdonald Sinclair*, Oxford University Press, 2001

Fergusson, J., *The Vitamin Murders: Who Killed Healthy Eating in Britain?* Portobello, London, 2007

Filby, F.A., *A History of Food Adulteration and Analysis*, Allen & Unwin, London, 1934

Foster, Sir William, (ed.), *The Voyages of Sir James Lancaster*, Hakluyt Society, 2nd edition, London, 1940

Fordyce, W., *New Inquiry into the Causes of Fevers*, Cadell, London, 1773

Furedi, F., *Culture of Fear: Risk-Taking and the Morality of Low Expectation*, Cassell, London, 1997

Fussell, G.E., *The English Dairy Farmer1500–1900*, Cass, London, 1966

Gamgee, A., *A Textbook of the Physiological Chemistry of the Animal Body*, London, 1880

Gandhi, M., trans. M. Desai, *An Autobiography or the Story of my Experiments with Truth*, Navajivan publishers, Ahmedabad, 1927

Gilbraith, C. and Walston, C., *Pembroke in Our Time*, Third Millennium, London, 2007

Gratzer, W., *Terrors of the Table: the Curious History of Nutrition*, Oxford University Press, 2005

Halliday, S., *The Great Filth: the War Against Disease in Victorian England*, Sutton, Stroud, 2007

Hanway, J., *Letters on the Importance of the Rising Generation*, London, 1767

Harrison, R., (ed.,) et al, *The Ethical Consumer*, Sage, London, 2005

Harrison, W., *The Description of England*, 1587, Cornell UP reprint, 1968

Hassall, A.H., *Food and its Adulterations*, Longmans, London, 1855

Hawkins, R., *Voyage into the South Sea in the Year 1593*, Hakluyt Society, London, 1847

Hempel, S., *The Medical Detective*, Granta, London, 2000

Hentzner, P., *A Journey into England in the Year 1598*, Strawberry Hill, 1757

Horder, Lord et al, *Bread*, Constable, London, 1954

Kemp, R., *Enquire Within Upon Everything*, London, 1865

Lacey, R., *Hard to Swallow*, Cambridge University Press, 1994

Land, T. & Heasman, M., *Food Wars*, Earthscan, London, 2004

Lind, J., *A Treatise of the Scurvy*, Navy Records Society, London, vol. 57, 1965

Lloyd, C., (ed.) *The Health of Seamen*, Navy Records Society, London, 1965
Loesecke, W. von, *Drying and Dehydration of Foods*, Chapman and Hall, London, 1955
Lovell, R., *The Complete Herbal*, Oxford, 1655
Malthus, T., *Essay on the Principle of Population*, Penguin, London, 1970
Marinetti, F.T., *The Futurist Cookbook*, trans. S. Brill, Trefoil, London, 1989
McCulloch, J.R., *A Statistical Account of the British Empire*, Knight, London, 1837
Maclaren, A., *Training in Theory and Practice*, Macmillan, London, 1866
Millstone, E., *Food Additives*, Penguin, London, 1986
Mitchell, B.R., *British Historical Statistics*, Cambridge University Press, 1988
Morris, T.N., *The Dehydration of Food*, Chapman and Hall, London, 1947
Nestlé, M., *Food Politics: How the Food Industry Influences Nutrition and Health*, University of California Press, Berkeley, Ca., 2002
Nestlé, M., *Safe Food: Bacteria, Biotechnology and Bioterrorism*, University of California Press, Berkeley, Ca., 2003
Newton, J.F., *The Return to Nature*, London, 1811
Oxford Dictionary of National Biography, Oxford University Press, 2001
Pepys, Samuel, *Diary of Samuel Pepys,* Harper Collins, London, 1995
Pomerleau, J. et al, *Nutrition and Lifestyles in the Baltic Republics*, London School of Hygiene and Tropical Medicine, 2000
Riley, H.T., (ed.), *Liber Albus*, Griffin, London, 1861
Rumford, Count, *Of Food and Particularly of Feeding the Poor*, London, 1796
Salaman, R.D., *The History and Social Influence of the Potato*, Cambridge University Press, 1970
Seddon, Q., *Spoiled for Choice*, Evergreen, Finchingfield, 1990
Shelley, P.B., *An Essay Upon the Vegetable System of Diet*, Linden Press, London, 1940
Shelley, P.B., *A Vindication of Natural Diet*, in *The Prose Works of P.B. Shelley*, E. Murray (ed.), Clarendon Press, 1993
Sheridan, R.B., *Sugar and Slavery*, Caribbean University Press, 1974
Singer, Dr. C., *A Short History of Medicine*, Clarendon Press, Oxford, 1928
Slare, F., *A Vindication of Sugars against the Charge of Dr Willis*, London, 1715
Smiles, S., *Lives of the Engineers*, John Murray, 1874, vol. 1
Smith, A., *Inquiry into the Nature and Causes of the Wealth of Nations*, Dent, 1960
Smith, D., (ed.), *Nutrition in Britain*, Routledge, London, 1997
Smith, E., *Victorian Farnham*, Phillimore, London & Chichester, 1971
Smith, W., *A Sure Guide in Sickness and Health in the Choice of Food and Use of Medicine*, London, 1776
Smyth, J.C., (ed.), *The Works of the Late William Stark, M.D.,* London, 1788
Strype, J., *Ecclesiastical Memorials*, vol. 2, London, 1822
Stuart, T., *The Bloodless Revolution: Radical Vegetarians and the Discovery of India*, Harper Collins, London, 2006
Sturt, G., *A Small Boy in the Sixties*, Harvester Press edition, Hassocks, Sussex, 1977
Sturt, G., *Change in the Village*, Duckworth, London, 1912
Tame, C. and Botsford, D., *Not Just Tobacco: Health Scares, Medical Paternalism and Individual Liberty*, FOREST, London, 1996
Taylor, A.J.P., *English History, 1914–45*, Oxford University Press, 1965
Thirsk, J., *Food in Early Modern England*, Hambledon Continuum, London, 2007
Tryon, T., *Letters Domestic and Foreign*, London, 1700
Turner, J.S., *The Chemical Feast*, New York, 1970
Watson, R., *Chemical Essays,*, London, 1787, vol. 3
Wheelock, J.V., *The Food Safety Crisis*, Bradford, 1989
Whistler, D., *Disputatio medica inaugurales de morbo puerili Anglorum*, London, 1684, Cambridge University Library, microfilm

Williams, P., *The Later Tudors,* Oxford University Press, 1995
Williamson, C., *The Natural History of Coffee, Thee, Chocolate and Tobacco,* London, 1682
Wohl, A.S., *Endangered Lives: Public Health in Victorian Britain,* Methuen, 1983
Woodall, J., *The Surgions* [sic] *Mate,* Griffin, London, 1617
Woods, R. and Woodward, J., (eds.), *Urban Disease and Mortality in Nineteenth-Century England,* New York, 1974
Young, A., *Farmer's Tour Through the East of England,* London, 1771
Zipf, G.K., *Human Behavior and the Principle of Least Effort: an Introduction to Human Ecology,* New York, 1965

Papers and reports

Authored, UK
Boyd Orr, J., *Food, Health and Income: Report on a Survey of Adequacy of Diet in Relation to Income,* Macmillan, 1936
Gregory, J. et al, *Dietary and Nutritional Survey of British Adults,* HMSO, 1990
McCance, R.A. and Lawrence, R.D., *The Carbohydrate Content of Foods,* Medical Research Council Special Report Series no. 135, HMSO, 1929
McCance, R.A. and Shipp, H.L., *The Chemistry of Flesh Foods and their Losses on Cooking,* Medical Research Council Special Report Series no. 187, HMSO, 1929
McCance, R.A. and Widdowson, E.M., *The Chemical Composition of Foods,* Medical Research Council Special Report Series no. 235, HMSO, 1940

Other, UK

Annual Abstract of Statistics, 2006, Office of National Statistics, 2007
Annual Abstract of Statistics, 2007, Office of National Statistics, 2008
Consumer Eastern Europe, 2005–6, Euromonitor, London, 2005
Cycling Towards Health and Safety, BMA, Oxford, 1992
Family Food a Report on the 2005–6 Expenditure & Food Survey, HMSO, Norwich, 2007
Family Spending, 2006, Office for National Statistics, 2007
Foresight report: *Tackling Obesities: Future Choices,* 2007, http://s3.amazonaws.com/foresight/17.pdf
National Diet and Nutrition Survey, Ruston et al, 2004, HMSO, Norwich
Parliamentary Papers, 1828, vol. ix
Parliamentary Debates, 3rd Series, vol. 154, 7 July 1859
Parliamentary Debates, 3rd Series, vol. 156, 29 February 1860
Report on the Health of the City of Liverpool During 1915, Liverpool, 1916
Social Trends, 1994, HMSO, London

Authored, Overseas

McRory, M.A. et al, *Overeating in America: association between restaurant food consumption and body fatness in healthy men and women ages 19 to 8* in *Obesity Research,* 2000, vol. 7
Roth, D., *A century of Change in America's Eating Patterns,* in *Food Review,* vol. 23, issue 1, US Department of Agriculture, 2000

Other, Overseas

The Challenge of Obesity in the WHO European Region and Strategies for Response, WHO, Denmark, 2007
Dietary Levels of Households in the US, United States Department of Agriculture, 1968
Energy and Transport in Figures, European Commission, Brussels, 2002
EU Transport in Figures: Statistical Pocketbook, European Commission, Brussels, 2000
Impediments to Efficiency in the Agro-Food Chain in Bulgaria, Romania and Slovenia, OECD, Paris, 1998, Agricultural Policy Papers, 1998–2002
Recommended Dietary Allowances, National Academy of Sciences, Washington D.C., 1974
Soft Drinks in Poland to 2008, Datamonitor, Brussels, 2005
The Surgeon-General's Call to Action to Prevent and Decrease Overweight and Obesity, US Department of Health, 2001
Ten State Nutrition Survey, United States Department of Health, Education and Welfare, 1970
Trends in Europe and North America, UN Economic Commission for Europe, Geneva, 2003
Walcyng: How to enhance Walking and Cycling, European Commission, Brussels, 2000
White House Conference on Food, Nutrition and Health, Final report, 1970, conclusions
World Agriculture: Towards 2015/2030, Food & Agriculture Organisation of the UN Rome, 2002

Publications of learned societies and others

Halliday, S., *Nutrition Labelling*, 1975, Winston Churchill Memorial Trust
Morton, J.C., *Town Milk* in *The Journal of the Royal Agricultural Society of England*, 1868
Public Health, vol. 9, 10 January 1897, *Journal of the Incorporated Society of Medical Officers of Health*
Royal Society Letters Book, vol. 1

Journals

American Journal of Clinical Nutrition, 2005, vol. 82 (Supplement 1)
American Medical Recorder, 1825, vol. 8
The Analyst, November 1906
Archives of Internal Medicine, 2000, vol. 160
British Journal of Psychiatry, vol. 181, July 2002
British Medical Journal, vol. 291, 27 July 1985, vol. 292, 12 April 1986
Economic History Review, vol. 9, no. 2, 1956
European Journal of Clinical Nutrition, 2004, vol. 58 (3)
Journal of Interdisciplinary History, 1980
Journal of Nutrition Education and Behaviour, 2002, vol. 34
Journal of Paediatrics, January 1989
The Lancet, 8 August 1829; 22 August 1829; 8 January 1831; 18 May 1839, 16 December 1848; 4 January 1851; 26 April 1851; 6 March 1852; 15 January 1853; 4 July 1857; 14 October 1865; 18 February 1889; 24 August 1935; 11 August 1979; 16 February 1980; 20 November 1982; 4 June 1983; 24 September 1983;

15 October 1983; 25 August 1984; 1 December 1984; 27 July 1985; 23 August 1986; 20 August 1988; 25 February 1989; 11 November 2007
Medical History, October 1960; *Medical History Supplement*, 11, 1991
New England Journal of Medicine, 13 April 2006, vol. 34, no. 15

Newspapers and magazines

The Daily Telegraph, 20 October 2002
The Evening News, 6 March 1950
Food Chemical News, 12 June 1995
The Guardian, 6 September 2007; 15 November 2007
The Magistrate, vol. 63, no. 10, Winter 2007
Meat Trades Journal, 13 April 1975
Punch, 28 November 1906
Illustrated London News, 10, 17 and 24 September 1892
The Independent, 17 November 1996
The Independent on Sunday, 27 May 2007
The Observer, 11 November 2007
Sunday Times, 6 May 2007; 27 January 2008
The Times, 20 March 1851; 28 March 1935
Wall Street Journal, 26 August 1999

Index